Living Orthodoxy

Living Orthodoxy
IN THE MODERN WORLD

Orthodox Christianity
& Society

Edited by
Andrew Walker
&
Costa Carras

ST VLADIMIR'S SEMINARY PRESS
CRESTWOOD, NEW YORK 10707
2000

LIVING ORTHODOXY
IN THE MODERN WORLD:
Orthodox Christianity & Society

First published in Great Britain 1996
Society for Promoting Christian Knowledge
Holy Trinity Church, Marylebone Road, London NW1 4DU

St Vladimir's Seminary Press
575 Scarsdale Rd., Crestwood, NY 10707
1-800-204-2664

ISBN 0-88141-212-0

PRINTED IN GREAT BRITAIN

Contents

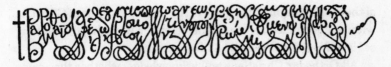

Bartholomew by the grace of God Ecumenical Patriarch, Bishop of Constantinople, the New Rome.

The book we have in our hands, made up of twelve messages drawn from living Orthodox theology, very suitably bears the title *Living Orthodoxy*. It is truly a harvest-offering of love by the authors to those who share our faith. It represents a conscientious effort to bring the unchanged spirit of crucified, resurrected and above all Pentecostal Orthodoxy close to an English-speaking environment, where each of the writers has been called, either as one of the clergy, or as a layman, to fulfil his diaconate of service.

In a period of religious indifference and metaphysical aridity, it is extremely significant that the twelve articles touch on very topical issues and treat them in an accessible manner so that Orthodox witness may, in accordance with the wish I have often humbly expressed, become the possession of every sincere reader. We have no sense of triumphalism, but the growth, alike qualitative and quantitative, of Orthodoxy in English-speaking lands, which is not a feature of all Christian confessions, lays on us the responsibility that we 'should be ever ready to give an account to any that asks concerning the hope that is in us' (1 Peter 3.15).

We are particularly joyful that those who have participated in this book of essays, based on a living experience of Orthodox theology, demonstrate its ecumenical spirit, that of unity in diversity, and of harmony between very different voices. Any reader will grasp that the common characteristic of the articles that follow is the experience of liturgical life and more specifically of the holy eucharist. The spiritual worship of the Orthodox Church is expressed in every language in the same manner, because the glory of the king's daughter, the glory of the Church as bride of Christ, is within, surrounded and embroidered by the wrought gold clothing of Holy Tradition (Psalm 44.14 Septuagint).

All Orthodox Christians will acknowledge, whether they came into the Church at birth or by later personal decision, that the unique experience of worship in our Church is translated into a personal transfiguration of the interior human being. When cultivated in the internal spiritual life of Orthodox Christians, it penetrates their whole approach to life and their attitude to the world.

For this reason we paternally recommend this work, not only as useful material for reading, but as a true joy, from which will come a confirmation of the ecclesiastical conscience of the Christian. This is the blessed 'Amen' of assent in our lives.

To conclude, we wholeheartedly give all those who will read this book our paternal and Patriarchal blessing, and call down on all the grace and boundless mercy of the Lord.

Bartholomew of Constantinople, in fervent prayer towards God.

Acknowledgements

This book has been made possible through the generosity of the
Hellenic Cultural Centre (a confederation of eleven organizations,
based in Britain), which originally organized the symposium,
Orthodoxy in Our Lives, early in 1992. In particular, we would like
to thank Lydia Carras, who, as chairman of the Hellenic Cultural
Centre, initiated the project, and Maria Wenneker, representative
on the Hellenic Cultural Centre of the National Trust for Greece,
who organized the lectures themselves. Costa Cleanthous and Niki
Beveridge have been very supportive while chairing the Hellenic
Cultural Centre during the preparation of this book.

We are the grateful beneficiaries, through the Hellenic Cultural
Centre, of financial support from the same source as that which
assisted the translation of five works by modern Greek Orthodox
theologians into English (published in a series by St Vladimir's
Seminary Press), as also the collected essays on the history of the
Church of Cyprus by Benedict Englezakis (published by Variorum).

The chapter by Metropolitan Anthony is an edited version of
three talks which he gave at the Russian Orthodox Cathedral in
Kensington, London. We would like to thank the London parish of
the Diocese of Sourozh for their permission to use this material.

Dr H. Tristram Engelhardt Jr wishes to express his gratitude
to Father George Eber of St Anne Institute, Tulsa, Oklahoma, for
his patience in re-reading numerous ancestral drafts of his chapter.

The chapter by Costa Carras is based on an extended essay on
the doctrine of the Holy Trinity in relation to political thought and
action, which appeared in Vol. 3 of *The Forgotten Trinity* (BCC,
1990).

Andrew Walker's chapter is a revised version of a talk given at a conference of the Russian Orthodox Diocese of Sourozh at Hawkhurst in 1993 and published by the diocese in 1995.

We would finally like to thank Simon Jenkins for assisting us in the editing process, and SPCK for agreeing to publish the book with enthusiasm.

Introduction

There is a view quite prevalent in ecumenical circles that Orthodox Christians spend so much time in Church services that they never face up to the great issues of the day, whether political, social or moral. Such a view is reinforced by the media, which typically characterize the Orthodox as exotic or oriental creatures who have never seriously reformed their traditions or come to terms with the modern era stemming from the Enlightenment. The favoured word whispered behind the backs of Orthodox Christians is 'primitive'.

The Orthodox could react to such charges with counter-charges of their own. The modern world, they might say, has reneged on Christian traditions because of faith in rational solutions to problems and a commitment to progress. Standing as we do at the door of a new millennium, where faith in Enlightenment certainties has diminished in the lengthening shadow of the nuclear bomb, ecological mismanagement of the planet, and growing alienation and terror in our inner cities, modernity can no longer be held up as the arbiter of all that is good, decent and hopeful.

Furthermore, if being primitive means that we adhere to the 'apostolic deposit of faith' handed down through the Scriptures, councils, and Fathers of the Church, then we plead guilty as charged. We might also insist that spending a great deal of time in Church is not an escape into fantasy or unreality, but a turning to an encounter with God who meets us in the divine Liturgy and calls us to at-one-ment with him for the life of the world.

However, as fair as some of these counter-charges may be, it is true that the Orthodox Church faces many crises at the present time which threaten its Christian witness in the world. There is, for

1

example, a marked secular streak in Greek society augmented (these days) by tourism and the mass media. The Church in Russia, having survived the Soviet era with a host of martyrs, now has to come to terms both with Western influences and a Slavophile resurgence at home.

With the exception of Greece and Cyprus, the Church in the Orthodox heartlands has little continuous experience of living under democratic systems and, beyond this, there lies the immense problem of facing up to cultural and religious pluralism – of which one example is the tragedy of former Yugoslavia. The Orthodox Diaspora, on the other hand, is a minority Christian presence in Western societies which are culturally heterogeneous, but largely indifferent towards any organized religion.

In the light of the challenge of the modern world to the Orthodox Church, the Hellenic Cultural Centre was concerned in its 1992 symposium, *Orthodoxy in Our Lives*, to address some of the problems as well as to inform, in a conciliatory and open way, Orthodox Christians and members of other Christian bodies of Orthodox approaches to contemporary issues. Naturally, these issues were raised and discussed in the particular context of Orthodox Christians living in Western Europe, since the Hellenic Cultural Centre, a confederation of cultural organizations, has been active for many years in the Greek and Greek Cypriot community in Britain.

In the event, the series of lectures under the patronage of Archbishop Grigorios of Thyatira, was so successful that it was felt that the original five speakers – Metropolitan John of Pergamon, Bishop Kallistos of Diokleia, Metropolitan Athanasios of Hercegovina, Bishop Basil of Sergievo, and Dr Jamie Moran – should be joined by others in preparing papers for a book on Orthodox approaches to contemporary problems. As a result, we have augmented the original talks with contributions from Metropolitan Anthony of Sourozh, as well as pieces from lay men and women, most of whom live in Great Britain. We are particularly pleased that our distinguished authors represent many Orthodox jurisdictions: the Patriarchates of Constantinople, Antioch, Moscow, and Belgrade.

We make no apologies for opening the book with a number of papers on the Orthodox ethos and the centrality of prayer and worship to its life. Part of our 'primitive' image stems from the fact that we consider worship to be the highest calling of human beings. Inevitably, however, while the later chapters range from politics to psychology, ecology to consumerism, family life to bereavement, art to ethics and prophecy, we have not been able, in this one volume, to cover all the contemporary issues which the Orthodox Church faces.

What does emerge from the following pages, we believe, is evidence that Orthodox Christians are responding to the challenges of the present day, and that Tradition, far from keeping a religion archaic, smelling of mothballs and hidden away like outdated clothes in a closet, is nothing less than the voice of the Holy Spirit to the Church, which needs to be heard afresh in every generation. In this respect it is true, without doubt, that the Orthodox Church needs to be constantly renewed by the Spirit in order to be faithful to the gospel and hence relevant to the world.

Emerging from these papers also, is what we might call a 'particular tone of voice', which we might call eirenic or dialogic. In this respect, it does not follow that the editors agree with all that the contributors have written, or indeed that the contributors will agree with each other in every respect. The Orthodox Church champions unchanging credal truths, but it also encourages freedom of exchange in wide areas of theological opinion, as well as practical action. This follows from the conciliar nature of Orthodoxy. Furthermore, as many of our authors realize, especially those living in Great Britain, dialogue is even more essential in this present age, because very often the Orthodox themselves do not know the treasures of their own Tradition. Consequently, questioning young people often need to be wooed back to the Church in which they were born with good arguments and evidence that Orthodoxy is relevant to their lives.

While it is true that the Orthodox Church has little experience of proselytizing in the West, we do need to give an account of the hope within us for those friends in other denominations who wish both to understand us and hear what we have to say about the Church in the modern world. This does not mean to say that our 'particular tone' will never have a polemical edge as we seek to challenge the secular apathy and consumer hedonism of this present age. Christianity is a serious calling, and while we wish to speak to all those who will listen in love, it is the truth that we wish to talk about as it is revealed to us in Christ.

Nevertheless, to adopt 'a particular tone of voice' is to declare that we seek fellowship rather than confrontation with others. For this reason we are most pleased, and think it truly appropriate, that the Ecumenical Patriarch, Bartholomew of Constantinople, should have contributed the foreword to this book, open as he has been to ecumenical encounter and Christian reconciliation. By the same token, we are also especially glad that Metropolitan Anthony of Sourozh has contributed both a major chapter on death and bereavement, and an envoi. His presence in Great Britain over the last five decades has been of the most crucial significance not only in establishing an Orthodox presence in Britain, but in sowing the Orthodox message in British soil with authority, profound insight and grace.

Finally, we would like to highlight an issue of current English usage which has not yet become a problem in many Orthodox countries. In contemporary Western culture, the words 'man' or 'mankind' are not always heard as including both men and women. In this respect, while we have not asked all our writers to translate *anthropos* as 'human', rather than 'man' (for sometimes correct usage does not always make for good English prose), we would like to reiterate what for a Greek and a Russian is self evident: *anthropos* is always inclusive of men and women. Consequently, 'man' and 'mankind' is always understood by Orthodox thinkers to mean all of humankind, and not only men.

Costa Carras and Andrew Walker

The Orthodox Vision of Wholeness

Gillian Crow

The Orthodox Church's reputation for clinging insistently to Tradition often gives the impression that it has no message to bring to contemporary society. Cut off, so it is thought, by geography, culture and a stultifying attitude of mind, which hides behind the word 'tradition' as an excuse for lack of change, it appears complacent and stagnating, without drive or vision; a showpiece for exotic and suspect rituals which obscure if not falsify the gospel.

'Western' Christianity, on the other hand, is moving fast, in ways which tend to provoke an increasing polarization between what is generally called liberalism, but which could better be termed modernism, and a resulting reactionary fundamentalism. To some extent cutting across Church boundaries, this polarization, exaggerated by media coverage to the detriment of the voice of traditional Christians of all denominations, nevertheless creates divisions running counter to the positive ecumenical advances which have become such an important feature of modern Christian life.

Such polarization and fragmentation may be lamented, but they are rarely understood as symptomatic of serious disorder. Against this attitude of division, Orthodoxy insists on wholeness as a basic concept of Christianity. This is expressed not only in terms of the unity implied by Christ's prayer, 'that they might all be one', but as an underlying principle which permeates every aspect of the faith. It is perceived both in contemplating the Trinity and in the eschatological vision of the Church and the world as they will be on that day, towards which the cosmos moves, when 'God shall be all in all'. It is this vision of God-given wholeness, handed on and in the process of fulfilment by the Church, which is at the heart of Tradition.

A Holistic Faith

The tendency to divide might at first glance appear inherent in Christianity, with a pedigree going back, so it seems, to the opposition of good and evil on the first pages of Genesis. This view comes dangerously close to seeing human beings created in a dualist mould, in which soul and body are seen respectively as the sacred and profane elements of the person. Later, the New Testament was interpreted in some quarters as opposing faith and works, and Church history went on to divide worship from doctrine, the Bible from Tradition, and one denomination from another.

In this way, fragmentation and individualism are often accepted as normative within Christianity, as they are in modern society. The understanding of wholeness as a Christian principle is marginalized or lost, to such an extent that the very word 'holism' is now often considered to have unchristian overtones, as if it were a modern invention, leaving people to look outside Christianity for many of the elements they ought to find there. Into the gap has stepped the New Age movement, which brokers a positive, holistic attitude to the created world and the environment as its own ideas, which are allegedly absent in Christianity. That in turn has the effect of making Christians suspicious of such concepts, perceiving them as pagan and alien.

Orthodox Christianity, on the other hand, remains a holistic faith in every sense of the word. Dualism, so Orthodoxy remembers – and in this respect it is nearer to Christianity's Judaic heritage than to Greek philosophy – is a pagan idea. The ancient vision of the Church, of creation, of the human person, of faith and worship, of

Scripture and Tradition, of prayer and action, was holistic. The holistic Tradition of Orthodoxy is an interwovenness of beliefs, practices, worship and life as the one whole faith of the Body of Christ. Faith expressed with the heart, mind and body in worship is to be lived out as a total vision of Christianity which cannot be compartmentalized.

That is a long way from the common perception of Tradition as something dead, and the modernist as the person with the vision and the drive to accomplish that vision, in direct contrast to the fossilized and fearful traditionalist who clings to outmoded beliefs and forms for their own comforting sake.

Orthodoxy does not accept such a time-bound view. It does not look to the past so much as live in the awareness of the eternal 'now' of the undivided Church in heaven and earth, in which modern Christians are contemporaneous and in communion with the saints and Fathers of earlier ages. The Body of Christ, sharing the mind of Christ, is one living reality. Orthodoxy is therefore uncomfortable with such terms as 'Church Militant' and 'Church Triumphant'. The Church is one, and even if the visible part of it may not yet have fulfilled its divine potential, that potential still remains. The Church is alive with the breath of the Holy Spirit and capable of expressing the divine spark afresh in every century, in whatever ways and directions the Spirit wills. This dynamic movement and action of the Spirit characterizes Tradition.

Freedom from fear is the hallmark of the dynamism of the Spirit. The Orthodox keeper of Tradition is not someone who clings to medieval beliefs through fear of letting go of what is no longer seriously tenable in the present age. He or she is a person who recognizes from experience certain truths as central to the gospel message and way of life, and is not afraid to remain faithful to them despite ridicule or persecution.

It is easy to think that it is only ridicule, and not persecution, which is encountered today. The Orthodox churches of the former

Communist bloc have suffered levels of physical persecution in this century which outdo in scope anything devised under Diocletian. Their martyrs have witnessed to a faith which was not the comfortable self-enhancing modernism which seeks to reconcile religious adherence to modern society, nor the Success Gospel promise of worldly well-being; such attitudes could hardly have withstood militant atheism. They came face to face with the challenge of accepting or rejecting the resurrection, and only through their experience of its truth were they able to give their lives, and in doing so demonstrate that truth to others in a wholeness of faith and action.

Instead of separating faith from works, the sacred from the secular, belief from worship or the material from the spiritual, Orthodoxy sees a mystery of unity. Standing in awe before the God of love, the Church experiences the fact that faith and worship are a wholeness, that the human person is a wholeness, that life should not be divided into religious and non-religious spheres as if the infinite God could be shrunk to manageable dimensions. The Christian is called to transfigure the whole of life and the whole of creation.

The wholeness of faith and worship goes beyond the *lex orandi lex credendi* ('the law of prayer is the law of belief') often quoted. The beauty of Orthodox doctrine, with its emphasis on love and joy, is reflected in services which overflow with light, colour and richness of sound. The singing, the colourfully vested priest surrounded by icons, candles and clouds of incense, are all offered as the Church's heartfelt response to the mystery of God's love.

The Divine Liturgy, a participation in the kingdom, is a superabundance echoing the gospel message and involving the whole person, both body and soul, and all the senses. It is a living out of the gospel message of God joining himself to created matter for all eternity through the incarnation, resurrection and ascension of Christ, who healed people's bodies as well as their souls and who took his own body into eternity. He is not a creator who divides the human person into lofty and disposable parts, nor one who views the earthly manifestation of his body, the Church, as nothing but a human institution.

Therefore, such aspects of Orthodoxy as Church ritual, the understanding of creation and the nature of the Church cannot be seen as peripheral and optional to Christianity. They are a vital part of the fullness of Tradition, without which the Body of Christ is disfigured and maimed.

Person, Creation and Church

Too often, contemporary Christianity seems to focus on the immediately apparent. The gospel is approached from the viewpoint of the human eye rather than from God's vision. The Church is seen only in terms of the organization on the ground, without reference to its eschatological perspective. People are judged without reference to the divine image at their core. Creation is exploited as a tool of imperfect humanity, instead of being cherished as the resplendent handiwork of God. Orthodoxy, by contrast, speaks in terms of the vision of the glorious potential of all things, which is not idle idealism, but freedom to grow Godwards instead of becoming enslaved to human limitations.

Three areas in particular illustrate the contribution which Orthodoxy can make to modern Christian understanding: the wholeness of the person, the wholeness of creation and the wholeness of the Church.

Orthodoxy understands the human person as a unique creature of soul and body together, both of which are capable of communing with Creator and creation, and both of which are offered eternal life.

Made of the earth's matter, humans have a kinship with the earth; they are as dependent on the food chain as any other creature.

11

Yet they are also made in the divine image, alive with God's spirit, his very breath; they have a kinship with God. They are therefore in a unique position in relation to both the created and the divine, in a situation of interrelation with the world and with God.

The earth was created for humanity and humanity was created for the earth. That is a vision – not just a holistic vision but a sacramental vision – of the place of humankind in the world and its unique vocation as priest of creation, offering it in love, thanksgiving and adoration to God, sanctifying all things, serving all things. It is a process of giving, not of taking. Each member of the human race is called to be a fellow-worker with God, blessing and consecrating the cosmos, offering back to him in love this world with which they are one. It is a eucharistic vision of creation, and humans are eucharistic beings.

The Orthodox reading of Genesis, which is seen neither in literalist terms, nor as an out-of-date fairy tale, but as a deep theological understanding of the human condition, awakens the Christian to the beauty of humanity as well as its shortcomings. Certain Church Fathers differentiate between the 'image' and 'likeness' of God, as used in Genesis, in which the human person is made. The image is seen as something which is given, while the likeness is the potential to be achieved by growing in spiritual maturity: 'the measure of the stature of the fullness of Christ', as the New Testament puts it. The image of God in a person is never lost, although it may be distorted or buried so deep that it is no longer apparent. The likeness remains a goal towards which each person can struggle, a goal made attainable for imperfect humanity through the grace offered by the Lord Jesus Christ.

Orthodoxy regards the created world as 'very good', according to the words of Genesis. It does not see humanity at the fall as descending into total depravity and a resultant tainting of all creation with evil. Rather it sees there the loss of humanity's original communion with God, and the world's consequent suffering at human hands. It looks forward eagerly to that day when the whole creation will be renewed and God will be 'all in all', restoring both humanity and the cosmos of which it is part to its intended glory.

Such an outlook, which is very different to what commonly passes for the Augustinian view, acknowledges humanity as both the pinnacle of creation and its steward. Humanity is not a tyrannical overlord whose charge to have dominion over the earth means the earth's enslavement, but instead is the master in Christ's image, the servant king and priest who kneels to wash the feet of his creatures, heals their ills and restores divine harmony to the wind and the waves.

In the current ecological crisis in which the world finds itself, those who have in the past understood the Genesis command to 'have dominion' as licence to dominate and exploit for humanity's own ends, have found themselves without a relevant environmental theology. Ecologists have preferred to look to other religions such as Buddhism for a sympathetic understanding. Many Christians have belatedly reacted by seeking a 'creation theology' to underpin what seems to them to be new and hitherto unchristened ideas.

Orthodoxy's understanding – not as such a compartmentalized 'creation theology', but simply part of its all-encompassing theology – has therefore an important role to play in this field. Since its ecology conference on the island of Patmos in 1988, the first day of the ecclesiastical year, 1st September, has been designated an annual Day of Creation when prayers for the environment should be offered throughout the Orthodox Church worldwide. This could usefully be taken up by other Churches, together with the wider dissemination of Orthodox views and publications on ecology. It is one area where the Orthodox Tradition, unseen so long in the West that its ideas seem 'new' rather than ancient, could put Christianity at the forefront of global thinking; where the Holy Spirit could be truly seen to be infusing the Church and through it leading the world towards fulfilling its divine potential.

The Orthodox understanding of both creation and the image of God in humanity is further revealed in icons. An icon demonstrates that matter is capable of becoming spirit-bearing. The word 'icon' means 'image', and the sacred painted images of Christ and the saints venerated in church and in the home are a sign of the incarnation. They express the wonder that created matter could be permeated by the divine, that the uncontainable and invisible God could take on a material body so that he could be seen, touched and painted. Icons are also reminders that the divine image within each person, towards which he or she has the power to grow in the Holy Spirit, is to be hallowed and venerated.

In practical terms, this is demonstrated in confession, which is not the recital of a list of misdemeanours, but an occasion for a person to look into the face of Christ as into a mirror and to see, honestly, him- or herself reflected there to a lesser or greater extent. The wise priest will not only try to correct those features which are distortions of the divine, but will go further to reveal to the penitent those features which are potentially true reflections of the Saviour. It is a moment when both body and spirit, which together have participated in sinfulness, can together receive divine healing.

The image of God in humanity is acknowledged in the course of Orthodox services when the priest censes all the icons in the church; not only those on the iconostasis and the walls, but the living icons, clergy and congregation. The glory and sanctity of the human person, even in its tentative, potential state, is also reinforced daily by prayer before the icons which remind the worshipper that all the people he or she will encounter during the course of the day are also icons of God, images of the Lord Jesus Christ. Whether they are respectable members of society or the beggar in the doorway, they are to be treated with exactly the same veneration as painted icons, as Christ calls his followers to minister to his image in others in the Parable of the Sheep and the Goats.

An icon portrays more than its subject's physical aspect. Through the traditional use of various techniques and conventions it depicts the whole person, body and spirit. It reveals Christ to be fully man, fully God. It reveals the saints not only in their ascetic struggle, but as having attained the victory, in the glory of their realized potential. That serves as a reminder of the reality of God's vision, of the potential greatness to which he calls everyone and which involves the complete person.

This precludes the false separation of the Christian life into sacred and secular compartments: the first limited perhaps to Sunday mornings and a few pious minutes of prayer each day, the second ruling every other aspect of living. Faith and spirituality are called to permeate daily life. Conversely, sin does not begin or end with the physical nature. Any sin committed by the body has first taken root in the heart, soul and will of a person, and evil thoughts can only be put into practice by the body. The two work not so much in opposition as in collusion.

Orthodox worship, both private and public, is necessarily a holistic event. All five senses are used, and posture is regarded as an integral part of prayer life. The casual armchair slouch of the person who considers the body of no significance if the soul is praying is alien to an Orthodox, who in standing, kneeling or prostrating dedicates every sinew to worship, in adoration, repentance, thanksgiving and self-offering. The sign of the cross is used as a physical way of praying the 'amen' at the conclusion of prayers, of dedicating one's life to the Trinity, of literally putting one's weight behind one's words.

The whole of life can be suffused with prayer. Orthodoxy is famous for the Jesus Prayer, which can be said more or less continuously in an act of consciously bringing oneself into the divine presence throughout the day. It can thus be a way of uniting the humdrum and the apparently secular to the sacred; of bringing eternity into the worldly situation; of coming face to face with divine love in order to bring it in turn to those one meets in ordinary life.

15

Seen in that way, it is by no means the purely mystical exercise or even 'Christian mantra' which some people would make of it, but another way in which wholeness is lived out in Orthodox experience.

The Orthodox use of fasting and feasting is another way of integrating the person, when the body joins with the soul in the life of prayer, according to its own capabilities. Christ linked prayer and fasting in the Gospels, and the Orthodox Church follows his words and example. The whole person enters into the preparation of discipleship and repentance which is Lent, not only through the deep theological prayers of the *Triodion*, the liturgical book for the season, but also through physical hunger which can awaken hunger for God, and the realization that one does not live by bread alone. In the same way, the whole person rejoices at the paschal banquet, the incomparable feast in which spiritual joy is reflected in the richness of traditional Easter foods.

The practice of fasting and feasting, like prayers before the icons, is also a way in which worship and the divine awareness are made evident in the home. The whole rhythm of life becomes one with the Church year, as the betrayal of Christ and the crucifixion are remembered at the weekly Wednesday and Friday fasts, and the resurrection is celebrated every Sunday.

The symbolism of the Church is also repeated in the home. The house is blessed with holy water at Epiphany (which Orthodoxy keeps as the feast of Christ's baptism in the Jordan). The family is regarded as a colony of the kingdom, and the house as a house church. This is demonstrated during the marriage service, when the bride and groom are crowned king and queen of their new household. The crowns also represent the crowns of martyrdom, of that sacrificial love which gives of itself unreservedly. The couple are given an icon which will form the foundation of their home's icon corner, a focus of divine presence where they can pray together. Family prayers before the icons are a feature of many Orthodox homes.

16

It is the mother's role to light the votive lamps and cense the icons, just as she will probably be the person who provides the vegan foods of the fasting seasons and the customary festal dishes. In other words, she is 'priest' of the home, the hallower of life, the person who maintains the rhythm of the Church's year in the family.

The spiritual dimension of eating finds its ultimate fulfilment within the Tradition in the sacrament of Holy Communion. The Orthodox Divine Liturgy is not chiefly a remembrance of the Last Supper, nor an earthly mock-up of the wedding banquet of the kingdom, but participation in the one event. The whole Church on earth and in heaven is present, and is made visible to the worshippers in the icons. As at the annunciation, by the power of the Holy Spirit, God joins himself to physical matter: the bread and wine become the body and blood of Christ.

All the sacraments are occasions when everyday material substances such as water, bread, wine and oil become vehicles of the Spirit. Water, normally used for physical cleansing, becomes able by the operation of the Holy Spirit to cleanse from sin. As an element essential to life, but also capable of bringing physical death, it effects spiritual death and rebirth. The person who dies with Christ also rises with him from the baptismal font to participate potentially in the new life of the resurrection. Orthodoxy sees the whole of life as sacramental, capable of being changed by the Holy Spirit into the presence of the kingdom. The world, society and secular life is to be transfigured by Christ's living presence in the Christian.

Miracles are understood as occasions when by the grace of God the conditions of the kingdom are fulfilled; when human faith, compassion and love are joined to the divine, allowing God to bring his healing power to restore part of his creation to its intended splendour and wholeness. They are occasions when the divine potential becomes reality. This is a long way from the view often put forward, both by unthinking believers and their sophisticated detractors, of gratuitous supernatural events performed by a Father

Christmas-like figure, who doles out magic at the whim of his gullible followers.

The virgin birth and the resurrection have come under attack by certain modern theologians, to whom they appear unnecessary, perhaps offensive relics of a bygone world-view. A God who is confined by the sceptics to the realm of the spiritual, or who is even the product of human psychological processes, has no immediate affinity with the material world and cannot disrupt natural laws. God is kept in his place, which is conveniently far removed from the world.

Orthodox experience, from the Gospel events to present examples, speaks otherwise. It speaks of a God who, loving the whole person, heals, redeems and brings into eternity the goodness of creation. Every atom of matter is cherished, beginning with those which constitute the Body of Christ and ending with the whole cosmos on that day when God shall be all in all. Until then, the Body of Christ is manifested each Sunday, the day of resurrection, when the Church comes together to celebrate the Divine Liturgy.

An Orthodox church celebrates only one Liturgy a day. If to a non-Orthodox this seems a mere detail, it only underlines an important difference of attitude. Details matter, being part of the whole. Certainly one has to distinguish between ritualistic hair-splitting which is the product of human custom and authentic inspired Tradition. In this case, the detail has theological importance: the parish constitutes the wholeness of the Church, the visible Body of Christ in a given place, and therefore cannot be divided into 8 o'clock, 9 o'clock and 10 o'clock sittings.

An individual or a member of an isolated family group travels to church knowing that it is not an ordinary journey from one location to another, but a coming together to constitute a body, the Body of Christ on earth. To assemble as the Church is therefore already a sacramental act, making visible the mystery of the incarnation.

The Royal Priesthood of All Believers

The Church is the gathering of the *laos*, the whole people of God. A lay person is not, as in the popular usage of the word 'layman', an amateur or an ignoramus. Instead, a lay person has the highest status, which all the baptized share: 'a chosen race, a royal priesthood, a holy nation, God's own people', as St Peter says in his first epistle.

Orthodox Tradition guards the concept of the royal priesthood of all believers. At chrismation – the second sacrament of initiation which is administered immediately after baptism – the newly baptized person, anointed with the holy chrism, is 'sealed with the gift of the Holy Spirit' as king, priest and prophet, a member of the *laos*, which is 'God's own people'. This confers to all the baptized, including infants, full membership of the Church in which there is 'neither Jew nor Greek, slave nor free, male nor female', in St Paul's words.

Each person, made in the image of God and living in a continuing movement of growth towards the likeness, the divine potential, is a holy member of the Church, dedicated to the absolute calling of taking up his or her cross to follow Christ to the self-sacrifice of Calvary and beyond to eternal life. Each person is called to be completely open to the Holy Spirit given at baptism. Each person is called to be a witness to Christ, with the totality of life and, if necessary, of death, as so many Orthodox have found in Eastern Europe in the twentieth century, as they have rediscovered the correlation between the words 'witness' and 'martyr'. The *laos* is a wholeness, the Body of Christ in which each member is irreplaceably unique, but also a vital part of the one living organism which has as its head not an earthly hierarch but the Lord Jesus Christ.

In this exalted and beautiful vision of the meaning of 'laity', the sacramental priesthood is included. This priesthood can only develop within the universal priesthood of all believers, because it is a position of service, not of power or superiority. The priest is the person chosen and delegated by the *laos* to serve at the altar, but the laity concelebrate with him and he still remains a member of the *laos*. That is made clear in the way he serves the Liturgy. He stands at the head of the congregation, facing east with them, and not on the far side of the altar in the place where only Christ has the right to be. He represents the laity and he also represents Christ, but not in the sense of an *alter Christus*. In an Orthodox Liturgy, Christ remains the only celebrant, just as he remains the head of the Body and the head of the Church.

Tradition regards hierarchical structures as positions of responsibility and service rather than power. The Orthodox bishop standing in the centre of the church surrounded by his flock, as happens at many services, is a familial image of a father surrounded by his children. Church structure has been described as an inverted pyramid, supported ultimately by Christ through the bishops and presbyters, in contrast to the perceived Roman structure of the Pope at the apex of the triangle. Orthodoxy is unequivocal in its rejection of the papal model. Tradition, going back to the first Church Council in Jerusalem, sees the Church in conciliar terms, with each bishop having an equal charism, and this principle of conciliarity has been cherished by Orthodoxy down to the present.

The equality of dedication and mutual reverence of the royal priesthood of all believers, straight from the New Testament, is as exciting and revolutionary as any modernist agenda. However, it has to be said that it is in practice often forgotten by the Orthodox themselves. Both clergy and non-clergy are often wrongly inclined to equate ordination with professionalism. Furthermore, although the whole *laos* may be said to concelebrate the Liturgy, reception of communion by the people has tended to be the exception rather than the rule, and is often actively discouraged, so that the doubtful human custom of infrequent communion has come to be confused with authentic Tradition.

It is also a commonplace for hierarchs to address their flocks as 'dear brothers and sisters', and having done so to think they have discharged their obligation to see them in those terms. History has given power to bishops and they have rarely been conformed to the authority of the servant king whom they were supposed to represent. Nevertheless, the vision, the image of the Church as divinely intended, the potential not yet realized but attainable through grace, remains like an ancient icon beneath the accretions of worldly pollution. In striking instances it still shines brightly.

The place of women is another area in which tradition's vision of the wholeness of the Church is waiting to be rediscovered. Orthodoxy does not have a good record for treating its members as 'neither male nor female'. The vital role of women in the Gospels, the honour accorded to those in the early Church who were given the title 'equal to the Apostles', has not been sustained. Although there has been talk for some time of restoring the New Testament institution of deaconesses, which Orthodoxy kept until the thirteenth century, this has not yet been implemented. Discussion of the ordination of women, a topic which has reached Orthodoxy from outside, rather than arising spontaneously within it, has barely taken place. The status quo has been accepted for the most part unthinkingly, in another confusion of Tradition with traditionalism, that blind lethargy of acceptance without any prayerful thought.

The vision of the Church as a model which the world was intended to follow has very often been replaced by the sad spectacle of an institution challenged by the lead of secular society. However, many people are now acknowledging the part which women – the silent, dogged babushkas – have played in keeping alive the Church in Russia during the years of Soviet persecution. St Paul's words remains true that the communion of saints is a wholeness, realized in eternity but still potential on earth, in which there is truly neither male nor female.

21

The struggle to be a saint of God, expressed by the Russian St Seraphim of Sarov in the last century as the acquisition of the Holy Spirit, is the goal of the Orthodox life. Sainthood, like Tradition, may seem to today's culture to be a word from the past with little relevance to the consumer society. Like the idea of holistic living, both conjure up an unworldly image which invites a certain mockery.

It is often forgotten that it is the Christian vocation to expect the same mockery as the Master. Growth towards the potential which God wills both for the human person and for the Church, within the wholeness of Tradition, is an all-absorbing, exciting process, but it inevitably remains at odds with secular aspirations. It is the pearl of great price, entrusted as a treasure to the Orthodox Church, but at the same time a vocation towards which the Church must still grow.

2

Living in the Future

Bishop Basil of Sergievo

I would like to begin by quoting from two sources which are not Scripture. One of them is a poster in a school room, a poster which has on it a picture of a pre-war locomotive and says in bold letters: 'Modern life is rubbish!' The other comes from a recent Sunday supplement, in which I read: 'Nostalgia is *the* mental health problem of the future.'

It is certainly true that nostalgia is big business: one only has to think about the music of the sixties, fifties or forties. You can find somebody who loves almost anything from the past. We in Britain have our fair share of theme parks, country museums and Civil War re-enactments. Even the VE Day celebrations of 1995 had a strong element of nostalgia in them. But does this nostalgia, this looking back to the past, have any connection with what we experience in our own return to the Tradition of the Orthodox Church?

From Nostalgia to the Presence of God

My own experience suggests that nostalgia has very little to do with what people are looking for when they become Orthodox. What they seek is something which enables them to look ahead, and to do so with confidence. And yet they do this quite consciously by joining a community which thinks of itself as the Church of the Councils, as being truly apostolic in the sense that simply by being itself it is the Church of the Apostles. They seek that unbroken continuity which the Orthodox Church claims. But continuity with what?

If we look back to the origins of the Church, we find that in the New Testament, Christ begins his proclamation of the gospel, of the 'good news', by saying: 'Repent, for the kingdom of heaven is at hand'. What he does – the miracles, the healings, the exorcisms – are all just pointers to that fact. They are nothing in themselves: others are healing people as well, others are casting out demons, and there is nothing unusual about this. But when Christ does it, it is a sign that the kingdom of heaven is drawing near, that it is 'at hand'.

Again and again in the parables, Christ stresses that the kingdom which he is introducing begins with small things. He uses the image of leaven, of a mustard seed; the kingdom is like a coin, it is like a pearl; it is something small, which when you see it, when you really appreciate it, proves to be extremely valuable.

And yet this is not the only thing he says about the kingdom. He also looks forward to the coming of the kingdom, to its coming with power. 'Verily I say unto you that there be some of you that stand here which shall not taste of death till they have seen the kingdom of God come with power' (Mark 9.1). When Christ speaks to his disciples after the resurrection, he tells them what this means. At the beginning of Acts, he says: 'But ye shall receive power after that the Holy Spirit has come upon you'. That power is then linked with Pentecost, with the gift of the Holy Spirit, but it is also linked with the coming together of the community. It is extremely important to note that in the description of what happened at Pentecost, it is said that the Apostles, with the disciples, were together 'in one place'. We associate that moment with the gift of tongues, the ability to preach the gospel in many languages.

However, at this point I would like to ask a question: when did the first celebration of the eucharist take place? We have in the Gospels a description of the Last Supper; we also have an account in the epistles of Saint Paul of the eucharistic practice of the early Church. But when did the Apostles, for the first time, celebrate this eucharist which we celebrate today? I remember years ago, when I was doing some research in the Bodleian Library at Oxford, coming across the works of an eighteenth-century Roman Catholic patristic scholar. He sought to demonstrate that the first eucharist had taken place at Pentecost. I was struck by the force of his argument, and looking at the New Testament it would appear, although we are not told this, that this is the most likely moment for the first eucharist to have taken place.

In this case it would be no coincidence that in the liturgical practice of the Russian Church, at the very heart of the eucharistic celebration, during the *epiclesis* itself, the prayer for the descent of the Holy Spirit on the gifts is actually interrupted, opened up, and into it is inserted the troparion, or hymn, of the Third Hour. That troparion refers specifically to Pentecost: 'O Lord, who didst send down Thy most Holy Spirit upon Thine Apostles at the third hour, take him not from us, O Good One, but renew him in us who pray unto Thee.'

And so at this central moment in the eucharist, our prayer is that Pentecost will in some sense be repeated; that it will be made new in our midst. As a result, we can say that every Liturgy is in some sense a renewal of Pentecost, every Liturgy breaks down the distance, in time and space, between this present moment and that moment in the past when the disciples were gathered together to receive the gift of the Holy Spirit. Our eucharistic celebration becomes one with that of the Apostles, one because the eternal Spirit of the one God is present with the community at that moment, and can draw it together into oneness across not only spatial barriers, but even the barriers of time. The Holy Spirit draws us into a oneness which is in the end an image, an icon of the oneness of God.

And so there is a clear relationship with the past, between each and every eucharistic celebration and the gathering of the Church at Pentecost. However, it bears no resemblance to nostalgia; instead it is reality, it is the presence of God in our midst.

The Pentecostal Mystery of the Liturgy

I would like now to look at certain other aspects of the realization of that Pentecostal mystery in the eucharist. What I say will certainly be very familiar to priests and deacons, and it will probably be familiar to those who serve in the sanctuary, but to others perhaps it will not. I am thinking about the preparation for the Liturgy which takes place before the initial blessing, 'Blessed is the kingdom...'.

In the course of the *proskomidia*, the preparatory service, the priest first cuts out and places on the paten a cube of bread which is called 'the Lamb', and which in the course of the service will be consecrated for our communion in the Body of Christ. Then from another loaf he cuts a small pyramid of bread, puts it on the right side of the Lamb – on the left side as he himself looks at it, but, of course, on the right side of the Lamb from the Lamb's point of view – and he does this in memory of the Mother of God.

And then, on the left side of the Lamb, he continues in effect to recreate the Church out of particles of bread. He begins with John the Baptist, and here immediately we remember the sequence of icons on the icon screen, with Christ in majesty in the middle, Mary on his right side, and John the Baptist on his left. Then in addition to John the Baptist, he cuts particles for the Old Testament prophets, then for the Apostles. I have always found this extremely significant: he doesn't begin with the Twelve, but says: 'For Peter and Paul, for the Twelve, for the Seventy, and for all the holy Apostles'. The apostolicity of the Church is something much greater than simply the Twelve, or even the Seventy.

Then he goes on to remember the holy hierarchs; then he remembers the martyrs, beginning with St Stephen; then our God-bearing Fathers and Mothers; then the selfless physicians, Cosmas and Damian, Panteleimon and others; then the ancestors of God, Joachim and Anna, together with other saints who belong to the

26

memory of the local church. And finally, he remembers with the ninth particle, the saint whose Liturgy is being celebrated, either St John Chrysostom or St Basil the Great.

Having created on the left side of Christ nine categories of saintly figures from the past of the Church, below them he begins to cut out particles for the living and the dead. In other words, this whole image of the Church is brought together from the past: from Old Testament days, through the days of the Incarnation, into the early Church, into the history of the Church, and down to the present time. This whole historic panorama is represented in particles of bread on the paten.

During the Liturgy, these particles are 'topped up' with particles cut from the prosforas, which the Orthodox faithful give in with the names of people they have remembered. This whole collection – this icon of the Church in bread – is then carried through the church at the Great Entrance and placed on the holy table. When, during the Liturgy, the Lamb is consecrated for communion, it is the Lamb surrounded by the Church. We pray for the descent of the Spirit not simply upon the Lamb, but upon all those present. We ourselves are present on the paten, next to the Lamb, in the particles of bread which represent us. So this Pentecostal mystery, which is made new in the living Tradition of the Church, is played out in bread in the course of the eucharistic celebration.

The Eschatological Mystery of the Liturgy

There is also another aspect of the Liturgy which will help to fill out the picture which I would like to develop here. For this, we need to turn to St Maximus the Confessor, the seventh-century theologian and ascetic writer. If we look at the way in which St Maximus understands the development of creation, we find that he sees it beginning with God's creative act, then moving on through a period of movement and development, and receiving its final form

27

in accordance with the ultimate purposes of God. For St Maximus, the development of creation follows this pattern: *genesis, kinesis, stasis*. So the world as created by God is a *directed* event. Even in his understanding of the Scriptures, one can see this same directedness built in. For example, St Maximus says that the Old Covenant is a shadow, the New Covenant is an icon, but the truth – in relation to which this shadow and this icon exist – will come into being only in the age to come.

What, then, is the relationship between the Liturgy which we celebrate and that age to come? In the conventional, late Byzantine interpretations of the Liturgy, as reflected for example in the work of the writer Nikolai Gogol in the nineteenth century, one finds the whole of the eucharist interpreted as an image of the life of Christ. Thus the moment of Christ's birth is reflected in the service of preparation before the opening words, 'Blessed is the kingdom...'. And at the very end of the Liturgy, the blessing of the people with the chalice corresponds to the ascension of Christ.

But this is not the only interpretation possible. Maximus gives another view entirely. For example, whereas for Gogol the preaching and the reading of the Gospel corresponds to Christ's preaching, in Maximus it corresponds to the preaching of the Apostles after the resurrection. This is very significant, because it enables Maximus to see in the movement of the bishop at the Little Entrance first into the sanctuary, and then from the altar to the throne behind the altar, the ascension of Christ to sit at the right hand of the Father. Already, at the very beginning of the Liturgy, Christ's ascension to the Father has symbolically taken place. And so, when the bishop descends from his throne to play his part in the Great Entrance, this corresponds to the second coming of Christ in glory, while the dismissal of the catechumens shortly afterwards represents the last judgment and the separation of the sheep and the goats. In other words, already at the Great Entrance, the age to come is being portrayed before us in the Liturgy.

This has important implications. We tend to think of the 'commemoration' of the Last Supper, the *anamnesis*, as bridging the interval between our present age and the time of Christ. But from the vantage point taken by Maximus the Confessor, it is clear that the 'commemoration' moves backwards from the end of time. In other words, it embraces in itself the whole of history. The celebration of the eucharist as an image or icon of the messianic banquet introduces us to the reality of the age to come. It does not simply look back to the Last Supper, but embraces both the Last Supper and the age to come, from the point of view of the latter.

So it is not simply a question of our being one with the events of Pentecost, being one with the Church of the Apostles. It is also a question of our being one with what will be, with what has yet to be fully realized in this world – and with what cannot be fully realized in this world. I think that here we can begin to see the significance of the dismissal of the catechumens in a new way. The dismissal of the catechumens creates the eschatological community; it creates the community of the last times. It is the critical moment of the Liturgy. The local community of the Church is now reduced only to those who are within, who can in all honesty say, 'Come, Lord Jesus', and mean it with their whole hearts. They are prepared for that moment which stands immediately before them, for which they long and for which they live. It is as if the local community of the Church is on the point of tipping over into the world to come, on that very brink of what God will bring.

Years ago, when it was possible seriously to contemplate the advent of nuclear war, I imagined how you might hear on your radio that nuclear missiles had already left the Soviet Union, headed in this direction. I discussed with a friend and priest what one would do in such a situation. His answer was very interesting: 'I would simply go to the church and begin to celebrate the eucharist.'

How right he was. One would then be ready for whatever happened, because the eucharist, by its very nature, stands at the end of the world. Because of the very nature of the Church, which is bound up with the nature of the eucharist, the Church is always ahead of its time. To the extent that we truly live in the Church, we belong to what will be. And the Church achieves this, not by struggling in this world, but simply by being what it is, by being what God wants it to be. To the extent that the Church is itself, to the extent that it lives in Christ, and is one with Christ, it is not only one with the Church of the Fathers and the Apostles, it is one with the Church of the end of time.

The Church's Calling as a Go-between: the Diaconate

Now what does this mean in practical terms? Does it mean that as a Church community we live in some separate realm, that we are somehow cut off from the world? Clearly the answer to that question must be both 'yes' and 'no'. The Orthodox Church is a Church with definite boundaries, for example, in not accepting communion with other communities. But Christian baptism, by itself, also creates a line between those who have received Christ and have been received by Christ, and those who have not received Christ and have not been received by Christ.

But while these realities – the Church and the world – are distinct, they also are connected. I would therefore like to look at another aspect of the Liturgy which, it seems to me, is of great importance for our understanding of how they are connected. This is the role of the deacon. It is a great privilege when a diocese has a good number of deacons, and without a doubt the nature of the Liturgy is seen with greater clarity when a deacon is taking part.

Some aspects of what I have in mind here can best be grasped by looking at Maximus the Confessor's understanding of the architecture of the church. Imagine that we are in church now, with its icon-screen. Behind the screen is the sanctuary and in it is the altar, which is hidden from the nave, the body of the church. In the

Mystagogy, which is an explication of the deeper significance of the movement of the eucharistic Liturgy, St Maximus also comments on the structure of the church building itself. He says that if the body of the church represents the human body, then the sanctuary represents the soul and the altar within the sanctuary represents the human *nous*, the human spiritual intellect.

At the same time, if the body of the church represents the visible world, the sanctuary represents the invisible world; if the body of the church represents earth, the sanctuary represents heaven; if the body of the church represents this world, the sanctuary represents the world to come, the kingdom of God. Now the significance of a deacon is that it is he, of all the ministers, who moves back and forth between these two worlds most frequently.

If you have had a chance to be in Russia and to take part in a large celebration, you have probably seen a very competent deacon moving much more quickly than anyone else back and forth between the sanctuary and the people. This liturgical role of the deacon, which is seen so clearly here, is something which the Eastern Church has faithfully preserved. While the diaconate disappeared almost completely from the consciousness and the liturgical practice of the Western Churches, in the Eastern Church the deacon's role has been much more appreciated. For the deacon functions as a mediator between two worlds.

If this role is reflected liturgically in his going back and forth, his 'between-ness' is also reflected in the way that he is neither priest nor laity. He is able on the one hand to enter through the holy doors, and yet in his funeral he is buried as a layman. He is able on the one hand to lead the people in prayer, to tell them to bow their heads or do this and that, but at the same time he is able to turn to the clergy to tell them to do this or that. The deacon works in two worlds all the time, and does so effortlessly. This is reflected in the etymology of the word 'deacon' itself. As I discovered recently myself, the word *diakonos* – 'deacon' – and *diakonein* – 'to serve as a deacon' – are related to the word for 'movement' – *kinesis*. The deacon is the one who moves back and forth between two people or two places.

Now if we look at the New Testament, there are interesting examples of this kind of 'deaconing'. Unfortunately, they are obscured in the English translations, but they jump out of the text as soon as you have the Greek in front of you. If you look, for example, at Christ's first miracle, in Cana of Galilee, you will see that the deacons play a very important role. They do not appear in the Authorized Version, where they are called 'servants'; in Greek, however, they are 'deacons'. Mary says to these servants, to the deacons: 'Whatsoever he saith unto you, do it' (John 2.5).

Now these deacons are those who go back and forth between the guests and the master of the feast, and so Jesus tells them: 'We are running out of wine, so go and fill those pots with water and take them to the master of the feast.' This is a completely natural movement, because this is what the deacons would be doing anyway. They would be taking the various dishes and things to drink to the master of the feast, and then the master would look around the room and say: 'take them over there – they do not seem to have anything to drink,' or: 'those guests look like they might enjoy some of this – carry it over there to them.' In this way, the master of the feast would have the whole feast under his control. But it is the deacons who would do the to-ing and fro-ing.

Again, in the temptation in the desert, after Satan is unsuccessful in tempting Christ, we read, 'Then the Devil leaveth him and behold, angels came and ministered unto him' (Matthew 4.11). What it really says is that angels came and 'deaconed' unto him. They acted as his deacons. In other words, they brought him what he needed in order to survive in the desert.

This means that the diaconate is by its very nature a kind of bipolar reality. And this can lead to a certain ambiguity even in the sayings of Jesus. For example, in Matthew 20.26, Christ says:

'Whosoever would be great among you, let him be your minister [your deacon]. Even as the Son of Man came not to be ministered unto [not to be 'deaconed' to] but to minister [to be a deacon, to act as a deacon himself].' Christ refuses the role of being ministered to. He will do the ministering.

However, Christ also says: 'If any man serve me [literally, if any man act as my deacon] let him follow me, and where I am there shall also my servant [my deacon] be. If any man serve me [if any man be my deacon] him will my father honour' (John 12.26). Christ refuses – and yet he also insists – to have someone serve him as deacon. The point that is being made here is that when Christ acts as deacon he ministers the gifts which the Father has given him to those whom he serves, but when the deacon who follows Christ ministers, he ministers the gifts which Christ has given him to others. Christ has his deacons, he has his ministers, but they too are carrying the gifts of God outward into the world.

Among the earliest comments which we have on the Liturgy are those found in the writings of Ignatius of Antioch. I would like to quote from these, because it seems to me that for an understanding of what the deacon is and what the diaconate means for us in relationship to living in Christ in this world, these are very important passages. For example, in his Letter to the Magnesians, Ignatius says:

> I exhort you, be zealous to do all things in harmony with God, with the bishop presiding in the place of God [in other words, in the place of the Father] and the presbyters in the place of the council of the Apostles, and the deacons, who are most dear to me, entrusted with the service of Jesus Christ.
> Letter to the Magnesians, 6.1

The service here is the *diakonia* – with the 'deaconing' of Jesus Christ. In other words, when Ignatius looks at the Liturgy, he does not see Christ in the bishop or in the priest, he sees Christ in the deacon. Again in the Letter to the Trallians, he writes: 'Likewise, let all respect the deacons as Jesus Christ, even as the bishop is the type of the Father, and the presbyters as the council of God and the college of the Apostles.'

For him, the picture is quite clear, for in his Letter to the Philadelphians, he encourages them to 'appoint a deacon to go as the ambassador of God to the Church in Antioch'. This is the appropriate role of the deacon, to serve as a 'go-between', linking the church in Philadelphia and the church in Antioch. So the deacon provides an image of Christ in the eucharistic service as understood by St Ignatius.

The point I wish to make here is this. The life in Christ which was given to us at Pentecost, and which is given again in that renewal of Pentecost which is the eucharistic Liturgy, the very heart of our experience of Church life, the very heart of our experience of Orthodoxy, is a Pentecostal life. It is a life in which the role and presence of the Spirit is absolutely essential for our being what we are called to be. And at the same time, it is a *diaconal* life, because the Church exists in a mediatory way between God and the world, as Christ himself acted in mediation, between God and Man.

In that sense, our life involves a bearing of gifts, but it also involves the offering of gifts. In the miracle at Cana, the deacons, in their diaconal role, bring the wine to the master of the feast. They also offer it to him to find out what should be done with it: 'where do we distribute it, what do we do with it?' So there is a two-way process here of mediation – an offering and a giving.

The Spirit at Work in the World

In our particular situation, we are asked as Christians – and not simply as Orthodox – to offer the whole of creation in our own person back to God. This is true for each one of us individually, and as the

34

Church. The creation has been given to us; now we are asked to give it back. But in that world which we have been given, the Spirit is already at work. I have spoken of the Pentecostal gift that descends on the Church in the course of the Liturgy. But the Spirit blows where he will throughout creation, and I would like to conclude by pointing out how in our own liturgical practice this reality is acknowledged and accepted.

I would like to begin with baptism, because we think of baptism as being the uniting, the making one, of a person with the death and resurrection of Christ. But think of the questions which are asked before the baptism takes place. First come the renunciations, and then finally the person to be baptized is asked: 'Hast thou united thyself with Christ?' Unless that person can say 'yes' – in other words, unless that uniting has in some sense already taken place – the baptism cannot go ahead. In other words, even before baptism, the Spirit of Christ, which is the only power able to unite us with Christ, has already been at work in this person.

The same ambiguity is found in the service for the reception of converts by Chrismation. Absolution, the sacrament of forgiveness, takes place just after the person has been physically led forward into the centre of the church by the priest, and only after absolution does Chrismation take place. Yet we give absolution only to those who are already members of the Church. In other words, through the work of the Spirit in that person, entry into the Church has somehow already taken place before the Chrismation itself. That entry into the Church is an inner reality which is then taken up sacramentally into the communal life of the Church.

Even in ordination, a true vocation, a vocation which comes first from God and has then been recognized by the people, is required before the ordination can go forward. Only then, when we know that the calling of God is active in that person, making him a reader, subdeacon, deacon or priest, only then can that person be ordained. And here we should note carefully that the candidate for the

35

diaconate is led through the holy doors – through which only the ordained may go – before his ordination.

The same thing is true of marriage. Unless the couple are already one, unless they have already committed themselves to one another in Christ, they cannot be crowned in church. All these instances are ways in which our own sacramental practice says that the Spirit of God is working both outside and inside the Church, to bring people into life in Christ.

All this teaches us that unless we can recognize the Spirit at work outside our own Orthodox community – in the culture in which we live, in the families to which we belong, in the work situations in which we spend so much of our time, and in other Christian communities – we will not be in touch with reality. Orthodoxy, if it is about anything, is about the real world. And in that real world, God is present, Christ is present, the Spirit of God is present, working to bring people to a fullness of life which we cannot give. Only God can give this life. But if in all humility we accept the gifts which we – not through any virtue of our own – have been given, we may be able to enter into this process in some small way, always remembering that the true actor, the true initiator in all of this is, in fact, God himself.

3

The Eschata in Our Daily Life

Metropolitan Athanasios of Hercegovina

In Greek, we call the first things *protologia*, and the last things *eschatologia*. Neither term can be directly translated into English. The technical term for the latter is 'eschatology', that which concerns the end of time, the last things. But *protologia* I do not think has even a technical translation in English. It concerns what is at the beginning of time, or before the beginning of time. I could speak in simpler terms of a prologue and an epilogue to a book. The reality of our lives is not a book, however, even if that book is the Bible.

A short while ago there was translated into Serbian a copy of Milton's famous *Paradise Lost*. I was present at the presentation of the book, and although I could not say anything about it as a poet, I could say something about Milton's theological approach to the whole issue. I would like to begin by comparing the approach to this matter by Milton on the one hand and by the Orthodox Christian Tradition on the other.

Milton's approach is protological, which means that he looks at the Bible with the emphasis on the beginning of time – on creation, and on its initial state – whereas I would like to see the Bible eschatologically, with the emphasis on the end of time and the final state. To put it in different and simpler language, according to Milton, something happened in the past, and that which happened in the past determines what has happened ever since. In contrast, the attitude of Orthodox Christian theology is that whatever may have happened in the past is one thing; what is to happen in the future is far more important.

When this matter came up with my theological students at the seminary where I teach, I tried to give them a metaphor from a world which Europeans know well, namely football. Allow me to pursue the same metaphor now. Take the attitude in a football game of Maradonna, Linneker or Stoykovich. Their opponents put in a goal or two in the first half, and that of course to some degree determines the style of play of their team. Maradonna, or whoever, has not yet shown what a good player he is. At some point, however, he suddenly, with great flair, puts in a first and then a second goal, and at half time they are equal. People then say that if Maradonna can do that in just two simple shots in the first half, what on earth will he do if he actually starts to play hard in the second half?

The Bible is the playground of the wonder and the miracles of God, and yet the most important thing in the Bible is not the wonders of God, the creation, the saving of the people of Israel and so forth, but rather that it is turned towards the last times, towards what God will do. He, who with so little effort, has already done such great things in past history.

So what God did at the beginning is less important as far as the Bible is concerned, than what he will do in the future – at the end of time. That beautiful book, the Song of Songs, is a book about two people in love, in which the beloved leaves, and yet still draws his lover to himself. This is indeed like our relationship with God, only we are still in the first half; God is drawing us after him into a deeper communion.

Understanding Time

I will now turn to the understanding of time, both in antiquity, and according to the biblical revelation. Antiquity in general – except for the people of Israel, to whom the biblical revelation was given – looks on the past as better than the present, and as the determinant of the future. There was once a paradise which was gradually spoilt:

our desire is to return to that paradise. So it is, for instance, with Odysseus. He too wishes to return to his paradise lost, his island, rather in the same way that Milton looks on it. The end must return to the beginning in a circular movement.

But the biblical understanding is exactly the opposite. Our nostalgia – unlike that of Odysseus, which is the nostalgia of all human beings – is for the future, for what is to come. It is turned not towards the past, but to what is ahead of us. Paradise is not behind us but in front of us. We seek for the person whom Adam lost in paradise, and that person – in the fullness of his glory – we shall find ahead of us.

Take the example of the prodigal son, who having departed from the house of his father, and having failed miserably in life, one day has the nostalgic longing to return to his father's house. On his return, he is met by his father who has already left the house in order to meet his son. My question is, was it the nostalgia to return to the past that drew the son back, or the understanding that his father would come out to meet him? Both must be true. But from the biblical point of view, it is the movement of the father towards the prodigal son which is the most significant. This then is what I mean by the eschatological attitude of the Orthodox Church.

This attitude is illustrated by icons in the Orthodox Christian Tradition, where there is no perspective as in Western art, going into the picture. Instead, the perspective is from the person in the picture towards the viewer. This might be called the 'reverse perspective' of Orthodox iconography, and no doubt for those artists who have gone through schools of fine art it may seem a very naive sort of perspective. But the thing to grasp is that God and the saints come out to greet us as if heaven is already here to enrich our everyday lives.

The ancient view, which we have already discussed in relation to regaining paradise, depended on a recollection of some event in the past. The Orthodox attitude is to a greater extent dependent on calling on the Holy Spirit, who comes to us from the future. The Orthodox liturgical Tradition unites the recollection of the past, the *anamnesis*, with the *epiclesis*, that is the calling on the Holy Spirit. Recollection, the past and history are not abolished, but are rather redefined by the *epiclesis*, which we must always understand eschatologically.

The end of time, to recapitulate, determines the beginning, and not the beginning the end. In the book of Revelation, this is summed up in the famous phrase: 'I am the Alpha and the Omega, the Beginning and the End' (Revelation 21.6). St Maximus the Confessor, who wrote in the seventh century, said that when we make the plan of a house, it is not the first drawings which determine the house. Instead, it is the vision of the architect of how the house will be at the end which determines the beginning, that is the drawings.

What St Maximus said – although I am simplifying his sophisticated philosophical language – is that the mystery of the incarnation of Christ possesses the power to explain the enigmas of the Bible and also to explain and help us understand creation. He who has known the mystery of the cross and the tomb will have reached this point of understanding. However, he who has entered the mystical power of the resurrection will have understood the very purpose of God in his creation and in the revelation of the Bible.

The whole experience of revelation, of the incarnation, did in fact give a great thrust forward to the concept of historical movement and the process of historical change. Before the Bible, and in particular the New Testament, we do not have the same sense of historical time or of development in history. The ancient and the Greek world feared history in this sense. They were afraid of what was new and unexpected, and accepted the past as a stable certainty. That is why what was most important to them was the cosmos, the beautiful stability and perfection of the world, which the ancient Greeks explored.

The great Indian civilization also had a very similar attitude in avoiding historical development. For Gautama Buddha, the whole process of becoming is something to be escaped from, and it is in escaping from it that we can reach nirvana. Whether nirvana is being or non-being is not the important point. The important point is that it was crucial for the Buddha that we leave the process of history, the process of becoming.

For the Bible, history is one of God's great blessings. It is the result of creation and it is what gives meaning to the life and drama of man. But although the Old and New Testaments gave this impulse and encouraged the idea of progress and the creativity of man in history, they could not and did not stop at that point. Without eschatology, history would merely be a succession of events which would have no meaning and no conclusion. The significance and importance of history are not disputed, but we do not stop with the concept of history. If the prodigal son had gone back home and his father had not come out to meet him, then the return would have been in vain.

The incarnation of Christ in history is an affirmation of history. Simultaneously, however, with the eschatological reality of the resurrection, we are freed from the bonds of a historical record which is always moving on, always evolving. That is why St Maximus, in the passage already quoted, said that it is the resurrection which gives meaning to creation, and it is the resurrection which gives meaning to the incarnation itself.

Eschatology in our daily life means to believe in the resurrection, to believe in the eternity of life. I do not mean by that, an eternal life of the soul or of the world. In the language of the gospel, it means something more than that, namely an *anakephaleosis*, a life for all, in a summing up of all history. It is the Holy Spirit which, by coming to the Church and entering into our daily lives, brings to us this eschatological sense.

The Holy Spirit and the World to Come

However great a painter, a poet, or a footballer like Maradonna may be, however much he or she may have developed their talents, such gifted people usually understand that what they do at a particularly crucial moment is the result of inspiration. It is not the direct result of any talent or gift, or of any training or study that they have made in the development of their talents. It is a universal human experience that truly great works and truly great achievements are the result of inspiration.

However, this does not mean that we do not have to prepare, study or develop our talents. It means that the inspiration which refers to the *eschaton*, to the end of time, is something more than all that. That 'something more' in our daily life is the presence of the Holy Spirit.

If we celebrate a Liturgy and the Holy Spirit is not present, then what we do is a mere ritual. Even an important event such as a martyrdom, as in the case of St Polycarp of Smyrna, would be little more than the passion and death of any man, if the Holy Spirit were not there to bless it. In Dostoyevsky's *The Brothers Karamazov*, Alyosha the monk says to Dimitri (the sinner, in effect) that they are very much the same. Alyosha may be a monk, and one or two steps up the ladder ahead of Dimitri, but it's all very much the same. There is very little difference between them.

I believe that modern European civilization, which has progressed so far, and which is so wonderful in many respects, is only a very short distance apart from our backward Balkan life. Where there is an absence of the oil of mercy, where there is an absence of the salt of faith, where there is an absence of the charisms and fruits of the Holy Spirit, where there is not the still, small voice in the breeze, as with Elijah, then all our achievements are as nothing. The basic hunger and thirst of human existence remain unfulfilled.

Even if man does not sin or fall into evil, he remains a prisoner of being, a prisoner of nature, a prisoner even, if you wish, of the whole universe – for that is still nature, and without the Holy Spirit, man would remain its prisoner. Eschatology means that man is not in prison either in the circle of time or in the evolution of events, because Christ came from beyond time, from the eschaton, in order to break the chains of time and history. The Holy Spirit continually keeps open the gate to the coming world, to paradise.

Christ, in his incarnation, brought the kingdom of God to man, and in his resurrection raised the human body next to God's throne. That is a matter of history, a historical event, and it is the greatest affirmation of human history. And yet, if the Holy Spirit had not been sent as a second comforter, to keep the heavens open, and also the place at the right hand of the Father open to us, then the event of Christ becoming man would remain an event imprisoned in history, in the historical records. Or, at most, there would have been a process of making history eternal. The Orthodox Christian experience of the end of time, however, is not an experience of making history eternal. This would be an eternity of the same thing, an exhaustion of spirit.

A Marxist whom I know in Belgrade, and who has not yet become a Christian, said: 'You speak to me about Christian mysticism, and that reminds me of a cat who is sitting in the sun and is just bored with life'. I replied to him that what he thought of as Christianity is not Christianity. It is the joy of the game, the joy of meeting, the joy of the embrace. It is the taste of love, which however much you may enjoy it leaves you unsated. You do not ever feel sated, but you feel as if you want to pass through your own physical limitations. God, by his eschatological action, has freed himself for us, so that we should not be shut up in him.

The experience of true love is an eschatological experience. The experience of hope is also an eschatological experience, an experience of the end of time. The same is true with the experience of expectation, and this comes from the fact that man is not what he appears to be, but what he shall be. Man is by his very nature an eschatological creature. If we do not accept this, and it is our privilege as free creatures not to accept it, then we condemn man to imprisonment, even if the boundaries of the prison are huge, even if they are the galaxies, even if they are eternity. Love wants man to be free, to be unbounded, to be an eschatological creature turning to the end of time.

Two experiences of the disappointment of human love can be seen in Dostoyevsky and Marcuse. Dostoyevsky says that if you love man, you feel it with all your being, but all the time you feel that even if you love man, so long as you cannot love God you are impotent to achieve what you wish to achieve. The love of God keeps open the eschatological dimension of the love of man. That is why the two loves, for God and man, symbolically form the cross. These two loves, towards man and God, are not merely ethical commands, they are the ontological foundations of man, and yet also a cross for man. If we remove either the vertical or the horizontal segments of the cross, all that we are left with is a beam. If we separate the love of man from the love of God, we do not find the eschatological dimension which love itself demands, while the love of God is indeed impossible without the love of man.

Herbert Marcuse – a German Marxist who lived in America and tried to combine Marx and Freud – has one of his heroes say in a prayer to God: 'O God, save me from myself'. With Christ's becoming man, God came out of himself in a movement of love. He is the ecstatic God – and this word 'ecstatic' literally means 'moving out of oneself' in the Greek. This is a God who moves out of himself, an ecstatic God, as Dionysius the Areopagite says, who comes out of himself to meet us going out of ourselves to meet him.

That is why I say that love is an eschatological experience, an eschatological type of life. When I speak of love in this sense, however, I mean a crucified love. That is why for us Christians, love experienced eschatologically in our everyday life means a cross.

A Christian must be a restless spirit, a revolutionary spirit, a man who is continually living on the chance, on the impulse. So that is why I say that man is not just *homo faber*, man the craftsman, or *homo sapiens*, man the thinker, but *homo ludens,* man the player. Not even *homo religiosus,* the religious man that Eliade talks about, but *homo ludens*, the player, who is at the same time a person giving and seeking love: a man of communion. In the Greek, 'communion' and 'society' are very similar words. Thus a man of communion should also be a social being who is interconnected with others.

Communion means, in the strictest sense, at least two people permanently open to each other, and that for ever without end. If we believe that communion ends, and thus loses its eschatological sense of reaching to the end of time, then communion starts to be debased, even if it is not totally destroyed. God in his being is the eternal communion. This is what the Holy Trinity means, the one communion of three beloved persons among themselves.

The creation of the world is a calling to us to come into that communion. History is a movement, a journey, towards that very end. If we have had an eschatological foretaste of the true God who loves us, we can only keep it if we also love our fellow human beings. Then we understand that communion, or society in this sense of 'communion', will not cease. That of all things under the sun, the only truly new thing is this communion of love which is also everlasting, because it comes from the end, the eschaton, and is God's communion.

Paradoxically, from this fact of communion I would draw the inference that as Orthodox Christians we are always in a tragic position in our relation to the world. This is as true for our contemporary situation as it was in former times. Our history, even when it is successful, is always a crucified history in this world. But the Christian sense of a crucified history or tragedy is not the same as that of ancient Greece. Without tragedy, human beings cannot come out of themselves. But God came into this tragedy and was crucified, and in that way we have indeed come out of the tragedy. The tragedy of the cross became the resurrection. The resurrection does not abolish the reality of the cross, but the crucifixion is not deified in itself. It can never be, for it is not the end, but the gateway to the resurrection, which is the end realized in history – although history still has to run its natural course.

This knowledge is the knowledge which is given to us by the Holy Spirit. That is why Christians in such early Christian texts as the *Teaching of the Apostles*, said, 'May the Holy Spirit come and this world pass'. It did not mean that they were against the world, it meant that they were not prepared to be enclosed within the world, even a world created by God. 'I am wounded by your love,' says the beloved in the Song of Songs, and he or she who is wounded by love is without consolation. However, this being without consolation is a blessing.

Let me give you an example. When I was growing up under Communism, the Communists told us what a wonderful world they were creating: that it was the kingdom of God on earth. These promises, this vision, troubled us. Fortunately, the same happened much earlier to Dostoyevsky. In fact, the first victim of Communism was the first man, Adam. When Satan whispered to him that he could become the equal of God, why did Adam fall into the trap? Because in one sense, man *is* created to be equal to God. The lie of the Devil and the lie of Communism were persuasive because they struck a true chord in human beings. They use this to try to fill humans with something that is wrong.

That is why St John of Damascus said that Adam fell into sin through stretching out in a mistaken way towards God. And indeed, speaking as a Serbian Orthodox Christian, my personal experience tells me that the Devil is a very powerful agent, with a dynamic capacity to draw us. All of this, however, pales into insignificance when compared with the vision of meeting the God who comes out to meet us. When, with bitter tears for my sins, I had that experience – which was indeed an experience of bitter dissatisfaction even with my success – then I realized that the Devil is in fact very weak, and that man is stronger both than the Devil and the archangel. And because Christians were living in a regime which imposed itself, not only by force but also with a very attractive ideology, I understood then why the Devil is so aggressive in our lives. He is aggressive because he is by no means certain that he can win man over.

By contrast, God is not aggressive towards us. Sometimes he even withdraws, because he is so sure that man is drawn towards him. Love is not aggressive, and neither is truth or eschatology. When we accept these realities, we live in the certainty that everyday life is eternal. We do not wish to lose that certainty given to us by the anchor of faith, which, as St Paul says, we have thrown into the third heaven. Yet we have in fact been tormented not just as individuals, nor as peoples – Greeks, Serbs, Russians – but we have been tormented through seeking the anchor of historical certainty, the certainty of success and of effectiveness.

Living in Eschatalogical Time

In the last resort, we understand that God shows his love for us in that we are not successful and he does not permit us to be so. The love of God wants us to be free, free from every idol. Even God can be our idol, and the worst idol of all is ourselves. As St Andrew of Crete said, in his Great Canon at the beginning of Lent: 'I have become an idol to myself'. St John ends his epistle by saying: 'My children, preserve yourselves from idols'.

The Orthodox Christian eschatological stance towards life, which is simultaneously liturgical and ascetic, is a stance of crucified love that leads to the resurrection. The resurrection does not come if we do not pass through the experience of crucifixion. That is why the eschata in our daily life are not feelings of happiness in a church service, which leave us feeling satisfied and secure. In fact, religion in itself is a dangerous phenomenon. It can be an excuse for wrongdoing, an alibi against unbelief, a substitute for crucified love. This is so because it is possible for man, with the great abysses which lurk inside him, to return inside himself and look on himself as the final end or purpose of his life. In doing that he will lose the fact of the loving and suffering God.

We can replace Christ in our daily life as we can replace God with all number of 'gods'. Our eschatological experience, however, is that Mary in the Gospels was right: only one thing is needful for the experience of Christ, and that is to follow him, as in the book of Revelation the martyrs followed Christ. This does not mean that we stand back and become inactive in history. It does not mean sloth, but expectation. It means an expectation of continual crusade – not with power, but with God-given weakness.

In all our weakness we should remember that the Holy Spirit is with us and in us, calling, 'Abba, Father'. In this epicletic attitude – that is, calling on the Holy Spirit – in this situation which is both liturgical and ascetic, it does not make a great difference who are the saints and who are the sinners; who are the virtuous and who are the fallen; who is higher up the ladder and who is lower down. In what way were the thieves on the right and on the left of the crucified Christ so different? The difference was that while both had sinned and both saw the end staring them in the face, only one thief saw it as personal and salvific. He cried out, in a true moment of repentance – of eschatological *epiclesis* – 'Remember me, O Lord, in thy kingdom'.

Here then is the cross between commemoration and *epiclesis*, a biblical dialectic between history and eschatology. But it is not a dialectic for dialectic's sake – not a dialectic for some evolution or some revolutionary change – but a dialectic of crucifixion and resurrection, a dialectic of love and faith.

I end with the thoughts of St Mark the Ascetic, which can be summed up in this way: the eschatological perspective is a continual light on our lives. God will not send us to hell because we are sinners and have done particular sinful deeds, nor will he send us to paradise because we have done good deeds, but because of faith which is because of love. He will judge us, or rather we will judge ourselves, from our response to love: love coming out to meet us, love shining through from the end, which is God himself.

This stance, this open response to love, can be described as eschatology present in our daily lives. It is hard for us to act like this. Many times even as Christians we prefer certainty, control and safety, but these are illusions and barriers to eschatological presence. As St John Chrysostom, one of the greatest of the Fathers, said: 'When you are uncertain, when you have nowhere to lean or to stand firm, then indeed you are paradoxically more certain because it is only God who is your support and your strength.' This is not a stance of hopelessness, nor is it angst. It is more like the openness that a child will have towards another child, or a child will have to its parents, knowing that it is loved because it also loves.

For many children, of course, this love simply fills them. It gives them sweetness and joy, and as these children become adults, this love will inevitably meet the experience of the cross. If they are faithful in their love, and if they come through the cruel experience of the cross to resurrection, then they will return to a childlike openness. They will be living in eschatological time.

4

Orthodox Tradition and Family Life

Sister Magdalen

'Every step in our Christian life is inseparably related to the fundamental dogmas of our faith.' How can this statement, made by Archimandrite Sophrony, be applied to family life? Christian life is lived in a community of one sort or another.[1] A monastic family, because of its greater degree of separation from the world, is freer to define its daily life in accordance with its aim of prayer and spiritual endeavour. Monasteries exist for this very reason. However, in the world, the situation may not be so straightforward.

Orthodox Christians in every country are a minority group, living in cultures whose values and consequent activities are not all compatible with following Jesus Christ. This means that in their family life there is an element of challenge from differing outlooks as they strive to live out their faith from day to day. Everyone, in fact, lives by what he or she believes about ultimate realities. Those who do not believe that the commandments of Jesus Christ are a reflection of divine and absolute reality will have other goals than those of the Christian. For many of them, earthly and even material aims will provide life's purpose, or else leave life empty and purposeless. Those who try to live as Orthodox Christians find themselves steering a path which aims to avoid two pitfalls: that of proudly disdaining the surrounding culture, and that of being seduced into ways that are alien to the Gospel.

Each family is unique, and each person has his or her own measure. I cannot thus describe a 'typical' family. Rather, I hope to show how the ways of the Orthodox Church can be applied in the family today. It is not unusual in the Orthodox Tradition to find monks or nuns writing about family life. As well as the personal experience of family life that someone called to monasticism has had, there is also the fact that monasteries are often centres of pastoral care for families. This is natural because all of us are trying to live the same Christian life. Our situations differ, but there is one spiritual ideal.

It is not an easy task to raise a Christian family nowadays, but no one should despair that it has become impossible. Christianity has always, in every epoch and place, posed a challenge for fallen man; St Silouan says that if the world can no longer produce saints, it will be brought to an end.

The Foundations of Family Life

The fundamental ontological category of Orthodox Christian theology is the person or *hypostasis*. This implies that it is the personal aspect, in God and in humankind, which defines our being and our life: the absolute and eternal life of God himself, and the life of man who is made in God's image. Archimandrite Sophrony says that 'differences in theological interpretation of the principle of the person-hypostasis in the divine being constitute a watershed, a demarcation line, not only between the various religions but between Christian confessions too.'

Theological accuracy on this issue has been seen by holy men and women to be vital, not simply so as to produce a 'correct' theology manual, but because, being such a basic issue, any distortion of it may have drastic consequences. If we imagine a circle with a wide diameter, we can visualize how a minute turn at the centre results in a significant movement at the circumference. If God himself, or humankind, are not envisaged as they really are, then human ideals become mirages, leading eventually to death. This does not mean that in order to 'obey the truth' (Galatians 5.7)

51

everyone must be an expert dogmatic theologian – that would exclude most of us – but it does mean that we use as guides for our life the saints who have known God as he is. As the first model of true humanity we have Jesus Christ the God-man, as he is described by those who have lived in Christ.

The Church, as the Body of Christ, of which the baptized are members, is thus the foremost experience of true human life, because true human life means to live in the image of God-in-Trinity, in loving communion with each other and with God. This is the basis of family life, whether or not anyone in the family is able to articulate it theologically. A baby cannot discourse on maternal love, but a baby knows, even better than any discourse could explain, whether or not he or she is receiving sincere maternal love. At baptism, the Orthodox Christian, or in the case of infants, the godparent, proclaims the traditional Nicaeno-Constantinopolitan Creed as his or her own vision ('I believe in...'). For this belief, which is initially based on trust, to become experientially confirmed, theological diplomas are not a prerequisite. What is necessary is to follow, in as full a measure as we can, the way of life taught and practised by those who could say 'I believe', because they knew, having lived in the Holy Spirit of truth.

Living in our turn as members of the Church, in the time and place given to us by God, we benefit from the teaching and experience of holy men and women, past and contemporary, just as one who is making a hazardous journey would benefit from clear maps and trusted guides. Christ is the unique way, as well as the destination. Living in this certainty should not lead Christians to any pride – it is Christ himself who instructs us to learn humility from him – but to gratitude to God who has revealed himself and shown a sure pathway to the kingdom. Christians believe that there is no time or place in which this ceases to be true. How, then, can today's Orthodox Christian families reflect these beliefs in their lives?

In practice, what I have been speaking of means that family life includes a dimension that might be termed liturgical. Yesterday and tomorrow become ever-present in this time scale. It is, for example, not irrelevant to see how a sixth-century saint recommends us to keep the fast, or to include the hope of the kingdom of heaven as an element when weighing up a painful moral decision. When a Church feast is celebrated, those attending are brought into the event itself, to experience now its eternal value. They are given the chance to be actually present as a contemporary; they are not simply reflecting on the past. For example, at Christmas, the choir sings: 'Today the Virgin gives birth to him who is above all being'. Orthodox Christians are known to have long services, which some people consider impractical in contemporary Western society. But liturgical life and everyday life are not in separate compartments in the life of a faithful Orthodox Christian. Liturgy is life and all of life is liturgical.

This liturgical pattern of life involves all family members, including the youngest children. In the Orthodox Church, there are no particular services for children, any more than there would be for, say, adults of differing intellectual ability. The services touch the whole of man and are not merely intellectual experiences. Sight, smell, touch, taste, hearing, emotions, are all blessed. The living presence of God can be sensed by a child even while it lies within the womb, as the case of John the Baptist shows. Thus, babies are baptized and brought for Holy Communion as full members of the Body of Christ.

The services, and even in many cases the rubrics, are handed down from the saints over the centuries, with little variation from generation to generation or from country to country. Even those who are illiterate can become familiar with them. Children, too, can grow into an intellectual understanding of what is taking place in church – as far as each one's natural abilities allow – by living in the presence of the Holy Spirit. The degree of participation, of course, varies with the spiritual state of each person; but that is a matter of human freedom.

Rather than actually changing the services, contemporary communities make allowances for particular circumstances. For example, parish services are often shorter than those in monasteries; often small children are not brought from the beginning, or they are taken out for a while if they are too fidgety. Sometimes young people are known to complain that the language of the services is an ancient form that is too hard to follow, and some communities have re-translated texts accordingly. However, youngsters who are spiritually hungry often make the effort to learn some uncommon words (which takes less time to learn than, for instance, computer terminology), or they attend where the services are in a language they know. Often, the uniformity in services means that even in a completely foreign language people can follow prayerfully.

Liturgical life spills over into the home, or rather, as St John Chrysostom puts it, members of the Church can make the home into a 'micro-Church'. On the visible level, the same icons which adorn the church building bring the events and saints portrayed in them into the home. There is an icon corner where prayers are said. Families pray all together, parents pray with small children, and each person needs time alone with God every day. The verbal prayers used are of two kinds: those of the saints, so that one learns to pray as they did, and each one's own prayers, which are not necessarily in the 'best style'. Prayer may also be without words. At any age, prayer can be experienced as a person-to-person meeting.

Any and every activity can be blessed by prayer: cooking, washing, speaking with children, setting out on a journey, deciding financial questions... anything. As St Silouan said, 'Every act which cannot be preceded by prayer without our feeling troubled, is better avoided.'[2] In a home filled with prayer, God is 'tasted', prayer is as natural as breathing, and Holy Tradition is passed to the next generation less by preaching than by life and example, which is the most enduring lesson.[3] Prayerful love is the keynote of the Christian home.

Loving as Christ commands us is not always easy. Everyone needs help and the opportunity to repent of any failures and continually begin again. One way in which the Orthodox Church can help its members is through the sacrament of confession. Again, there is no age limit for this sacrament; I have known three-year-olds who confess sincerely. The norm is usually that from about seven years old people go regularly, that is, a few times each year, often during the fasts before the major feasts.

Confession is not anonymous, but, as with all sacraments, it is participated in by name, that is, with growing personal consciousness. The priest hears confessions as a representative both of God and of the whole Church community.[4] The relationship which each one can have with a spiritual father furthers the feeling of belonging in the wider community of the Church. For example, it often safeguards the relationships of teenagers with God even in cases where there is animosity between parents and children.

Sin is a reality of our daily life; but the positive application of our freedom is also a fundamental reality, whose true meaning we can learn day by day. In this quest, a spiritual father is a link between the Tradition of the saints and each one's life in today's world. Following well-trodden paths does not imply merely a mechanical repetition of the past, because people's circumstances vary, and more importantly, because each one of us is a unique being, called by God's personal love into personal existence.

It is the spiritual fathers – as well as the parents, where children are concerned – who decide how, and in what measure, to apply the Church's practice in particular cases. The person is more important than the rule. The rule provides a standard which we may not simply dismiss because it dates from long ago, or because it is difficult to apply, or because it involves discomfort or ascetic struggle. A failure to reach the standard can be healed by repentance. An example of this is that since the first millennium, the Orthodox Church has allowed for divorce – as a last resort, of course, and not lightly – and second, or occasionally even third marriages, whose rites are penitential in character.

Spiritual life is not considered to be the prerogative of monasteries. Indeed, parish services and home prayers use the same service books as the monasteries, and monastic books, such as the famous anthology on prayer, the *Philokalia*, are read by lay people. The family, no less than the monastery, is a school where one can learn life's great lesson: how to love God with all our being, and our neighbour as ourselves. 'On these two commandments depend all the law and the prophets' (Matthew 22.40). In other words, they are, quite literally, what life is all about.

Christ enjoins perfection on all of us (Matthew 5.48). Those who hear his call before they are married will try, not least by prayer, to seek out a partner who shares the aims of the gospel. They can choose to mark their daily life with prayer, hospitality, Christian forbearance, help for the less fortunate, care for the environment, and by avoiding greed and the other passions. Their whole relationship will be guided by the spirit manifested in the teachings of Christ and his apostles. They can, to give a concrete example, organize their holidays so that they are free in Holy Week. (In a practising Orthodox family, the feasts of the Church year are events around which life is scheduled, as far as work and school timetables permit.)

In some cases, one of the spouses does not belong to the Orthodox Church.[5] In others, the partners do not share the same degree of commitment to the ways of the Church. From apostolic times, married Christians have been in such situations (1 Corinthians 7.12ff., 1 Peter 3.1f.). There is no way that a Christian should wish to impose faith on other members of a family. Differences in outlook arise where there are non-believing (or less practising) adults in the family, and also in the context of the upbringing of children, to which we now turn once again our attention. What does the Orthodox Tradition have to say to contemporary parents?

The Upbringing of Children

The gospel calls us to feed the hungry and clothe the naked. Apart from the obvious meaning, itself an important element in Christian service, there is also a spiritual meaning. We are to share spiritual nourishment and clothing. This reminds us of St Paul's description of the baptized as those who have 'put on Christ', or who are clothed in Christ (Galatians 3.27). This aspect of caring for children is the most vital part of their upbringing, even more vital than overseeing their physical and psychological development. Again, I stress that the spiritual dimension includes every aspect of the person, down to the question of how they dress and what they eat.

It is the order of priorities that is important for a Christian family. The commandment to love God is the first; thus the first concern is each child's personal relationship with the Absolute, Personal Truth. The Church's pedagogy is based on this foundation. For example, when mother and child are churched forty days after the birth of a baby, the child is dedicated to God in his or her own name.[6] The mother receives back the child, picking it up from the floor of the church. The message of the service is clear: this child is first of all called to be a child of God and co-heir with Christ, the Son of the Father (Romans 8.17). The parents' task is to bring the child up 'in the discipline and instruction of the Lord' (Ephesians 6.4), and to teach him or her how to know God personally.

Knowledge of God is personal. God is personal love, and we can only know him by loving him, which cannot be brought about by constraint. The Eastern Church's doctrine of synergy, which describes how man can freely co-operate with uncreated grace, and how this is what saves man, applies directly to the role of parents. We might use the analogy of fishing, and say with the old proverb: 'Give your son a fish and he will eat well today. Teach him how to use a fishing rod and he will eat well all his life.' Or to take another analogy, from horticulture: those who teach children are not so much occupied with counting flowers on the plants, as with watering their roots.

Freedom does not, of course, mean 'being allowed to do what you feel like'. This misunderstanding of freedom prevails in Western culture, and leads, visibly, to slavery to selfish passions, to the idea that I have a right to something if I desire it. Freedom really means our human capacity to determine, by the use of our own will, our destiny. In our daily life, this implies our potential to discern right from wrong and to fulfil what is right. In this God-given human attribute, man's person, or *hypostasis*, is akin to God.

Those who are truly free are those who love. A primary task of parents is to teach love, and love is learned more easily by those who have the experience of being loved. 'Nothing so furthers teaching as this: loving and being loved', said that wonderful pedagogical guide, St John Chrysostom (Homily 6). To do the best one can for one's children means to foster as well as one is able their growth in likeness to God. This is not simply a pious duty; Christian parents are called to be fellow-workers with God in the creation and formation of new persons, new sons and daughters of God. Personhood in the fullest sense belongs to the saints; they are the most truly human beings. A lesser aim for the children in a Christian family would ignore the most vital elements of reality both human and divine.

In daily life, this means that each child is to be treated as unique. The child's real worth stems from his or her personal existence, and not from any particular talents or personality traits. Indeed, it may be harmful to confuse personhood and personality, because the latter often includes characteristics that are negative and 'passionate' –

that is, a destructive distortion of human energies. The true person, as God wills and calls him or her by name (Revelation 2.17 and Philippians 4.3), is the 'I' which loves God and other people, not the 'I' which demands the gratification of sinful desires. A strong personality may be one full of egoism. Christian parents, above all by example, will try to encourage humility, service, unselfishness and obedience, as well as courage and self-discipline.

St John of Kronstadt, along with other ecclesiastical writers, urges great attentiveness so that children learn to distinguish between right and wrong from a young age.

> Do not neglect to uproot from the hearts of children the tares of sins, impure, evil and blasphemous thoughts, sinful habits, inclinations and passions; the enemy and the sinful flesh do not spare even children; the seeds of all sins are to be found in children too. Show them all the danger of sin on the path of life; do not hide sins from them lest through ignorance and want of comprehension they should be confirmed in sinful habits and attachments, which grow stronger and stronger and bring forth corresponding fruits when the children grow up.
> St John of Kronstadt, *My Life in Christ* (Holy Trinity Monastery, Jordanville, 1984).

In training their children, parents will try to be guided even in everyday decisions by prayer for enlightenment and discernment. Is the answer to be 'yes' or 'no'? Is a lesson necessary now or should I wait until another time? Is this a moment to show indulgence, or to show anger? (Anger, not meant here as the passionate state of irritation or rage, but as a pedagogical tool when gentle words of explanation, warning or reproach have not sufficed.) 'Lord, enlighten me!'

Parents are recommended to pray every morning in words such as these: 'O Lord our God, thou knowest this thy child, his heart, his needs, his future. Guide me at all times, and do not let me harm him by any error in my dealings with him today.'

If a faithful Christian parent has to impose his will on a child, it will be for the sake of the child – for example, to avert danger or to ensure that the child learns obedience. Authority in parents is one of the factors providing security for a child; Scripture itself teaches honour and obedience to parents. But authority should not mean 'power', or the suppression of a child's individuality; it is for guidance, not for tyranny. Obedience, itself an expression of love, develops with maturity. At the beginning it has to mean: 'do as you are told'; by adulthood it means: 'prefer the will of another out of love'.

St John Chrysostom, writing in the fourth century, suggests mealtimes as a good occasion to speak with children and to introduce stories and examples from Scripture and the lives of godly people into their lives. A Christian family will make occasions to be together, to eat together, to speak together.

It is worth every effort and sacrifice to give time to listen to children. How can parents give them the vital experience of being unconditionally loved and treasured if their own timetable allows perhaps ten minutes of 'quality time' per day? When a conflict of opinion arises, how can parents deal with it fairly if argument is the only form of dialogue they have had with the child for a fortnight? Such practical issues cannot be neatly solved by any recipe. But neither can they be ignored by parents for selfish reasons. Parenthood means giving children a lot of time over many years.

A good relationship with children makes real dialogue possible. In the case of older children, this is their anchor as they learn to use more and more freedom of choice, so that they can leave home ready to find and do the will of God in every situation. If parents feel something had better be forbidden to a teenager, they will be able to explain, and sometimes also to make compromises or set conditions, so as to develop the child's sense of responsibility. Their opinions will only have weight if they have a real relationship with their children. Christian discernment about all that the world has to offer cannot be learnt in a straitjacket.

Parents of teenagers especially, will spend much time in prayer for their children, and they will struggle to emphasize essential matters, such as faith in Christ as God, or prayer, even at the risk of a period of relative negligence on 'secondary' issues.[7] To give a concrete example, a parent may decide against insisting that an adolescent go without meat on a Friday, and may even avoid mentioning it at all, if that seems best in that particular case at that time. Nothing of eternal value is achieved by using force against another. God himself has this problem with all of us...

The venerable Elder Porphyrios used to say, when parents complained that their children would not listen to them: 'It's because you tried to tell your daughter before you'd told the Mother of God', or, 'if you can't speak to your child about God, speak to God about your child', or, 'it's because you yourself are not at peace and at prayer – put yourself right and everything will change in your house.' Spouses who communicate well between each other will also set a healthy tone for communication between generations.

Practising Orthodox teenagers may differ from the average teenager today, but this is principally because, unlike the majority, they have a relationship with God. They have many tastes in common with their contemporaries. One mother once told me: 'The walls of my son's room tell you all about him. On one side the football posters, on the other side the icons.' St John Chrysostom wrote for parents, in his book, *On the Education of Children*: 'Bring up an athlete for Christ, and teach [your son] to have, living in the world, fear of God from his youth.'

Externally viewed, there are many areas of overlap between Christian daily life and the life of our fellow-citizens. In the second-century Letter to Diognetus, the writer says:

The difference between Christians and the rest of mankind is not a matter of nationality, or language, or customs. Christians do not live apart in separate cities of their own, speak any special dialect, nor practise any eccentric way of life... They pass their lives in whatever township each man's lot has determined; and conform to local usage in their clothing, diet, and other habits. Nonetheless... their community does exhibit some features that are remarkable, and even surprising... They obey the prescribed laws, but in their own private lives they transcend the laws.
Letter to Diognetus (translated by M. Staniforth, *Early Christian Writings*, Penguin 1995).

In families where there are school-age children, the main area of overlap is the school environment. However, the values the school tries to inculcate are not necessarily always in accordance with the Spirit of truth. Peer pressure can also create value-conflicts for the child. This is a domain where Christian parents need a lot of effort: to know the school, to attend the school functions, to ensure that any issues can be fearlessly discussed at home, to show appreciation for the school's positive contribution to the child's development, to offer hospitality to the child's school friends, and so on.

Often the children of a Christian family – and not only in the case of immigrants from another country – find themselves leading a kind of double life. In a sense, Christians in the world are doing just that – they belong to the earthly and the heavenly spheres – but children need help to hold all their experiences together under God.

Thus we return in thought to the Church's services, which do precisely that. There are even prayer services for particular situations: for the sick, for the blessing of homes and cars and crops, for travellers, for times of distress, at the deathbed, for the beginning of a child's schooling and so on. The Divine Liturgy itself includes petitions for many specific occasions and needs.

The services also make intercession for all the world, and there is, equally, a universal dimension in Christian family life. Followers of Christ are called to be the 'salt of the earth' (Matthew 5.13). The 'savour of Christ' (2 Corinthians 2.15) really can be an ingredient in contemporary family life. When it is, the family itself benefits, and those who come into contact with the family benefit; but also, because humans share one nature, all of humanity can benefit. Each family can contribute to the transfiguration of the world by abiding in the grace of God, which is living and active today and for ever.

5

Lent and the Consumer Society

Bishop Kallistos of Diokleia

For the Christian community, both Eastern and Western, the season
of Lent – the seven weeks before Easter – is traditionally regarded
as a high point in the Church's year. It is a *kairos*, a time of decision
and opportunity, a period specially set apart. But specially set apart
for what? How in our contemporary consumer society are we to
understand the purpose of 'the Great Fast' or 'the Great Forty Days',
as we Orthodox call Lent? What relevance, if any, does this Great
Fast have for the ecological crisis that confronts all of us today?

Flying Kites

In Greece, at any rate in the past, the first day of Lent – 'Clean
Monday', as it is termed, for in the Orthodox Church Lent
commences not on Wednesday but two days earlier than in the West
– was observed as the earliest open-air celebration of the year.
Families went out into the country, climbed the hills, and flew kites.
Here, then, is an image for the beginning of the Lenten Fast, to set
side by side with the Western ceremonies of Ash Wednesday.

Obviously, the two are very different in their implications. Ashes,
poured out on our heads and marked on our brow, with all that this
signifies – a sense of mortality and penitence – constitute certainly
an essential part of the total meaning of Lent. But that is not what
Greek Orthodoxy chooses to emphasize at the outset of the Fast.
On the contrary, we are encouraged to associate Lent with fresh air,
with the wind blowing on the hills, with the coming of spring. Lent

is a time for flying kites – a time for adventure, exploration, fresh initiatives, new hope.

In this connection, surely it is no coincidence that the season of Lent comes, not in autumn when the leaves are falling and the days grow shorter, and not in midwinter when the trees are stripped bare and the ponds are frozen, but in spring when the ice is breaking up and there is new life everywhere. In fact, the original sense of the English word 'Lent' was precisely 'springtime', as we can see from the words of the medieval poem:

Lenten is come with love to towne,
With blosmen and with briddes rowne.[1]

'Spring is come with love to the world, with blossoms and with bird-song.' It may seem strange to think of Lent as a time for falling in love, but perhaps that is part of its meaning. The link between Lent and springtime is also apparent in the Orthodox liturgical texts:

The springtime of the Fast has dawned,
The flower of repentance has begun to open.

Repentance – *metanoia*, 'change of mind' – is not just ashes, but an opening flower.

Such is the context in which Lent should be placed: it has to do with the flying of kites and the start of spring. It has also to do with freedom. It is significant that there is one major feast of the Church's year which almost always falls within Lent: the annunciation, on 25 March. This is precisely a feast when we celebrate the liberty of choice exercised by the Blessed Virgin Mary.

When the archangel Gabriel announced God's plan to Mary, he waited for her to reply: 'Here am I, the servant of the Lord; may it be with me as you have said' (Luke 1.38). This response on Mary's part was not a foregone conclusion; she could have refused. The Holy

Trinity respects our human freedom. In the words of the second-century Epistle to Diognetus, 'God persuades, he does not compel; for violence is foreign to him.'[2]

So it was exactly in the case of the Holy Virgin: God did not become human without first seeking the willing agreement of the one who was to be his mother. Her voluntary consent was an essential prerequisite. 'We are co-operators (*synergoi*) with God', says St Paul (1 Corinthians 3.9), and this applies pre-eminently to the Virgin Mary. At the annunciation she was a *synergos*, a fellow-worker with God – not simply a pliant tool, but an active participant in the mystery. As St Irenaeus (d. *c*. 200) puts it, 'Mary co-operates with the economy'.[3]

Here, then, is another clue to the meaning of Lent. As well as being a season for exploration, a spiritual springtime, it has to do with the way in which we use our human liberty of choice. Lent is a time when we learn to be free. For freedom, as well as being spontaneous, is also something that has to be learnt. If you were to ask me, 'Can you play the violin?', and I replied, 'I'm not sure, I've never tried', you might feel that there was something odd about my answer. For I am not free to play Bach's sonatas on the violin unless I have first learnt, through a prolonged and arduous training, how to handle the violin.

On the moral level, it is the same with our exercise of freedom. As a human person in God's image, I am not truly free unless I have learnt how to use my freedom rightly, and this process of learning presupposes obedience, discipline and self-denial. Freedom is not only a gift; it is a task. It is what Russian spirituality terms a *podvig*, an ascetic exploit. As Nicolas Berdyaev (1874-1948) rightly asserts, 'Freedom is not easy, as its enemies and slanderers allege: freedom is hard; it is a heavy burden.'[4] But it is also a privilege and a joy.

These, then, are three 'soundings' which may help us to navigate our ship through the Lenten archipelago. Already it has become abundantly clear that Lent is not just concerned with our use of food and drink. Let us now try to broaden our appreciation of the Great Fast by considering, first, a parallel from the Old Testament; second, the way in which the Lenten Fast emerged in the early Church; and third, the particular and distinctive importance of the Fast in today's world. This will show us that Lent is concerned, first, with the offering of the world back to God in thanksgiving; second, with baptismal initiation and with the Church's missionary witness; and third, with the way in which we relate with our fellow humans and with the material environment. If we wished to sum up the meaning of Lent in three words, those words could be sacrifice, schooling and sharing.[5]

Sacrifice

In the Old Testament, the people of Israel were instructed to offer to God each year a tithe, a tenth part, of the produce of the earth: 'You shall tithe all the yield of your seed, which comes forth from the field year by year' (Deuteronomy 14.22). The part was offered in token of the whole: by rendering back to God the first fruits of what he had given to them, the Israelites called down his blessing upon the total harvest. It was a way of acknowledging that the earth is God's, while we are only the stewards of his gifts; and so, in offering tithes, we are giving back to him in gratitude that which is his own. And this act of giving back was felt by the Israelites not as a loss but as an enrichment. The harvest festival was a time of joy and gladness: 'You shall rejoice before the Lord your God, you and your son and your daughter, your manservant and your maidservant, the Levite who is within your towns, the aliens, the fatherless and the widows living among you...' (Deuteronomy 16.11).

This idea of tithing was applied by the early Christians to the Great Fast. The season of Lent was seen as a tithe of the year, a tenth part specially dedicated to God.[6] Through the observance of

Lent we acknowledge that the whole span of our life, and all the moments of time within it, are God's gift to us; and by offering a part we invoke his blessing upon the whole. Lent, then, signifies the sanctification of time. Lenten asceticism affirms that time is not simply under our control, to be exploited selfishly as we think best, but it belongs to God; we are only the stewards of time, not the overlords. The Lenten Fast is thus a way of rendering back to God that which is his own, and so we may apply to it the words used in the Divine Liturgy immediately before the invocation (*epiclesis*) of the Holy Spirit upon the gifts of bread and wine: 'Your own from Your own we offer You, in all things and for all things.'

Moreover, just as the Israelites experienced the offering of tithes as a time of rejoicing, as an enrichment and not a deprivation, so it can be also for us. Lent is a time of joy, as we affirm clearly in the hymns used on Clean Monday, the first day of the Fast:

> With joy let us enter upon the beginning of the Fast.
> Let us not be of sad countenance...

> All mortal life is but one day, so it is said,
> To those who labour with love.
> There are forty days in the Fast:
> Let us keep them all with joy.

Lent, then, as this parallel from the Old Testament indicates, is a time of offering and sacrifice. We offer to God in sacrifice a tenth part of the year, and with this tithe we offer ourselves, our whole life, all our days and hours. This offering of self and of time, if it is to be meaningful, needs to be costly: 'I will not offer to the Lord my God that which has cost me nothing' (2 Samuel 24.24). Any true observance of Lent commits us to an effort that is at times painful, involving as it does a degree of self-denial that goes far beyond our normal inclinations. Yet this does not mean that Lent is

predominantly a period of gloom and self-mortification. Our
Christian feast of tithes, like the Jewish harvest-offering of the first
fruits, is a time of rejoicing.

Sacrifice, that is to say, is not primarily a matter of giving *up*
but of *giving*. The main emphasis falls not upon what we deny to
ourselves, but upon what we offer to God and to our neighbours.
And the effect of our making a gift to God – a gift which God then
accepts – is to re-establish the personal relationship between
ourselves and him. Such exactly is the aim of all sacrificial offering:
to restore communion. This notion of Lent as a time for the
restoration of relationships needs to be kept constantly in view, and
we shall have more to say about it later.

How shall we apply to ourselves individually this understanding
of Lent as an offering of tithes? We can apply it first of all to money.
Certain Western Christians offer to God throughout the year a tenth
part of their income. I doubt if many Orthodox Christians do that
as a regular practice; but at least during Lent we might try to set
aside a tenth part for God's use. That, however, is no more than a
beginning; for God invites us to offer not merely what we have but
what we are. We are to give our time as well as our money.

More intensively than at other periods of the year, we are to set
apart time for God through prayer, and time for our neighbour
through acts of service and *diakonia* – visiting the sick, the
housebound and the lonely, inviting the stranger to our home,
catching up on our backlog of letters and writing to all those whom
we have been too long neglecting. Could we not offer to God in this
way at least a tithe of our waking hours: say, twelve hours each
week of Lent?

Schooling

Moving from Old Testament times to the early Church, we can ask
the question: how did Lent start? What was its original purpose and

meaning? Lent, as we know it, is closely linked with the mystery of baptism. Baptismal immersion, as St Paul teaches, signifies that we are 'planted' or united with Christ in his death and burial, and therefore united with him in his resurrection (Romans 6.3-5). For this reason, during the early centuries of the Church, the chief moment in the year when baptism was conferred was the night of pascha, as the Church celebrated the burial and the resurrection of the Saviour. Baptism was not, as so often today, a private family occasion, but it was a public event in which the total community participated.

In modern Orthodox practice, the ancient paschal vigil has been moved forward from Easter midnight to the morning of Holy Saturday; and a different vigil service has replaced it at Easter midnight. The service on the morning of Holy Saturday – Vespers, followed by the Liturgy of St Basil – still has an unmistakably baptismal character. There are fifteen Old Testament readings, at least four of which refer symbolically to baptism (readings 4, 6, 14 and 15).

During these readings at the paschal vigil in the early Church, the bishop and clergy went to the baptistery with the candidates for baptism and their sponsors, and the candidates were duly immersed in the font and marked with the holy chrism. Then, as the readings came to an end, the newly-baptized, arrayed in white robes and holding lighted candles in their hands, returned in procession into the church with their sponsors and the bishop and clergy, as the whole congregation joined in the chant, 'All of you who were baptized into Christ have put on Christ. Alleluia!' (see Galatians 3.27).

The same chant is employed today on Holy Saturday in place of the *trisagion*. The epistle and Gospel readings that follow in current use both refer explicitly to baptism. The epistle (Romans 6.3-11) speaks of baptism as death and resurrection with Christ, while the Gospel (Matthew 28.1-20) ends with our Lord's missionary command to go and make disciples of all nations, baptizing them in the name of Father, Son and Spirit (Matthew 28.19).

Now the Lenten Fast, in both Eastern and Western Christendom, is directly connected with the period of final preparation that led up to this great baptismal celebration at paschal midnight. In many places during the fourth century, the catechumens – those receiving instruction for baptism – underwent in the forty days immediately before their initiation at pascha a time of intensive training, with rigorous fasting, vigils and prayer, with exorcisms and daily sermons.

Their pre-baptismal instruction would in most cases have commenced months or even years earlier, but now in the concluding weeks all was recapitulated and re-emphasized. In fourth-century Jerusalem, the catechumens, during these forty days, were expected to come daily to church for about three hours. How many of today's baptismal candidates would accept a discipline as demanding as that?

In the early centuries of the Church, to a degree far surpassing the imagination of most of us, there was a vivid awareness of mutual solidarity throughout the total Christian community. Believers felt, not in a theoretical way but with sharp immediacy, that they were members one of another in the one Body, and that the joys and sufferings of each were the joys and sufferings of all (see 1 Corinthians 12.26). So it came about that many of those already baptized felt directly involved in what the catechumens were doing. They too wanted to share in the final training of the baptismal candidates, so that when paschal midnight arrived they might renew their own baptismal commitment in union with those newly receiving initiation.

In this way, the entire congregation came increasingly to participate in the forty days of fasting, vigils, prayer and instruction that the catechumens underwent. The pre-paschal forty days became each year a decisive event in the personal experience of every Christian, a shared event, a time of spiritual schooling for the community as a whole.

So it was that the original one-week fast immediately before pascha – kept by many Christians during the second and third centuries – developed in the fourth and subsequent centuries into the forty-day observance of Lent as we know it today. Lent has, therefore, a fundamentally baptismal orientation, which we often overlook and which we need to retrieve. The Lenten Fast is an annual opportunity for us to reflect afresh on the centrality of baptism in our Christian experience, and a call for us each to renew our baptismal promises. In the Great Forty Days we are to remind ourselves of the truth affirmed by Vladimir Lossky (1903-58): 'Baptismal grace, the presence within us of the Holy Spirit – inalienable and personal to each one of us – is the foundation of all Christian life.'[7]

Such is the message of Lent. In the words of St Mark the Monk, writing around the time of the fifth century:

> However far someone may advance in faith, however great the good he may attain... he never discovers, nor can he ever discover, anything more than what he has already received secretly through Baptism... Christ, being complete and perfect God, has bestowed upon the baptized the complete and perfect grace of the Spirit. We for our part cannot possibly add to that grace, but it reveals and manifests itself increasingly, the more we fulfil the commandments... Whatever, then, we offer to him after our regeneration was already hidden within us and came originally from him.[8]

Recalling, then, the origins of Lent in the early Church, we come to appreciate that Lent is not only our feast of tithes, when we offer time back to God, but it is equally our re-immersion in the waters of initiation, when we rekindle our loyalty to Christ the baptizer.

It is an invitation to reaffirm, not just through words but through actions, our rootedness in baptism as the foundation of all our Christian life; it is a season of self-exploration during which we become actively conscious of the indwelling presence of Christ and the Holy Spirit that exists 'secretly' or 'mystically' within our hearts from the moment of our baptism. Lent is a time to ask ourselves St Paul's question: 'Do you not know that you are God's temple, and that God's Spirit dwells within you?' (1 Corinthians 3.16). Lent is a time for each of us to become what we are: baptismal God-bearers.

At the same time, Lent is more than that. As well as renewing my own baptismal commitment, I need also to ask myself: what am I personally doing to bring others to faith and baptism in Christ? Today in most of our churches there is no organized catechumenate. Why is this so? Why are the catechumens so very few in our Orthodox congregations? Where are they? Do we find a dynamic missionary zeal in the contemporary Orthodox Church? (When I speak of missionary work, I mean of course not proselytism among other Christians, but the conversion of unbelievers.)

Furthermore, whether we are clergy or laity, each is to see evangelism as her or his direct responsibility. What am I myself doing to preach the gospel 'to all nations'? In the Liturgy of the Presanctified Gifts, performed on weekdays in Lent – a service with many baptismal undertones – the celebrant comes out during the Old Testament readings with a lighted candle in his hand, and he says: 'The light of Christ shines upon all'. We are each to ask ourselves: What have I done since last Easter to communicate this light to others?

Lent, then, is about baptism and mission. It signifies a reawakening of our baptismal initiation, a revivified missionary dedication. It is to say both: 'who am I?' and 'here am I'. Recalling our identity as baptized Christians, we ask ourselves: who am I? And, responding to Christ's missionary command, we affirm with the prophet Isaiah (Isaiah 6.8): here am I.

73

Sharing

How, in the third place, are we to understand the distinctive value of the Lenten Fast in today's world? Contemporary society, as we are all acutely conscious, is marked by a twofold breakdown in fellowship or *koinonia*: a breakdown in the human community, and a breakdown in the cosmic community. On the human level, we see not only a growth in lawlessness and violence – accompanied in many countries by a widening economic gap between the rich and the poor – but also, most fundamentally of all, an ever-increasing threat to the survival of the family, which is the primary social unit on which all other forms of society are based.

On the cosmic level, we have tragically weakened the life-giving bonds which unite us to our material environment. As we destroy the rainforests and create holes in the ozone layer, we would do well to recall the words from the 'Service When in Danger of Earthquake', found in the Orthodox *Euchologion*, or *Book of Prayers*: 'The earth, although without words, groans and cries out: Why, all people, do you pollute me with so many evils?'[9]

In the face of this twofold breakdown, Lent is an attempt to reassert our true relationship both with our fellow humans and with the created order. The first aspect, our interdependence as members of the human race, is asserted in a striking manner through the selection of Scripture readings in the period immediately before Lent. Exploring the choice of texts, we discover what my history teacher at school used constantly to repeat to us: 'It all ties up, you see, it all ties up.'

1. Shortly before Lent, we celebrate on 2 February the feast known in the West as 'The Presentation of Christ in the Temple', or 'The Purification of St Mary the Virgin' (Candlemas). In the Orthodox Tradition, this is called 'The Meeting of our Lord and God and Saviour Jesus Christ'. When the infant Christ is brought to the

temple on the fortieth day by his mother and St Joseph the foster-father, and is received by Simeon the Elder and Anna the Prophetess, this is seen as symbolizing the meeting of the Saviour with his chosen people (see the Gospel reading for the day, Luke 2.22-40, especially verses 27-32). Thus, not long before the actual beginning of the Great Fast, the Lenten *leitmotif* is already established: meeting, encounter, relationship. I am truly a person – a *prosopon* or 'face', to use the Greek term – only if I meet and face other persons, if I look into their eyes and allow them to look into mine. I need you in order to be myself!

2. Three weeks before the Great Fast, we start to use the special service book for Lent, the *Triodion*, on what is known as 'The Sunday of the Publican and the Pharisee' (Gospel reading: Luke 18.10-14). The Pharisee's fault is that he refuses to recognize the publican as his brother. In his unloving rejection of the publican, the Pharisee denies the essential relationship of *koinonia* which unites him to his fellow humans. He exemplifies exactly the predicament from which, during the Great Forty Days, we are striving to escape.

3. The next observance, seven days later, is 'The Sunday of the Prodigal Son' (Gospel reading: Luke 15.11-32). The parable of the prodigal is basically the story of the loss and the recovery of personal relationship. At the outset, the younger son goes astray because he thinks in terms of things rather than persons. 'Give me the share of the property that falls to me', he says to the father (Luke 15.12). He is not interested in his personal relationship with his father, but only in the property that he expects to inherit. And the result of this repudiation of personal relationship on his part is that he finds himself 'in a far country' (Luke 15.13), alienated, in exile, lonely and self-isolated.

The path of repentance that he has to traverse involves a restoration of personal relationship, a return to his father, his family and the community of his home. His return is sealed by a great feast, and the purpose of every feast is precisely to express *koinonia* and fellowship. Food is a mediating bond, and so each common meal is an affirmation of community. When the elder son refuses to join the feast, what he is doing is to exclude himself from relationship and community. This is clear from the way in which he refers to the returning prodigal; he does not call him 'my brother', but says to his father, 'this son of yours' (Luke 15.30). Until he can learn once more to say 'my brother', the elder son will inevitably remain out in the cold, self-excluded from the human community – in short, an 'unperson'; for without mutual love there is no true personhood.

4. On the following Saturday there is a special commemoration of the dead, all-embracing in its scope:

> To those who died in faith on the mountainside or the road, in the tombs or the desert, monks and married people, young and old: grant to them all, O Christ, a dwelling with your saints.

> To the faithful who were taken from this life suddenly, at a time that they expected not, in the midst of joy or sorrow, of prosperity or misfortune: give rest, our Saviour, to them all.

> To those destroyed by cold, killed by falling from their horse, overwhelmed by hail, snow or thunderstorms, crushed by rocks or suffocated in the earth, give rest, O Christ our Saviour...

The community of which we are members, so we proclaim on this 'Saturday of the Dead', is not obliterated or severed at our departure from this life. The risen Christ has destroyed death: in him we are all alive, and in him we are all one. Thus, in our prayers on this Saturday for those who have died, we testify that the *koinonia* to which we belong is a single and undivided fellowship of both living and departed.

5. On the next day, eight days before Lent, we observe 'The Sunday of the Last Judgment, or 'The Sunday of Meat-Fare', as it is also known, for it is the last occasion on which meat is permitted until we reach Easter Sunday. In the epistle reading (1 Corinthians 8.8–9.2), the theme is once more personal relationships. Persons are far more important than rules about fasting, St Paul insists: 'Food will not commend us to God' (1 Corinthians 8.8). What matters is not the strictness with which we observe regulations concerning food, but the degree of sensitivity that we show towards the distress and uneasiness of our fellow humans. If by eating 'food offered to idols' I 'wound the conscience' of another person, then it is better for me to abstain from such food, even though eating it is not in itself sinful (1 Corinthians 8.10-12). The decisive criterion is mutual love, not the observance or non-observance of fasting and abstinence.

In the Gospel reading, the parable of the sheep and the goats (Matthew 25.31-46), exactly the same point is implied. The determining principle of the last judgment is not the rigour of our ascetic self-denial, but the practical compassion that we show to our neighbour. At the second coming, I shall not be asked how strictly I fasted, how many vigils I kept, how many prostrations I made. I shall be asked: Did you feed the hungry? Did you give drink to the thirsty? Did you take the stranger into your home, did you clothe the naked, did you visit the sick and those in prison? That is all I shall be asked.

In both the Scripture readings for this Sunday, then, there is set before us a clear and unmistakable order of priorities. Persons come first, rules of fasting come afterwards. Our Lenten abstinence will be worse than useless if it does not bring us closer to our fellow humans. A fast without love is the fast of demons. What is the use of our abstinence, protests St Basil the Great (d. 379), if instead of eating meat we devour our brother or sister through cruel gossip?[10] It is better to eat meat, and at the same time to be kind and humble, than to eat nothing but lentils and to be a sour rigorist.

6. Last of all in the pre-Lenten period, there comes 'The Sunday of Forgiveness', on the day immediately before the start of the actual Fast. The epistle reading (Romans 13.11–14.4) takes up the same theme as the previous Sunday's epistle. 'Let not him who eats despise him who abstains, and let not him who abstains pass judgment on him who eats' (Romans 14.3). If we fast in a spirit of censoriousness, we deprive our fasting of any spiritual value. God is interested not in my diet but in my relationships with other persons.

The same point is underlined, in a much more fundamental and far-reaching manner, in the Gospel reading for this Sunday (Matthew 6.14-21). Here Jesus emphasizes the crucial importance of mutual forgiveness: 'If you do not forgive others their trespasses, neither will your Father forgive your trespasses' (Matthew 6.15). The meaning here is not that God denies forgiveness to us, deliberately withholding his pardon. On the contrary, God is always eager to forgive us; but if we on our side are not willing to extend forgiveness to others, we simply render ourselves incapable of receiving into our hearts the forgiveness that God is offering to us. Unless we ourselves forgive, we are not open to the divine forgiveness. God does not shut us out, but it is we who close the door in his face through our hardness towards others and our unrelenting resentment.

The message of the Sunday Gospel is re-enacted in visible form through the ceremony of mutual forgiveness that takes place in many monasteries and parish churches at the end of Vespers on the same day. The monastic superior or parish priest kneels before the congregation, asking pardon and saying, 'Forgive me, a sinner'; and then the others kneel before him, each saying the same words. The forgiveness is given on a one-to-one basis: each comes in succession and kneels before the superior or celebrant, who kneels likewise in return, and then the members of the congregation go round the church and kneel individually before one another, requesting and transmitting pardon.[11]

This ceremony of mutual forgiveness, so far from being merely a ritual form, can be and often is a profoundly moving moment, altering the lives of those who participate. Symbolic gestures of this kind have a decisive effect. I can recall occasions when this exchange of forgiveness on the threshold of Lent has served as a forceful catalyst, suddenly breaking down long-standing barriers and making possible a true re-creation of relationship. What the Vespers of Forgiveness surely proclaims, in actions that speak louder than words, is that the Lenten voyage is a journey which none can undertake alone.

'It all ties up.' The pre-Lenten period shows us plainly what is the true character of the Great Forty Days. The Lenten springtime is a season when, by God's mercy, our wintry heart thaws and we come back into relationship both with God and with each other. The two forms of relationship, Godward and humanward, presuppose each other. I cannot draw nearer to God unless I draw nearer to my neighbour, and I cannot draw nearer to my neighbour unless I draw nearer to God. Lent signifies in this way not only offering, not only mission, but mutual love.

The purpose of Lent is to break down barriers, so that we can more fully share our life with God and with each other. From one point of view, then, the aim of the Great Forty Days is 'decentralization', the displacement of my fallen self from the centre of my attention, so that there is room in my heart for others and for my Creator. Lent teaches each person to say, not simply 'I', but 'I-and-Thou'; not simply 'me', but 'us'. In our present-day consumer society, dominated as it is by selfishness and the lust for possessions, that gives to Lent a direct contemporary relevance.

Thus it becomes evident that fasting, which is often regarded as the chief feature of Lent, is not an end but a means. Fasting is valueless if it fails to bring about a restoration of relationships. In fact, in the Gospels, Jesus does not simply speak of fasting alone but often employs the doublet 'prayer and fasting' (see Matthew 17.21; Mark 9.29). If we fast, it is in order to render ourselves more apt for prayer, that is to say, in order to bring us back into relationship with God.

The early Christians expanded this doublet into a triad: along with prayer and fasting they emphasized the need for 'almsgiving' (*eleimosyni*), for acts of specific and practical compassion towards others. The money that we save through fasting and abstinence is never to be spent upon ourselves, but should be given to those in special need. Moreover, as we have already seen, what we are to share with others is not only our money but ourselves; we are to give our time, our companionship, our loving concern. So the reawakening of our relationship with God in prayer comes to fulfilment in the renewal of our relationship with others. Fasting, prayer and acts of compassion form a single whole.

Yet, even though fasting itself is not the primary purpose of Lent, at the same time fasting and abstinence – in the Orthodox usage no sharp distinction is drawn between these two terms – are not to be marginalized or dismissed as unimportant. In fact, the Orthodox are encouraged to fast with considerable strictness. If Lent is indeed to be a time of sacrifice, this must apply among other things to our eating and drinking. In the seven weeks from Clean Monday to Holy Saturday, Orthodox Christians are expected to observe what is basically a 'vegan' diet. Meat is forbidden, together with all animal products (eggs, milk, butter and cheese); wine and olive oil are allowed only on Saturdays and Sundays, and on a few other feast days; fish may not be eaten except on the Feast of the Annunciation and Palm Sunday.[12]

In practice, relaxation of these regulations is allowed with some frequency within the Orthodox Church today, especially for those living in families where the other members are non-Orthodox or even non-Christian. There are three useful guidelines to be kept in view. First, we should not fast in such a way as to damage our health or to make ourselves inefficient in our work. Secondly, we should not fast 'like the hypocrites' (Matthew 6.16), in such a way as to excite notice or to draw attention to ourselves. When we are eating in the home of others, it is often humbler and most Christ-like to accept what is set before us, raising no objections, rather than to demand an alternative that conforms to the rules. If our fasting embarrasses others or causes them extra work, something has gone badly wrong.

Thirdly, at the same time, our fasting should be more than merely casual and nominal. It should be sufficiently exacting for us to notice and to regret what it is that we are denying ourselves. Lent will have lost its value if it ceases to be a *podvig*, a struggle against our fallen selfishness. 'Through the Cross joy has come to all the world', we affirm each Sunday in a hymn at Matins. We cannot enter into the joy of the Lenten springtime except through cross-bearing.

Nevertheless, even though fasting, rightly practised, does indeed involve sacrifice and self-denial, it is not to be construed exclusively in negative terms. Its purpose is most definitely positive: not to chastise the body, but to render it spiritual; not to fill us with weariness and self-disgust, but to break down our sinful sense of self-sufficiency and to make us conscious of our dependence upon God. Fasting is certainly an ascetic *podvig*, but its effect is to bring about a sense of lightness and freedom, of wakefulness and hope. 'Thus says the Lord of hosts: the fast... shall be to the house of Judah seasons of joy and gladness, and cheerful feasts' (Zechariah 8.19).[13]

Walking Gently on the Earth

The sense of community which Lent seeks to establish is not limited to our relationship with God and our relationship with our fellow humans. It extends yet more widely. Lent is a time when we also restore our relationship with our material environment: first of all, with our own physical bodies, and then with the world of nature – with the animals and the plants, with earth, air, fire and water – with which our bodies bring us into contact. Lent reactivates our membership not only of the human community, but equally of the cosmic *koinonia*. 'Anyone who does not love trees does not love Christ', as Fr Amphilochios (1888-1970), the *gerontas* of Patmos, used to say. That, too, is part of the meaning of Lent.

'Every thing that lives is Holy', said that great prophet of eighteenth-century England, William Blake. Glossing his words, we may add that every thing that God has made is in some sense alive. Lent cleanses the doors of our perception, so that we recognize anew this intrinsic and universal holiness. The Great Fast teaches us, in the phrase used by the American Indians, to 'walk gently upon the earth'. Confronted as we are by an ecological crisis that is escalating on a horrific scale, we can recover through our observance of Lent a sacramental view of the universe.

In what way? It is all too easy to misinterpret Lent in a Manichaean sense. People seem to think that, because they are encouraged to fast, there must be something shameful about enjoying one's food. By the same token, when married couples are urged to abstain from sexual intercourse during Lent, they may be in danger of imagining that sexuality is a defilement. Such conclusions are erroneous and deeply harmful. 'God saw everything that he had made, and behold, it was altogether good and beautiful' (Genesis 1.31). Our bodies, as created by God, are essentially good; food and drink is God's gift, and so is sexuality; all material things are potentially a sacrament of his presence, a means of communion with him.

Why then are we told to fast and to abstain? The answer is that, although the world as God's creation is 'altogether good and beautiful', it is also a fallen world. More exactly, our attitude as humans towards the divine creation has been distorted by sin – both by the original sin that we all inherit and by the sins that we each

82

individually commit. Fasting and abstinence correct the distortion
in our relationship with the material world, purifying us from the
effects of sinfulness, and restoring our primal vision of the created
order. Asceticism is in this way not a negation but a vindication of
the innate holiness of all material things.

Fasting teaches us first of all to have a right attitude towards
our own body, with all its needs and impulses. Through fasting we
school the body to participate in the spiritual life, so that it becomes
– to use the phrase of St Maximus the Confessor (d. 662) – 'the soul's
messenger'. Our aim is not the body's repression but its transfiguration. Properly understood, asceticism is a fight not against
but for the body. Through ascetic self-restraint we reaffirm the
materiality of our body, but at the same time we seek to render that
materiality spiritual. Asceticism does not mean that we repudiate
the legitimate pleasure that is conferred through eating, and also
within marriage – on a much more profound level – through
sexuality. What fasting and abstinence do is to assist us in liberating
ourselves from greed and lust, so that both these things become not
a means of private pleasure but an expression of interpersonal
communion.

Recovering through the Great Fast a right attitude to our bodies,
we recover also a right attitude to the creation as a whole. We are
helped to value each thing for itself – not just for the way in which
it serves our own ends – and at the same time we are helped to see
the divine presence at the heart of each thing. The Christian, it has
been said, is the one who, wherever he or she looks, sees everywhere
Christ and rejoices in him: 'Lift the stone, and you will find me; cut
the wood in two, and there am I.'[14] That is the true aim of fasting:
it renders the creation personal and transparent, so that we regain
our sense of wonder before the sacredness of the earth. It assists
us to see all things in God, and God in all things.

In this manner, through fasting and voluntary self-restraint we
come close in spirit to the Blessed Virgin Mary at the moment of

the annunciation, and we reassert our freedom and personhood in God. So long as we are dominated by greed and lust, then in our relationship to material things we are profoundly unfree and depersonalized. Once we cease to see material things as objects and regard them as means of personal communion, once we stop grasping them compulsively and begin to offer them back to God in thanksgiving, then we become free and personal once more. At the same time, we make the all-important transition – so often emphasized by ecologists – from a way of life based on what I want, to a way of life based on what I need.

Such are among the kites that each Lent we are encouraged to set flying in the sky. The Great Forty Days proclaim a world-view utterly at variance with the standards of our consumer society. As the Lenten Fast returns each year, we can make it a season of inner springtime – an occasion, that is to say, for renewed sacrifice and self-offering; for renewed schooling in our baptismal commitment and for renewed missionary witness; for renewed sharing between self and neighbour, and between self and cosmos.

Lent, so far from being world-denying, is in reality intensely world-affirming. This is a fallen world, full of the ugliness and pollution caused by human sin and selfishness. But it is also God's world, a world full of beauty and wonder, marked everywhere with the signature of the Creator, and this we can rediscover through a true observance of the Great Fast.

6

Death and Bereavement

Metropolitan Anthony of Sourozh

I would like to begin by dispelling, if I can, the habitual attitude which modern men and women have developed concerning death. This is a feeling of fear and rejection, the feeling that death is the worst that can occur to a person and that at all cost survival must be achieved, even if survival has little to do with real living.

The Remembrance of Death

In earlier times, when Christians were nearer both to their pagan roots and to the tremendous, shaking experience of conversion, death was spoken of in terms of a birth into eternal life. It was perceived not as an end, not as the ultimate defeat, but as a beginning. Life was thought of as an ascent towards eternity, and death was felt to be that door which opens and allows us to enter it. This explains why so often the early Christians used to remind one another of death by words such as 'remember death', while in the prayers which St John Chrysostom has left us as a precious inheritance there is a petition in which we ask God to give us 'a remembrance of death'.

When such words are spoken to modern people, the reaction is usually one of rejection and revulsion. Do these words mean that we should remember that death is like the sword of Damocles over our heads, hanging by a hair, and that at any moment the banquet of life may end tragically? Do they mean that whenever a joy comes our way, we must be aware that it will have an end? Is it that we wish to darken the light of every day by the fear of an impending death? This is not what the early Christians felt. What they felt was that death is a decisive moment at which all that we can do on earth will have come to an end. We must therefore hurry to achieve on earth all that can be achieved. Remembering death is paradoxically an aim to achieve in life: to become the true person whom we were called by God to be; to reach as near as we can to what St Paul calls the full stature of Christ; to become as perfectly as possible an undistorted image of God.

St Paul in one of his epistles says that we must make haste to live because time is deceptive. We live all the days of our life as though we are writing hastily, carelessly, a draft of life which one day we will copy out in fair hand. It is as though we are just preparing to build, collecting all that will later be organized into beauty, harmony and meaning. We live this way year after year, not doing completely, fully or perfectly what we can do, because there is time ahead of us. We tell ourselves: later we will achieve something; later it can be done; one day the fair copy will be written. But years pass and we never do it.

This is not only because death comes, but because at every period of life we become unable to do what the previous period would have allowed us to do. It is not in our mature years that we can achieve a beautiful and meaningful youth, as it is not in old age that we can reveal to God and to the world what we might have been in our years of maturity. There is a time for all things, but once the time has gone, these things can no longer be done.

Victor Hugo said that there is fire in the eyes of the young, but there should be light in the eyes of the old. The time of the glowing fire passes, the time of light reaches us, but when the time of being a light has come, we can no longer do those things which can be done only in the days of our flaming. Time is deceptive. When we are told that we must remember death, it is not in order to give us a fear of life, it is in order to make us live with all the intensity which we could possibly have if we were aware that every moment is the only moment which we possess, and that every single moment of our life must be perfect: not a trough but the crest of a wave, not a defeat but a triumph. And so the remembrance of death seems to be the only power that makes life ultimately intense.

Those of us who have had occasion to live for a certain time with a dying person, with a person aware of the coming of death, while we were aware of it also, must have understood what the presence of death can mean in a relationship. It means that every word must contain all the reverence, all the beauty, all the harmony and love which was perhaps dormant within the relationship. It means that there is nothing which is small, because everything, however small, can be an expression of love, or a denial of it.

This is very important, because it colours our whole attitude to death. It may make it a great challenge, the thing that allows us to grow to our full stature and continuously try to be all that we can be without any hope to be better later if we do not care to be right today.

Dostoyevsky, in *The Brothers Karamazov*, speaks of hell. He says hell can be summed up in two words: 'too late!' Only the remembrance of death can allow us so to live that we should never be confronted with this frightening awareness: it is too late. Words or gestures that could fulfil a relationship can no longer be spoken or made. This does not mean that ultimately this cannot be achieved; but it can only be achieved in another way, at the cost of much pain.

Several years ago, an old man in his middle eighties came to see me. He wanted advice because he could not continue to live in the agony that had been his for some sixty years. In the course of the Civil War in Russia he had killed a girl whom he loved and who loved him. They loved one another dearly. They intended to be married, but in the course of the shooting she had suddenly run across his line of fire and it was too late to deflect his shot.

For sixty years he could not find peace. Not only had he cut short a life that was infinitely precious to him, but he had cut short a life that was blossoming and that was infinitely precious to the girl he loved. He told me that he had prayed, begged forgiveness of the Lord, gone to confession, made penance, received absolution and communion – done everything which his imagination and the imagination of those to whom he turned suggested, but he could never find peace.

In the inspiration of an intense, searing sympathy and compassion, I said to him: 'You can turn to Christ whom you have not murdered, to priests whom you have not harmed. Why haven't you ever though of turning to the girl that you killed?'

He was surprised. Cannot God forgive? Is he not the only one who can forgive the sins of men on earth? And indeed, of course, it is so. But I suggested to him that if the girl whom he had shot could forgive, could intercede for him, even God could not pass her by.

There is a story about the prophet Daniel in which Daniel prays, and God says to him that his prayer is in vain. This is because an old woman who has a grudge against him is praying against Daniel's prayer, and her prayer is like a strong wind that blows down like smoke the prayer which he hoped would ascend to heaven.

That was the image, perhaps, that came to me subconsciously. I suggested to him that he should sit down after evening prayers and tell this girl about these sixty years of mental agony, of a heart laid to waste, of the pain he had endured, ask her forgiveness and then ask her also to intercede for him and to ask the Lord to send peace into his heart if she had forgiven. And he did it, and peace came. So what is left undone on earth can be fulfilled. What has been a failure on earth can later be healed – but years of pain and remorse, of tears and loneliness, may be the price.

Now when we think of death, we cannot think of it as either a glorious or a miserable event. The vision given to us by God in the Bible and the Gospels is more complex than this. To put it in short:

God did not create us for death and destruction; he created us for eternal life. He called us to immortality – not only to the immortality of the resurrection but to an immortality that knew no death. Death came as a result of sin. It came because man lost God, turned away from him, looked for ways in which he could achieve all things apart from God. The knowledge which could have been acquired by communion with the knowledge and wisdom of God man tried to acquire himself. Instead of living in the familiarity of God, he chose his own independence.

The French pastor Roland de Curie wrote in a way that is perhaps a good image, that the moment man turned his back on God and looked into the infinite in front of him, there was no God for him, and as God is the only source of life, he could do nothing but die. This means that there is a tragedy in death. On the one hand, death is monstrous, death should not be there at all. Death is the result of our loss of God. On the other hand, an endless duration separated from God, thousands and thousands of years of life without any hope that there will be an end to this separateness from God, would be more horrible than the dissolving of our bodily frame and an end of this vicious circle.

So there is another aspect of death: narrow as the gate is, it is the only gate that allows us to escape the vicious circle of endlessness apart from God – a creaturely endlessness in which there is no space for our becoming again partakers of the life of God and ultimately partakers of the divine nature. This is why St Paul could say: 'for me to live is Christ. Death will be a gain, because as long as I live in this body I am separated from Christ.'

This is why he said in another passage that for him to die is not to drop from his shoulders the temporary life; for him, to die means to be clothed in eternity. It is not an end; it is a beginning. It is a door that opens and allows us into the vastness of eternity which would be closed for us for ever if death did not free us from our integration into earthly things.

In our attitude to death these two sides must play a role. When a person dies we can legitimately be heartbroken. We can look with horror at the fact that sin has murdered a person whom we love. We can refuse to accept death as the last word, the last event of life. We are right when we cry over the departed, because this should not be. This person was killed by evil.

On the other hand, we can rejoice, because new life, unbounded, free, has begun for him or her. And again, we can cry over ourselves, our bereavement, our loneliness, but at the same time we must learn what the Old Testament had already foreseen and foretold, when it said: 'love is as strong as death'. This is the love that does not allow the memory of the beloved to fade, the love that makes us speak not in the past tense of our relationship with the beloved one: 'I loved him, we were so close', but makes us think in the present tense: 'I love him; we are so close'.

In the New Testament, we find something even greater than this, because with the resurrection of Christ, death is virtually overcome. Death is overcome in more than one way. It is overcome because we know through the resurrection of Christ that death is not the last word and that we are called to rise again and to live. Death is also defeated in the victory of Christ over sin and over death itself in the harrowing of hell, because the most horrible aspect of death, as it was conceived in the Old Testament, was that the separatedness from God that had brought about death was made definitive, unconquerable, by death itself. Those who had died – and this applied to everyone – those who had died of the loss of God in death lost him for ever. The Old Testament Sheol was the place where God is not, the place of definitive, irretrievable absence and separation.

In the resurrection of Christ, in his descent into hell, in his harrowing of hell, this has come to an end. There is separation on earth and the pain of separation, but there is no separation in death from God. On the contrary, death is the moment and the way in which, however separate we were, however incompletely united or in harmony with God we were, we present ourselves before his face. God is the saviour of the world. Did he not say more than once: 'I have come not to judge the world but to save the world?' We stand before him who is salvation.

So death has a complexity – one could perhaps say an ambiguity – but we have no right, if we are Christ's own people, to allow ourselves to overlook the birth into eternity of the departing one because we ourselves are so deeply wounded by our bereavement and in our earthly loneliness. There is also in death a power of life that reaches out to us. If our love is faithful, if we are capable of remembering, not only with our mind but with our heart, those whom we have loved on earth, then, as Christ puts it: 'where your treasure is there will your heart be also'.

It is difficult, if not impossible, to speak of questions of life and death without being personal. We meet death in our lives first of all, not as a subject on which we reflect, although this happens, but mainly as a result of bereavement, either our own or someone else's. And it is this vicarious experience of death that serves as a background for us to reflect afterwards on the certainty of our own death, and on the way in which we relate to it.

My father was a shy man. He spoke little, and we spoke little to one another. On Easter Day he felt unwell for a short moment, so he lay down. I sat next to him and for the first time in our lives we spoke with total openness. It was not our words that were so significant. There was an openness of mind and heart. The doors were open. The silence was as open and as deep as the words.

And then I had to go. I said goodbye to everyone who was in the room, but not to him, because I felt that, having met as we had met, we could not ever part from one another. There was no goodbye. There was not even an *au revoir*, a 'see you again', because we had met, and that was for ever.

He died the same night. I remember coming back from the hospital where I worked, being told that he had died, walking to his room and shutting the door behind me. What I perceived was a quality and depth of silence that was not to any degree an absence of noise, an absence of sound. It was a silence that was substantial, a silence, as the French writer Georges Bernanos expressed it in one of his novels – 'a silence that was a presence'.

And I heard myself say: 'and people dare to say that death exists. What a lie.'

This explains why my attitude to death is perhaps so one-sided: why I see the glory of it and not only the pain and the bereavement. My experience refers to sudden death, to death unexpected, the death that comes like a thief in the night. If such experiences come your way, you will probably understand how one can still rejoice, while one's heart is in searing pain and agony, and how – to this we will come later – we can in our funeral service exclaim: 'Blessed is the road which thou treadest today, O human soul, because the place of refreshment is prepared unto thee.' This is also why we use the words of a psalm in the same service, as though the departed was speaking to us saying: 'My soul lives and I give glory unto the Lord'.

But more often than a sudden death we are confronted with a long or short terminal illnesses, or with old age that gradually brings us either to our grave, seen from one viewpoint, or to our freedom. This is the supreme encounter for which each of us, knowingly or unknowingly, longs and strives throughout his earthly life, our meeting face to face with the living God, our encounter with Life Eternal, our communion with him. This period of illness or of increasing old age must be faced and must be understood creatively and usefully.

One of the great tragedies of life, which brings great agony of mind to people, is when they see a beloved person grow older and older, lose his or her physical and mental faculties, seeming to lose what was most precious: a clear mind, a witty response to life, and such like. So often this process is put to one side. We close our eyes so as not to see, because we are afraid of seeing and of foreseeing.

And the result is that when death comes, it is a sudden death which not only has the horrors of an unexpected death, but has the additional horror of hitting us in our most vulnerable situation.

This is because the pain, fear and anguish have been growing in intensity within us while we were refusing to give them freedom of expression and any possibility of maturity. The blow is even more painful and destructive than that of sudden death, because apart from the horror and pain of bereavement, comes all the self-reproach and self-condemnation for not having done all that could have been done. To have done it would have forced us into truth, and into unveiling for ourselves and for the dying person the fact that death was gradually opening a door – and that this door would one day open wide and the beloved one would have to enter into it without looking back.

It is important for all of us, whenever we are confronted with this gradually approaching bereavement, to face it from the beginning and to face it in the wonderfully balanced way in which we can do it while the person is still alive and in our midst. For against the thought of the coming death there is the reality of a living presence. We can all the time lean on the security of this presence while we become more and more aware of the complexity of the coming bereavement. It is this balance between the power of reality and the frailty of thought that makes it possible for us to prepare ourselves for the death of people who are precious to us.

This preparation also entails – as I said earlier – an attitude to death which recognizes on the one hand the horror and pain of bereavement, but also recognizes the fact that death is a door opening into life eternal. 'To me to die is not to divest myself of temporal life, but to clothe myself in eternity', said St Paul. This period of preparation can be illustrated with a couple of examples.

My mother died of cancer over a period of three years. She was operated on unsuccessfully. The doctor told me about it and then added: 'But of course you will not say anything to your mother'.

I said: 'I will'. And I did.

I remember how I came to her and said to her that her doctor had rung and that the operation was not successful. We kept silent for a moment and then my mother said: 'And so I shall die'.

I said: 'Yes.'

And then we stayed together in complete silence, communing without any words. I don't think that we thought thoughts. We faced something that had entered life and made all the difference to life. It was not a shadow. It was not an evil. It was not a terror. It was the ultimate. And we had to face this ultimate without yet knowing what this ultimate would unfold itself into. We stayed as long as we felt we had to stay. And then life continued.

But two things happened as a result. The one is that at no moment was either my mother or I walled up within a lie, forced into a comedy, deprived of any help. At no moment had I to come into my mother's room with a smile that was untrue, or say words that were untrue. At no moment were we to play a comedy of life conquering death, of illness waning, of things being better than they were, when we both knew they were not. At no moment were we deprived of one another's help. There were moments when my mother felt she needed help. She would then ring the bell and I would come and we would speak of her dying, of my bereavement.

She loved life. She loved it deeply. A few days before she died she said that she would be prepared to live 150 years in suffering, but to live. She loved us. She grieved over separation: 'Oh, for the touch of a vanished hand and the sound of a voice that is still.'

And then there were other moments when I felt the pain of it, and I would come and speak of it to my mother. And she would give me her support and help me face her death. This was a deep and true relationship. There was nothing of a lie in it. Therefore, all that was true could find a place in it.

There was also another side which I mentioned earlier. Because death could come at any moment, and it would be too late to put right something that had gone wrong, all life has to be at every moment an expression, as perfect and complete as possible, of a relationship that is one of reverence and love. Only death can make things that seem to be small and insignificant into signs that are great and significant. The way you prepare a cup of tea on a tray, the way you put cushions behind the back of a sick person, the way your voice sounds, the way you move – all that can be an expression of all there is in a relationship.

If there is a false note, if there is a crack, if something has gone wrong, it must be repaired now, because there is the inevitable certainty that later it may be too late. Death confronts you with the truth of life, with a sharpness and clarity which nothing else can convey.

It is important for us, whether we face our own death or the death of another person, to become aware of eternity. Some thirty years ago, a man was taken into hospital with, as it seemed, a common illness. On examination, it was discovered that he was ill with an inoperable cancer. His sister was told and so was I, but he was not. He was vigorous, strong and intensely alive.

He said to me: 'I have so much to do, and here am I, bedridden and for how long?'

I said to him: 'How often you have told me that you dream of being able to stop time so that you can *be* instead of doing. You have never done it. God has done it for you. Now is your time to be.'

Confronted with the necessity of being, in what one might call a totally contemplative situation, he was puzzled and said: 'What shall I do?'

I said to him that illness and death are conditioned not only by physiological changes – by germs and pathology – but also by all those things which destroy our inner energies. This is what one may call our negative thoughts and feelings, everything that saps the power of life within us, everything that prevents life from gushing like a torrent that is clear and free. I suggested that he should put right not only outwardly but within himself all that was wrong in his relationships with people, with himself, in the circumstances of his life, and to begin in the present moment. And when he had done it in the present, to go back and ever further back into the past, clearing it all, making his peace with everyone and everything, undoing every knot, facing every evil, coming to terms in repentance, in acceptance, in gratitude, with his whole life – and his life had been hard.

So day after day, month after month, we went through this process. He made his peace with the totality of life. And I remember him at the end of it lying in his bed too weak to use a spoon and saying to me with shining eyes: 'My body is almost dead, and yet I have never felt so intensely alive as I feel now'. He had discovered that life was not his body, although his body was him, and that he had a reality which the death of his body could not destroy.

This is a very important experience. It is something which we must do in the course of all our life, all the time, if we want to be aware of the power of eternal life within us and, therefore, not be afraid whatever happens to the temporary life which is also ours.

Bereavement

Our first and most continuous contact with death is through bereavement. By learning to understand and live through the death of others, in them and in ourselves, we can learn to face death and eventually face our own death, first as a possibility – a certainty indeed, but a certainty which is often apparently so far removed from us that we do not call it certainty – and then as the very reality that comes upon us.

One of the immediate problems which a bereaved person has to face is the experience of loneliness, of being left behind by the only person, at times, who mattered, by the person who filled all the space, all the time, all the heart. But even if all the heart was not involved, the person who left us leaves a very vast space. While the person is ill we give a great deal more time to thought. Our activities are centred and directed. When the person dies, very often those left behind feel that their activities have no purpose, no immediate purpose at least, no centre, no directedness. A life that, however painful and agonising, was running like a stream, becomes a bog.

Loneliness also means that there is not one person with whom we can talk or listen to, or to whom we can be attentive; who responds and reacts, and to whom we react and respond. The person who leaves us is more often than not the very person who in our own eyes gave us our ultimate value: the person to whom we truly mattered, the person who asserted our existence and our importance.

I have mentioned more than once on the occasion of a wedding, the phrase of Leon Bloy, who says: 'To tell a person "I love you", is tantamount to saying "You shall never die".' This also applies in this context. The person who leaves us is no longer there to proclaim our ultimate value, our ultimate significance. This person is no longer there who can say 'I love you', and therefore we are no more affirmed or acknowledged eternally. This is something which must be faced. It is not something which must be or can be put to one side, forgotten or evaded. A void is created, and this void should never be artificially filled with things which are unworthy of what they replace.

We must be prepared to recognize that pain is one of the expressions of love. If we claim that we truly love the person who has now departed this life, we must be prepared to love them in and through pain, as we once loved them in and through joy – the joy of assertion, the joy of the common life. This requires courage, and I think there is a great deal that needs to be explained in this respect in our present day, when so many people, in order to escape the pain, will turn to tranquillisers, alcohol, or to entertainment of one sort or another in order to forget. What is going on in a human

97

soul may be overshadowed, but it continues to go on, and unless it is resolved, it leaves the person poorer, and not richer.

Another thing which a person bereaved must learn never to do is to speak of the love relationship that existed before in the past tense. One should never say 'We loved one another'. We should always say 'We love each other'.

If we allow our love to become a thing of the past, we have to recognize that we do not believe in the continuing life of the person who has died. If we do this, we must recognize that we are unbelievers and atheists in the crudest sense, and face life from a quite different angle. If there is no God, if there is no eternal life, then the death which has occurred has no metaphysical significance at all. It is an event of natural history. It is a victory of the laws of physics and chemistry, and the person continues to exist not as a person but as a part of nature. In each case, we must face squarely either our faith or our lack of faith and act accordingly.

Very often, those left behind feel that the loss of the person is not only their loss; it is a loss that bereaves everyone around them of something precious – of an intelligence, a heart and will, of one who acted rightly and beautifully. And the bereaved one dwells on this loss also. At this point we must remember – and this is essential – that everyone who lives sets an example: an example of how to live well, or an example of how to live badly. We must learn from everyone, living or departed, that which is wrong in order to avoid it, and that which is right in order to emulate it. Everyone who has known a departed person must reflect profoundly on the mark which this person's life has made on his or her life. They must reflect on what kind of seed was sown by the life of this person, and bear fruit.

There is a saying in the Gospel that 'unless the seed dies, it will not bear fruit, but if it dies, it will bear fruit thirtyfold, sixtyfold and a hundredfold'. This is exactly what can happen if we reflect with all our heart, mind and memory, with all our perceptiveness and sense of justice, on the life of those who have departed this life. If we have the courage to use that sword – which is God's own word – to divide the light from the darkness, to use all our discernment in sorting out the tares from the wheat, then, having collected all the wheat we are capable of discerning, each of us, every person who has known the departed person, can bear fruit from his or her life. We can live according to an example given and received, and emulate everything which is worthy of emulation in the life of this person.

At the funeral service we stand with lit candles. This signifies, I believe, two things. First, the one which is obvious: we are proclaiming the resurrection. We stand with lit candles in the same way in which we stand in church during Easter night. But we also stand witnessing before God that this person has brought at least a flicker of light into the twilight of the world; that this person has not lived in vain; this light we will keep, protect, increase and share out, so that it may illumine more and more people, so that it may grow thirtyfold, sixtyfold, a hundredfold if possible.

If we set out to live in such a way, to be the continuation of the earthly life of the departed person, if we set out to be the continuation of everything that was noble and good and true and holy in this person, then truly this person will not have lived in vain, and truly we will feel that we do not live in vain. There will be no space in us for hopes of prompt death, because we will have a function to fulfil.

We are left behind to make it possible for all we have seen, all we have heard, all we have experienced, to multiply and spread and be a new chain of light on earth. But if we can truly say that the person who has departed this life was a treasure to us, then where our treasure is there our heart should be. We should, together with this person who has entered into eternity, live as completely, as deeply as possible in eternity. For this is the only place where we can be together with the departed person. It means that as more and more beloved ones leave this earthly pilgrimage and enter into the stability and the peace of life eternal, we should feel that we belong more and more to that world, ever more completely, ever more perfectly, that its values become ours increasingly.

And if one of the beloved ones, one of the most treasured treasures is called the Lord Jesus Christ, then we can truly, while we are still on earth, like St Paul, long with all our hearts and minds, with all our flesh and heart, for the day when we shall be inseparably united to him.

Facing our own death is something which we do in ways very different according to age and circumstances. We perceive death differently in different situations and at different ages. Think of children who hear the word 'death'. They have perhaps a vague notion about it, or have perhaps lost a parent and grieved in loneliness. Their perception is that of bereavement, but not of death itself.

A child may be introduced to death in a monstrous way that will make him morbid or, on the contrary, in a sane and healthy way, as the following story shows. A most beloved grandmother died after a long and painful illness. I was summoned to the house, and when I arrived, I discovered that the children had been removed. After my question, the parents said: 'We could not allow the children to stay in a house where there was a dead person'.

'But why?'

'Because they know what death is.'

'And what is death?' I asked.

'They saw the other day a little rabbit torn to pieces by a cat in the garden, so they know what death is.'

I suggested that if that was the image of death which these children possessed they were bound throughout their lives to live with a sense of horror whenever they heard the word, wherever they attended a memorial service, wherever they saw a coffin – untold horror hidden in this wooden box. After a long argument, during which the parents told me that the children were bound to become nervous wrecks if they were allowed to see their grandmother and that their mental condition would be my responsibility, I brought the children back.

Their first question was: 'What really has happened to Granny?'

I said to them: 'You have heard her say time and again that she longed to join her husband in God's kingdom, where he had preceded her. It has happened to her now.'

'So she is happy,' said one of the children.

'Yes,' I said.

Then we went into the room where the grandmother lay. The stillness was wonderful. The old lady, whose face had been ravaged in the course of the last years by suffering, lay absolutely still and serene.

One of the children said, 'So that is death.'

And the other one said, 'How beautiful.'

Here are two forms of the same experience. Are we going to allow children to see death in terms of the little rabbit torn to pieces by cats in the garden, or are we going to let them see the serenity and beauty of death?

In the Orthodox Church, we bring the dead person to the Church as soon as we can. We pray in the presence of an open coffin. Adults and children approach it. Death is not something to be hidden: it is something simple and a part of life. And the children can look into the face of the departed person and see the peace.

We give a kiss to the departed person. And this is the moment when we must not forget to warn the child that when he kisses the forehead of a person that was always warm, it will be cold and we can say, 'this is the mark of death'. Life goes with warmth. Death is cold. And then the child is not horrified, because it has experience of things cold and things warm, and each of them have their nature, and each of them have their meaning.

Death

We now turn to the various services which are connected with death in the Orthodox Church. First of all, there are two services which are familiar to all Orthodox Christians. They are the short service in memory of the departed – the *panichida* – and also the funeral service of lay people. There are also other sequences which are less familiar: the canon which is read over a person whose departure from this life is difficult; the funeral service of a small child, and that of a priest. I want to single out a certain number of features which are basically common to all.

There are two sides to these services: a concern for the soul and a concern for the body. We have in common with all the Churches a prayerful concern for the departing or departed soul. But I believe that in Orthodoxy the attention paid to the body is very special and significant. In the *panichida*, all the attention is concentrated on the soul that is now in eternity, face to face with the living God, growing into an ever-deepening communion with him. In the funeral service, side by side with this concern for the soul which has departed, but is somehow still close to the earth, there is a deep concern for the body.

When we read the funeral service, the body is seen from two angles. On the one hand, we are aware that this body is doomed to corruption: 'Dust thou art and unto dust shalt thou return'. There is an acute pain in the thought and sight of this. We must find, in our attitude to the departed, a balance between the acceptance of reality and the certainty of our faith; between the sight of corruption and the certainty of eternal life; between the love for the place where rests what is left of a beloved body, and the certainty that the relationship of communion continues in God in eternity.

This is a first aspect of the participation of the body. We find in the various prayers, in the troparion and the canon, in the hymns of John Damascene, the reflection of this pain and this sense of

102

tragedy: a human body that was called to eternal life, killed by mortality born of the loss of God.

On the other hand, Holy Scripture uses the words 'body', 'person', or 'soul' on occasions to signify the whole person. And indeed the connection there is between the body and the soul, between the body and spiritual experience itself, is so complete. The testimony of St Paul is that 'faith comes by hearing, and hearing by the word of God'. A word is spoken, a word is heard, both through bodily means: the lips of the speaker, the ears of the hearer. And yet it reaches the heart, it reaches the mind, it reaches the core of a person in such a way that one word of God can transform the life of a person.

We also know how much all our senses participate in every event of our mind and heart; how much love is expressed by a mother to a small child by touching and nursing it; how much consolation can be given by the touch of a hand, how much love in all its forms finds expression through the body. And so, if we look at the body of a departed person, we do not see – as many say to console themselves, to blot out the pain – a clothing that has been discarded. It is not clothing and it is not discarded. It is a body which is as real, as really the person, as the soul. It is only together, body and soul, that we are a complete person.

This is brought out in an unexpected way, in a strange way perhaps, by St Isaac of Syria who, speaking of the body, says that the eternal destiny of man cannot be fixed before the resurrection of the body, because the body has as much right as the soul to choose and to determine the eternal destiny of the person. These words are mysterious to us because we cannot imagine how that can be. And yet, this body is me as much as the soul is me. And it is only in their togetherness that I can be seen.

Therefore, when we look at this body, we look at it with veneration. We see in it all the suffering and joy, all the mystery of life that has been that of the person. The body could be called the visible of the invisible. In that sense perhaps it is not in vain that in Slavonic, in the Church services, we use for the body the word *moshchi*, which is the word we use for relics.

And so, on the one hand we see this body so dear and so precious, wounded and conquered by mortality, subjected to death. And on the other hand we see it as a seed sown in order to rise again in the glory of immortality through the resurrection. And looking at it we cannot help seeing its connection with the Body of Christ.

St Paul used the phrase 'our life is hid with Christ in God'. Our bodily humanity is hid in the mystery of the Trinity, and this bodily humanity comprises our humanity. In Christ, in the Mother of God, we can see what our body is called to be: a glorious body. And so we are not divided but in a complex situation in which, heartbroken that we are separated, we look in wonder at the fact that a human body can die, and in faith and hope at a body which one day will rise like Christ's .

And then there is the soul. There are several prayers that precede the death of a person. These include sequences that are connected with preparation for death. First of all there is that preparation which consists of turning from things temporal to things eternal. St Seraphim could say before his death: 'Bodily I am nearing death, and in spirit I am like one just born, with all the newness, all the freshness of a beginning, not a finishing.'

This leads to the necessity of preparing for death through a stern and liberating process of coming to terms, making one's peace with everyone, with oneself, with one's conscience, with one's circumstances, with the present and the past, with events and with people, and indeed with the future, the coming of death itself. There must be a process by which we come to make our peace, as I think St Isaac of Syria puts it, with God, with our conscience, with our neighbour, even with the things which we have handled. This means that the whole earth can say to us: 'Go in peace'. And we too can say to all that the earth was to us: 'Stay in peace, and may God's peace and blessing be on you.'

One cannot enter into eternity tied, fettered by hatred, out of peace. If we want to be able to do this, in the short time which the coming of death offers us, it is essential that we should consider all our life as an ascent: an ascent into eternity, not a gradual decay towards death. This is an ascent to the moment when through the narrow gate of death we shall enter into eternity – not divesting ourselves of temporal life, but clothing ourselves with eternity, to use the words of St Paul.

If, in the *panichida*, there is a concentration of attention on the *departed* soul, in the funeral service, attention is also paid to the *departing* soul. According to Orthodox Tradition, for the first three days after the death of a person, his or her soul remains close to the earth, visiting familiar places perhaps, recalling to memory all that the earth has been; so that it is in full possession of all its memories that a soul will leave the earth and stand before God.

We therefore surround these three days with particular attention. Prayers are offered, *panichidas* are celebrated, our thought concentrates on all the complexities of our relationship with the departed person. And we also have our part to play. We also must untie knots within our soul. We also must be able to say to the departed person from the depth of our heart and of all our being: 'forgive me', and also say, 'I forgive you, go in peace'.

Perhaps it is here that we find the sense of the old saying that one should not speak ill of the departed. If we had truly, in all truth and reality, said to the person who has departed this life: 'I set you free; I will stand before God proclaiming forgiveness, let nothing that has happened between us stand in your way to fulfilment and eternal joy', then how can we go back and remember evil and bitterness?

This is not a way of closing one's eyes to reality, because if truly there has been evil in the life of a person, if truly there has been evil between us and the departed person, then how much we must pray to God to set both free – ourselves and the other one. How much we must pray to God to hear the words of forgiveness, 'go in peace', and to say the same words once and forever with an ever-increasing depth of understanding, with an ever-increasing awareness of an increasing freedom.

There are difficulties in the burial service. To start this service with the words, 'Blessed is our God', requires all our faith and all our determination. It stretches our faith at times to the limit. 'The Lord gave, the Lord hath taken away. Blessed be the name of the Lord', said Job. But it is not an easy thing when our hearts are rent and when we see the person whom we love above all, dead before our eyes.

And then there are prayers which are prayers of faith and prayers of reality and prayers of human frailty – prayers of faith accompanying the soul of the departed person, offered before the face of God as a testimony of love. This is really what prayers for the departed are: a testimony before God that this person has not lived in vain. However sinful and frail this person was, she has left behind a loving memory. Everything else will become dust. Love will survive all things. Faith will go and hope will go when faith is replaced by vision and hope by possession, but love will never go.

As we stand and pray for the departed, all we say is: 'Lord, this person has not lived in vain. What he has left on earth is an example and is love; the example we shall follow; the love will never die.'

I quoted earlier the words of Leon Bloy: 'To say to a person "I love you" is tantamount to saying "you shall never die".' To proclaim before God our undying love for the dead person is a way of affirming this person, not only in time, but in eternity. And when we stand with lit candles at the service we indeed proclaim our faith in the resurrection, but also we proclaim before the face of God that this person has brought a light into the world. 'Let your light so shine before all men, that seeing your good works they may give glory to your Father, who is in heaven.' This person has not shown merely a creative ligh‘, nor impressed us by genius, beauty or talent alone, but has allowed the light of God, the uncreated divine glory, to shine. This is something that will never die on earth.

Heartbroken we may well be, yet we still proclaim these words of faith: 'Blessed is our God'. At times, even more tragically resounds the Troparion of the Resurrection: 'Christ is risen from the dead, by death he has undone death and to those in the tomb he has given life', when before our eyes lies the dead body of a person whom we love. But there also is the voice of the Church speaking to us words of comfort and consolation: 'Blessed is the way thou treadest today, O human soul, for a place of rest has been prepared for thee.'

All the pain of the dying person is expressed in one of the troparia of the canon of the soul that has difficulty in departing from life: 'How painful it is to think of our separation', says the soul. Yet, here also is our certainty that death, which is our bereavement, is also a birth into eternity: that it is a beginning and not an end; that it is a great and holy encounter between God and the living soul, which can be fulfilled only in God.

7

An Orthodox Approach to Bioethics

Prof. H. Tristram Engelhardt Jr

It seems natural to speak of the ethics of different religious, cultural and ideological communities. Various books explore the ethics of Roman Catholics, Jews, Lutherans and others. It would therefore appear appropriate to give similar accounts of the ethics of the Orthodox, with books on Orthodox Christian ethics, bioethics, social justice and environmental ethics. The difficulty is that proper Orthodox conduct, Orthodox ethics, is understood quite differently from secular ethics and other religious ethics.

In Pursuit of an Orthodox Ethics

What for others is easily divided into a legion of various ethics – for example, bioethics, business ethics, environmental ethics, legal ethics – is for the Orthodox united in the right worship of one perfect God, who is a Holy Trinity of Father, Son and Holy Spirit. The ethics of the Orthodox is liturgical rather than discursive. It is an ethics founded in the transfiguring, liturgical worship of a God who transcends human categories, but who reveals himself in worship. In this transfiguring worship, the individual finds moral identity and the community finds its integrity. Orthodox ethics steps back from the babble of moral diversity and forward to communion with a trinitarian God. Consequently, Orthodox ethics often appears to be unengaged with popular social issues.

The Orthodox moral engagement also contrasts with ethics developed in the light and shadow of Western European philosophy.

Orthodox ethics is not just a body of teachings and dogmas. Nor is it simply a set of rules for proper deportment. Orthodox ethics offers deification rather than mere moral rectitude. It is an all-encompassing and all-demanding way of life. This deifying way of life, because of its focus on worship over analysis, on a transcendent God rather than discursive principles, is at best difficult to define. Rather than inviting definitions, Orthodox ethics invites engagement with the persons of the Trinity through a community united in eucharistic communion.

The significance of Orthodox ethics can be better gauged if one recognizes the differences between Orthodox ethics and Western moral philosophical accounts of ethics, as well as the intellectual and moral history that separates Orthodox moral concerns from the moralities of the secular West. These differences express themselves in different understandings of love of neighbour, appropriate human relationships, and proper responses to death and dying. The character of Orthodox moral concerns is especially highlighted in those issues of bioethics and healthcare policy that involve life and death decisions. Such decisions can only be made responsibly in the face of a recognition of the meaning of life and death.

This chapter will therefore illustrate the implications of Orthodox ethics through an exploration of the moral commitments that should guide the use of critical care – that is, the high-technology medical treatment provided in intensive care units.

Ethics: a Legion of Ambiguities

Secular ethics is broken into a diversity of ethics addressed by competing moral accounts. It is also marked by central ambiguities. Ethics has its roots in the Greek *ethos*, a word for 'custom' or 'habit'. Similarly, as opposed to *lex*, or 'law', morality derives from the Latin *mos*, or *mores*, a word for 'manners', 'customs', 'usages', and 'fashions'.

These meanings range from what is usually done, as in the sense of the ordinary manners of a people, to what ought to be done, in the sense of the canons of appropriate conduct. This last sense involves acceptable behaviour, much as we speak today of morals. Ethics in English refers to moral behaviour and moral principles, as well as to the study of moral values and proper conduct through philosophy and theology. Ethics in this last sense incorporates moral philosophy and moral theology. Given the varied character of these usages, this chapter does not draw a distinction between ethics and morality.

There are many ethics and moralities, which differ substantially from each other. We can distinguish four defining characteristics.

1. The Axiological Dimension – First, ethics differ with respect to the values they take seriously, as well as how they understand rightness and wrongness. The various ethics are separated by their 'axiologies', or orderings of values. An ethic that gives priority to freedom over equality is different from one that gives priority to equality over freedom. One that gives priority to freedom over prosperity is different from one that gives priority to prosperity over freedom. So, too, moralities differ depending on how they compare the present and future realization of that which is valued. The more a morality is future-oriented, the more it counts the realization of goals in the distant future on a par with the realization of values in the present.

2. The Explanatory Dimension – Ethics also differ in terms of their explanatory character, by how they justify the moral life, by their inherent rationales. Here, for example, are two markedly different ethical approaches:

- **Teleological ethics** – Some ethics are teleological in that they account for rights and duties, as well as right and wrong, in

110

terms of concerns with a *telos*, or a goal. In thoroughgoing teleological accounts, all moral concerns with the right are reducible to concerns with goods or goals. Utilitarian accounts are well known examples of teleological ethics. For the utilitarian, all moral concerns are reduced to maximizing utility, to maximizing the positive balance of benefits over harms.

- **Deontological ethics** – In contrast, deontological ethics explain morality in terms of the priority of the right over the good. The term 'deontological' derives from the Greek *deon*, a word meaning 'necessary', 'proper' or 'right', and is drawn from a root word meaning 'to bind or tie'. As this derivation suggests, deontological ethics recognize a claim of rightness and wrongness which is independent of utilitarian outcomes. Some actions are right or wrong, whatever the consequences.

  Deontological accounts such as Immanuel Kant's (1724-1804) give primary focus to what makes a moral agent blameworthy or praiseworthy, worthy of reward or worthy of punishment, worthy of happiness or unhappiness. These ways of understanding ethics are fundamentally different from teleological accounts, which focus on achieving some good such as happiness. Both, as we will see, differ from Orthodox ethics.

These two rationales for morality, the teleological and deontological, offer fundamentally different ethics. The very meaning of acting morally in the two kinds of ethics is different. A utilitarian account dismisses claims that certain actions or volitions are evil or wrong in themselves. All moral concerns are placed within a consideration of benefits and harms. In contrast, a deontological account involves moral concerns that cannot be articulated within a utilitarian framework – for example, the intrinsic blameworthiness of certain exercises of human will, apart from any consideration of consequences. Though utilitarian and deontological accounts may employ similar terms – such as rights, duties, right, wrong – these terms have substantially different meanings in the two types of ethics.

Though different moralities may appear to make similar claims about the importance of promise-keeping, the force of their claims differs, depending on the morality's ingredient rationale. Someone who is a 'rule utilitarian' will keep promises because he believes that, as a general rule, keeping promises will lead to the greatest positive balance of benefits over harms. However, he will tolerate exceptions to moral rules when, on the sum of all their consequences, they produce more benefit than harm. In contrast, a Kantian will keep promises because this is required by the very logic of moral agency. No exceptions will be allowed. Each approach involves a different moral rationality and sustains a different moral world.

There are also moral frameworks which focus not only on achieving the good, or on acting so as to be worthy of happiness, but on being an individual of virtuous character. In such a 'virtue ethic', moral concern is directed not simply to the consequences of actions, or the intentions of agents, but to the nature, integrity and moral strengths of a particular way of being a good individual, an individual with good moral character. However, there are different types of virtue ethics, depending on the nature of the virtue and character endorsed. A Samurai warrior whose chief virtue was *bushido* had an appreciation of moral character quite different from that of a courageous Viking. The virtuous life pursued by a Stoic was set within a complex framework of expectations quite different from that of an English gentleman. Virtues take content from the values they sustain and from the view of right and wrong that they endorse.

Virtues also invoke an integrity of life that speaks against attempting to reduce them to deontological or teleological moral concerns. In addition, virtue is understood in a variety of ways: as a mere habit or disposition to act in accord with the good and the right; as a moral excellence; as the power and operative influence of the good and the right. None of these senses of virtue and character is equivalent to the Orthodox concern with holiness, although the last sense intimates a recognition of the transforming, deifying, uncreated energies or grace of God. Virtue as holiness is not an isolated power, but the uncreated energies of God, union with God.

3. The Foundational Dimension – The varieties of ethics are also distinguished not only by the values they accent and their rationales, but also by the general foundations in which they are embedded. Natural law theories, for example, attempt to show the reasonableness of their claims by an account of human nature. Philosophers such as Immanuel Kant have appealed to the very character of rationality to justify their claims regarding the moral law and proper conduct. Philosophers such as David Hume (1711-76) have assumed a background notion of humans and their mutual sympathies so as to make plausible a particular web of moral claims.

In each of these instances, a surrogate for the grounding of life and morality in God is sought in rationality, human sympathies, an understanding of virtue and integrity, and so on. In each of these instances, the anchor for morality fails in fact to be the source and grounding of all reality, but is instead some isolated fragment or piece of reality.

4. The Social Dimension – Finally, the differences among ethics can be highlighted by noting the moral community, which is central to their framework of proper behaviour. For the utilitarian Jeremy Bentham (1748-1832), who was concerned about happiness for all beings who experience pleasure and pain, the moral community includes all organisms capable of sensation. For Immanuel Kant, who was concerned about the blameworthiness or praiseworthiness of moral agents, the moral community encompasses all and only moral agents, a class including beings other than humans, but not necessarily including all humans. For the Orthodox, the cardinal community is that of the Trinity, to whom the bodiless powers and the saints are obedient, and on whose relationship that of human beings should be patterned.

Ethics or morality thus has axiological, explanatory, foundational, and social dimensions. The first involves the content of the morality, the second its rationale, the third its deep justification, and the last the social framework which is its central focus. The character of a particular ethics or morality can usually be identified by reference to these considerations and their particular content. We can also use these reference points to identify how ethics differ from each other.

This helps us to appreciate that the various ethics are not species of one genus, but rather practices which at best share partial resemblances, or 'family resemblances' to use the term of Ludwig Wittgenstein. The various secular and religious moralities can then be recognized as differing substantially, although they appear to coincide in using similar moral terms, such as good and bad, right and wrong. The use of similar moral terms can often mask dissimilar understandings of the significance of morality and of the ways in which the moral life is organized.

Against this background, the distinguishing mark of Orthodox ethics is that it unites moral approaches that are otherwise sundered. For the person in worship of, surrender to, and union with the Holy Trinity, there is no tension between an approach that emphasizes what is right and another that emphasizes what end is good. An Orthodox ethic is both teleological and deontological. Morality is focused on discharging obligations and avoiding evil, where evil is not simply a non-optimal balance of benefits and harms, but the first-fruits of fallen, bodiless powers.

Orthodox ethics is also focused on realizing the good – indeed, on maximizing utility for all creation – through complete submission in love and obedience to God, whose Son submitted to death on the cross. Orthodox ethics is the pursuit of a holiness that has its rationale not in a consideration of the good or the right; or a favourable balance of benefits over harms; or the worthiness of particular finite agents; but in a God who alone is praiseworthy and the final focus of all duties, which in the end are completed in eternal worship. As God is one, the right and the good are in the end one in him. The integrity of the moral life is achieved not simply through pursuing virtue and realizing a good character, but in deification through the mysteries of the Church. The deep justification of Orthodox morality is found neither in nature nor human reason, but in God, the source of all nature and reason, who is beyond our nature and reason.

Unlike Orthodox ethics, secular ethics encounters a tension between the justification of morality and the motivation to act morally. A utilitarian account can justify morality in terms of the greatest good for the greatest number, but has difficulty in establishing why it would be rational for an individual to act radically against his own good in order to sustain the greatest good. Even a deontological account, such as Kant's, has difficulty in showing convincingly why an individual should be motivated to act radically against his own happiness (for example, to lose his own life) in order to avoid the rational sanction of being blameworthy. As Kant recognizes, the right, the individual good, and the highest good can only be fully united if one acts as if there were God and immortality.

In contrast, an Orthodox ethics discloses that the genesis of morality, the rationale of morality, its deep justification, and the motivation to act morally are indeed united in our relationship to the Trinity. Both what is good for the individual and the ultimate good are one, although that oneness is experienced only in true worship, and never simply known in rational discursive reflection. Orthodox ethics is neither governed by a body of merely human customs and traditions, nor derived from rational argument, nor expressed in merely discursive rational terms, but is rather an expression, in union with the Tradition from the Fathers, of a particular living relationship with a loving, transcendent God.

The West and the Secularization of Ethics

The Orthodox understanding of morality as sustained in a liturgical life contrasts with what became the dominant moral tradition of the West. This tradition saw the grounding of theology, and especially ethics, more in reason than in worship. The development of Western Christian and secular ethics involved a shift in the central context of moral concerns from liturgical communion with God to a discursive rational community with reality. The shift was from the mystery of the eucharistic community to the intellectualism of the academy.

As this occurred, there was another shift: the people who were regarded as moral examples were no longer those who were united with God in true worship and belief, but those who were engaged in the discursive exploration of values and obligations. These changes were subtle and slow. They produced deep, though often unnoticed, differences between Orthodox ethics and the received ethics of the West. These differences are frequently discounted, since they often do not appear as a clash of discursive propositions, but rather of different orientations to the project of being moral.

The differences have roots in a long history of growing apart. The early Western Renaissance, born of the Carolingian court at the end of the eighth and the beginning of the ninth centuries, did not simply embrace the *filioque* clause in the Creed, but came as well to embrace a confidence in reason that eventually flourished in the high scholasticism of the thirteenth century. The reflections born of that period led to the conclusion that from the knowledge of 'sensible' things, we can know of God's existence, have knowledge of God's essence, and by an examination of human inclinations have knowledge of the moral law, through disclosing a natural law. The view was not simply that created reality has an order, or that this order can be found in a human heart turned to God, or that this order has moral implications. It was that humans can know this order and its moral implications without opening their hearts to God in prayer.

In contrast, Orthodoxy recognizes the darkening of the human intellect because of the sin of Adam and Eve. It has different expectations regarding moral knowledge. It turns in worship and asceticism to God to be taught his statutes. It is not as if the Orthodox sought to set limits to secular philosophical reflections on the provability of God's existence or the knowability of the general lineaments of God's law. The possibility of such knowledge appears simply to have been regarded as a taken-for-granted element of the received philosophical science of the time. But there is a recognition, as St Gregory Palamas (1296-1359) underscored, that knowledge of the essence of God is impossible.

As a consequence, the primary focus of theology is on a living relationship in worship to a transcendent God who is totally other, not on a philosophical exploration of God's nature. Rather than searching out God's law through a discursive study of nature, culminating in a natural law ethics, Orthodoxy seeks to ground its ethics in a liturgical relationship with a personal God, whose being as persons of a Trinity is as salient as God's being as God. Still, even when men turn their hearts from God, there is the possibility of sharing a shadow of an ethics.

However, the difference between an ethics found in the liturgical worship of God and an ethics that can bind moral strangers not united in God is stark. It is as stark as the difference between an ethics found in liturgical worship of God and the various secular ethics that have attempted to secure moral content through various types of moral argument. The contrast is between an ethics found in worship and an ethics disclosed, established or justified discursively or contractually. The difference affects the Orthodox approach to contemporary moral challenges, including those posed by modern medicine.

The difference showed itself already in the fourteenth-century dispute between St Gregory Palamas and Barlaam of Calabria (1290-1348). This concerned not only the uncreated energies of God that deify human beings, but the growing tendency in the West to contrast what can be learned about ethics without God's grace and what can be known through it. Although for believing Western Christians, the context for moral knowledge had presupposed grace, ethics as the systematic exposition of proper conduct was now judged possible outside of a close relationship with God. Careful reflection or reasoning concerning the human condition or the nature of the world could by itself disclose how people ought to act. Ethics grounded in a natural law, open to human knowledge even without grace, became in principle a matter of secular philosophical study.

Where the East recognized a role for reason in elaborating what was known through grace, the West came confidently to advance a role for reason in disclosing a substantive morality that was independent of grace altogether. An epistemological dualism now contrasted what could be known by natural reason, and what could be known by supernatural revelation.

Even when scholasticism fell into disrepute, the ethics of natural law, developed in the High Middle Ages, continued to inspire Western secular moral reflections. After the Renaissance and the Reformation, a Europe divided confessionally, and battered by the bloodshed of the Thirty Years War and the Civil War in England, hoped that reason could by itself disclose how humans should live. The modern project of moral philosophy shouldered this task. An ethic for humans, so the various accounts argued, could be secured through inspecting the character of reason itself, through an exploration of the human condition, through an examination of human sympathies, through an assessment of human sensibilities, etc. Either by turning inward to the nature of reason, or by turning outward to human nature, canons for proper deportment could be disclosed without having to engage with any particular religious beliefs, commitments or worship.

This project, if successful, would have healed through reason Western Europe's fragmentation of faith, and would have provided a substantive secular morality binding all. If one could by rational argument show how people ought to act, then one could correct immoral people by showing them to be irrational. Moreover, when one imposed rationally established rules of conduct, one could claim the authority of reason for the force employed. In addition, coercive force used in imposing a rational morality would not be alien to those subjected to it. Such force would restore those coerced to conduct proper to their nature. Rationality would disclose a secular moral community binding all, establish its rationale, and give its content a foundation independent of a relationship to God. The fragmentation of Babel would be set aside by human reason, not through human repentance, divine forgiveness, and unity in Christ. The community of mankind would have been found in rationality – and not in grace, which appeared only to divide.

This hope, which reached its height during the Enlightenment, that reason would be able to unite Europe in a common moral understanding, actually produced as many secular accounts of justice, fairness, equality, rights and the good life as the Reformation had produced of the Scriptures and the nature of religious faith. The moral diversity of postmodernity, irresolveable in secular terms, mirrors the moral diversity of the polytheist world that preceded Christianity.

As we have already seen, moral theory is beset by a diversity of challenges: how to order the various goods for which humans have concern; how to balance the good and the right; how to understand proper moral community; how to articulate the rationale of ethics; how to disclose its deep foundations – or to claim that deep foundations are unnecessary. Since the choice of any particular moral understanding presupposes the endorsement of a particular ranking of values, 'discount rate' for values, and/or content for notions of moral rightness and wrongness, secular morality requires the guidance of a canonical moral account, vision, sense or set of intuitions, in order to know which account to endorse. Since this is exactly what is at issue – that is, the question of which moral account should guide – secular philosophy cannot discover its way out of the impasse of not knowing which moral vision should be canonical.

For a secular moral philosophical account to have content, it must at some juncture assume particular basic moral principles or axioms. The cardinal question – answered for the Orthodox by Holy Tradition – is which principles or axioms to assume. Since secular rationality for centuries aspired to a universal moral account, which could be articulated outside of any particular history, social context, or 'mere' tradition, an appeal to tradition would be the abandonment of the task secular rationality had set itself. Its project was and is therefore impossible. Either a secular account must arbitrarily accept a particular moral vision as ultimate and absolute, or it must beg the very question at issue. Secular thought cannot in a non-arbitrary fashion provide a canonical content for its ethics.

The postmodern cacophony of competing moral visions is thus not simply a sociological fact. It is an unavoidable epistemological condition for secular reason. The Enlightenment hope that philosophy could disclose the rules for proper human conduct has gone unfulfilled. Reason without grace, as the Orthodox anticipated, cannot restore the moral unity shattered by sin. Nor can it establish which moral principles or axioms should be taken as foundational. The Enlightenment discounted the role of the will in repentance and worship, while accenting the role of reason in disclosing moral truth. However, only in repentance, united in Christ through the community of the eucharist, can one unite the fragmented elements of morality. In the ruins of its failure to repent and turn to God's grace, and given the impotence of mere reason, secularity confronts postmodernity's inability to discover through reason a universal secular moral narrative, or to justify a canonical content-full account of proper moral conduct.

In contrast, Orthodox Christianity discloses moral solutions through a liturgical, transfiguring relationship to God, the ground of all being and value. That relationship is not sought through analysis and discursive reflection. It is sought and manifested in prayer, fasting, almsgiving, love of one's neighbour, and love of God. A canonical moral sense is disclosed not through philosophical reflection, but in Orthodox worship and committed love. The first and foremost moral examples are those who seek to be perfect by giving up all in the pursuit of Christ (Matthew 19.21), free their hearts from passion, receive illumination, and know God. As a consequence, Orthodox Christian ethicists can more reliably be found in the monastery than in the academy. The test of moral understanding will be the judgment of those who are the true theologians, those holy men and women who give their lives worshipfully to God.

This can only suggest that Orthodox ethics will be burdened, if not endangered, in any country or Church that spawns more academicians discursively reflecting on theology and ethics than it does holy ascetics, both celibate and married. The recent prayerful reflections of St Silouan the Athonite (1866-1938), Archimandrite Sophrony, and Archimandrite Vasileios, underscore this truth appreciated by the Fathers, defended by St Gregory Palamas, and which constitutes the unique character of Orthodox ethics. Only in a relationship through worship to the linchpin of reality – that is, God – can fragmented moral practices be made whole. The ethic of proper conduct, the guiding content of a proper moral sense, is to be found in a love of God and our neighbour that takes its authentic character from Orthodox worship that discloses and incorporates Orthodox belief. Moral knowledge is integral to Orthodox moral living and worship. It is distorted the more it is separated from an engagement in the tasks of holiness. Orthodox ethics is holiness, a communion with a God who is utterly other, but still Father. Such an ethics is a holy mystery disclosed within holy mysteries. It is an ethics that is to be lived, and can never be merely explained.

Critical Care Ethics: Orthodox Reflections

Orthodox ethics aspires to be one with that of the Apostles and the Fathers, and some people may therefore doubt that it has anything useful to say to contemporary moral challenges, especially those framed by the high-tech interventions of healthcare. Traditional Orthodox ethics sternly forbids abortion and physician-assisted suicide, but does not seem to speak to the particularities of high-technology medicine.

Although there is nothing morally new in our contemporary confrontations with death, they have taken on a new complexity, given the new technologies and the complex social structures that healthcare now involves. The risk of death, the costs involved in avoiding death, the quality of life to be achieved through medical interventions, and the length of life likely to be secured can now be more reliably weighed, one against the other. The likelihood of saving a life can now even be calculated through computer programs. The substantial advances in medicine and medical knowledge may suggest the need for a new ethic, and for the revision of traditional Orthodox approaches to death and dying.

However, it is precisely the Orthodox commitment to holiness realized in worship that makes a new ethic out of place. It is the very enduring character of Orthodox moral concern with holiness which transcends the particulars of contemporary high-tech medicine. Having said this, there are still issues to address.

The intensive monitoring, support and treatment provided in critical care units (that is, intensive care units, or ICUs) can increase the likelihood that severely ill patients will survive to leave hospital, return to their families, and resume their previous occupations. The difficulty is that one can rarely predict whether a particular intervention for a particular patient will with certainty be successful. Although medicine has developed ways of better gauging the likely success of therapeutic interventions, especially in critical care, uncertainty remains.

However, one can determine in general that patients with a particular disease and level of illness will have only a 5 per cent chance of surviving. One can then predict the likely costs of attempting to save such patients and, as a consequence, estimate the costs of saving a patient's life. One can also estimate the cost of the years of life likely to be secured. If there is a 5 per cent chance of saving a patient's life, and the usual cost of such treatment is $500,000, one will be saving lives at the cost of $10 million per life saved. If the patient has a disease, or is of an age such that the likely life expectancy is only five years, one will be securing life at the cost of $2 million per year of life saved.

For healthcare policy, decisions regarding critical care technology are of significant moment. In the United States, where approximately 7-10 per cent of all beds are in critical care units, about 1 per cent of the entire gross domestic product is consumed by intensive care. Moreover, about 8 per cent of the patients consume approximately 50 per cent of critical care resources.

The costs themselves draw secular moral attention, given their enormity in both absolute and relative terms. So too, does the probabilistic character of the questions posed: at what probability of success should one invest how much money to save a human life? At what quality of life to be secured? And for how many years of life likely to be lived? How low must the chance of success be, and how high the cost of treatment, for one not to be morally obliged to provide care to particular patients or classes of patients? Because secular morality possesses no univocal standards to guide, responses have been diverse and controversial.

Some Christian traditions have considerable resources for answering the moral questions posed by critical care. For example, when Roman Catholic moral theology confronted the medical developments and advances of the sixteenth century, it began to frame a distinction between ordinary and extraordinary care. In most cases, this reflected a distinction between proportionate and disproportionate care, appropriate and inappropriate care, as well as obligatory and non-obligatory care. Non-obligatory care was care that was either improper or beyond duty. For example, Dominicus Banez (d. 1604) regarded 3000 ducats as a level of expense at which treatment became non-obligatory for a man of usual means. In 1956, this figure was determined by an American Jesuit, Edwin F. Healy, to be equivalent to $2000.

For the most part, this tradition of moral reflection recognized that the *prima facie* duty to preserve life could be:

- **defeated** – in the face of financial, social, psychological and personal costs;
- **weakened** – the more hope of recovery dimmed, the length of life to be secured became insignificant, or its quality decreased.

One was obliged to provide medical treatment only if there was hope of recovering health. It was recognized that costs could be morally – and not just economically – prohibitive. If one tried to save physical life at all costs, one would be distracted from the more important task of securing eternal life. There was an implicit recognition that if one made saving physical life an overriding goal, one would have illicitly made physical life an idol.

In analyzing how the duty to stay alive can be defeated, the very thoroughness and attention to detailed analysis upstaged considerations of what it is to die well and of how dying well should be embedded in a life directed to holiness. The concern became more avoiding the guilt of a wrong decision than understanding what is involved in living and dying in accord with a right decision. That the Orthodox Church has not provided a similar moral theological literature should not be attributed to a lack of opportunity or a historically determined omission. If the ethics or morals of the Orthodox are found in the worship of God, one should expect to find matters as they are: extensive prayers to accompany the dying, but no developed discursive moral account of when it is appropriate to limit, withhold, or withdraw possibly life-prolonging or death-postponing treatment.

Instead, there is a concern to die in prayer and without pride. There is a literature about how to accompany the dead in prayers, especially during the first forty days after death. The focus is directed to the worship of God, such that the decision of whether or not to accept particular therapeutic interventions is not a matter of direct attention.

This absence of direct concern for such decisions is the result of a particular moral understanding or way of life, with a positive emphasis on union with God through the mysteries. Moreover, there is an emphasis on a particular community of care. For example, the Orthodox anointing of the sick follows the letter of James (James 5.14) in involving more than one priest. Ideally, seven priests carry out the anointing, placing the sick person in a community focused on holiness, where the guidance of a spiritual father is more likely. The emphasis is on spiritual attention and guidance, not on a set of discursive reflections or guidelines. The living and dying of the Orthodox can only be understood within the context of proper worship and belief. Treatment choices that are incompatible with this commitment fall short of the mark.

The Orthodox Christian response to the challenges posed by critical care should not be to look first at financial costs and likelihood of success, but rather at the extent to which the intrusions of critical care will distract patients, family and society from the tasks of living and dying in worship and prayer. The focus should be on whether the use of critical care will be an impediment to dying in repentance and spiritual peace, with the hope of being able to receive the holy gifts until one's last breath.

One must bear in mind that a critical care unit is usually a place where the anointing of the sick can only be undertaken under considerable constraints and limitations. It is an environment where participation in the life of liturgical worship through receiving the holy gifts may become impossible because of an all-consuming effort to realize a very small chance of survival. (For example, the patient may be intubated and otherwise absorbed within a shroud of invasive machinery.) Since a critical care unit is a place where one will often face challenges to confronting one's suffering and death prayerfully and in peace, critical care must be used with spiritual awareness and caution. A critical care unit is not a place where, without significant distractions, one can attempt with one's whole heart finally to repent of one's sins and in humility face death.

The very character of critical care technology, with its emphasis on human power and scientific promise, can distract from the humility with which Christians, following Christ, must confront their suffering and death. Christian love is a particular love, a love sustained in humility. It is not a love directed to conquering death through technology, but through deification. The use of technology to postpone death must be made part of this life of holiness.

In particular, the appropriateness of critical care must be judged by weighing the likely challenges it will pose to the Christian's task of living well and dying well. Such challenges count against using critical care when death is very likely, or the likely postponement of death very minor. The more intrusive the interventions involved in attempting to pursue a small chance of postponing death, the more one must be concerned about the spiritual risks of critical care. One should be concerned with things other than struggling against death through medical technology when death is very likely or very near. Yet in some circumstances, critical care may postpone death long enough so that one will have the opportunity finally in humility to repent.

The focus should be on providing and accepting healthcare so as to support the task of a good life and a good death. This does not involve a vague commitment to living and dying well, but requires a concrete commitment to repentance. This task cannot be understood in terms of a discursive principle or formula. Orthodox Christians must reach back to the true meaning of *euthanasia* (the 'good death') by underscoring the traditional tasks Christians should undertake in dying well – for example, prayer, repentance, almsgiving, and the reception of the holy things. They must underscore that the use of life-saving and death-prolonging technology can be part of a good death only if that technology is set within the larger context of a good life.

Orthodox reflections on the proper use of critical care technology can demystify high-tech medicine through the mysteries, thus avoiding the dualism of secular and religious moralities, which led to the fragmenting of Western moral thought. One must avoid the Western moral error of seeking in reason what can only be found in a worshipful relationship to God. To ask how to use critical care should be to ask about how to live and die in holiness. The moral enterprise must be placed centrally within the religious life of Christians.

Such an attitude toward death and the use of medical technology is wonderfully illustrated by the account of the death of Archbishop Ezekiel in 1988, as told by a monk from Mount Athos to David V. Hicks.

Ezekiel's illness had worsened, and he was rushed to the hospital and put into a private room. There, full of tubes and various monitoring devices and slipping in and out of consciousness, he was surrounded by his praying friends and brothers.

Suddenly, the Archbishop became fully alert and firmly instructed the young Monk, who was acting as his aide, to disconnect the tubes and monitoring devices and to help him put on his ecclesiastical robes. His friends protested, but the Archbishop insisted, and the young Monk began to help him get dressed as others ran to fetch the doctor. When the doctor arrived, he was much alarmed to see the Archbishop dressed and standing beside the bed, and he went over to him and told him in stern professional tones that he had to get back into bed, that he was behaving foolishly, that the hospital could not be held responsible for what might happen to Ezekiel.

When the doctor had finished, Ezekiel placed his hands on the doctor's shoulders and, with a gentle smile, said: 'You don't seem to understand, doctor. I am now going to meet my Saviour, and I want to enter His presence dressed as His servant.' With these words, Ezekiel died in the doctor's arms. (Homily given by David V. Hicks, 29th October 1995.)

The Archbishop understood the limits of medicine, the purpose of life, and the meaning of the resurrection, which transcends death.

The proper use of critical care must be found in a *metanoia* of both healthcare providers and receivers: the attempt of provider and receiver of health care to place all that they do within true worship and belief. Critical care should be integrated within a repentance from pride and recognition of our finitude, both against death and in the presence of the infinite God.

In life and death decision-making in critical care, it is a mistake to look for the letter of the law. The focus should be on the spirit.

Moral attention should address the task of turning with full worship, love and repentance to God, not on seeking precise rules regarding what can defeat an obligation to accept treatment. One must step away from the temptation of reducing the moral life to anonymous principles. However, there are side constraints that set limits. Christians are forbidden to take their own lives or the lives of others by euthanasia. These real and absolute restraints must be seen within the community of persons united to God in true worship and belief. Only by wholeheartedly placing critical care technology within a concern to pursue holiness can the dehumanizing risks of critical care be avoided.

Aside from proscribing euthanasia, one will find the letter giving little guidance to the Orthodox Christian in this area. Unlike the secular moralist, the Orthodox Christian has the Spirit for guidance, and need not be concerned if the letter appears sparse. Decisions about whether or not and under what circumstances to apply the invasive and isolating interventions of critical care medicine should be made with one's spiritual father, considering the canons and spiritual goals, not merely the physical and economic risks and costs. Insofar as possible, dying should be an occasion for final reconciliation with one's family, community and God.

Conclusion

The axiological, explanatory, foundational, and social character of Orthodox ethics contrasts with the various secular and religious ethics. Orthodox ethics has a moral content placed in a liturgical context that defines it over against other attempts to live the good life. Orthodox ethics is properly integral to Orthodox theology, which is most properly Orthodox worship. In its worship, Orthodoxy calls us to recognize that if we attempt to save this temporary life at all costs, one of the costs may be eternal life. One may have fatally distracted oneself from holiness.

Orthodox ethics requires placing medical technology, with its powerful secular allure, within traditional Orthodox concerns of prayer, repentance and deification. Orthodox ethics will often not directly answer the secular moral questions that seem most pressing. This should not be unanticipated. Orthodox moral concerns radically differ from those of secular ethics. They seek holiness even in death, not merely the good and the right. Orthodoxy, after all, requires us not to be good by the standards of this world. It calls us to be holy by a standard beyond this world. It draws no easy lines between obligation and supererogation. It calls us to be nothing less than saints.

8

Orthodoxy and Modern
Depth Psychology

Dr Jamie Moran

I have been asked to discuss the relation of modern psychology to
the Eastern Orthodox Christian tradition. The first problem this
poses is: which modern psychology? Like everything else in Western
society, psychology is prolix and fragmented, with huge differences
of philosophy, theory and practice. Indeed, many psychologists are
in fundamental disagreement even over what the 'data' of
psychology should be, much less the best way to approach the data.

I have therefore chosen to focus on what is called 'depth
psychology' or 'dynamic psychology'. This is the psychology forged
out of clinical practice and the profound philosophical questions
about human life that this raises. Even here, the variety of
perspectives demands a strategy of selection. Therefore, I have
decided to highlight what I see as the basic convergences of depth
psychology and Orthodox Tradition and then the basic divergences.
I hope in this way to show that there are profound similarities, and
yet also equally profound differences. This similarity/difference is
actually of quite marked significance in itself, for it raises questions
about the tension and interplay of God's workings in the Church
and outside the Church in the world.

Convergences Between Orthodoxy and Depth Psychology

The branch of modern psychology called depth psychology is
associated with clinical and therapeutic interests, but also impacts

more widely in the surrounding culture in its effect on ethics, world view and life generally. From an Orthodox perspective, depth psychology can be seen as a search for a depth which is lacking in so much of Western life, especially as it has come to be lived since the European Enlightenment. In the light of this, it can be affirmed that psychology is the special domain of the Holy Ghost, who 'searches and proves the deep things of God and of man'.

Though the divine image in us may be directly modelled on 'theandrism' (a divine-human reciprocity) of the incarnate Logos, as St Maximus contended in the seventh century, there is no doubt that the life, growth and transmutation of this image, its protection and ultimate destiny, is in the hands of the Holy Ghost. There is a saying that 'what the Son effects, the Holy Spirit perfects'. Thus it can be said, from an Orthodox perspective, that Western man's hunger for depth reflects the absence of a strong orientation toward the pneumatological in Western religion, no less than in Western secularization. Depth psychology is a response to the hunger in all human beings for a depth which ultimately springs from the image of God, and whose promptings, cries and crises are directly related to the ever-present but hidden reality of the Holy Spirit in all people's lives in their depth.

I will list baldly what I think are the points of convergence and divergence between modern depth psychology and the psychology that is both tacit and explicit in the pneumatological approach of Orthodoxy. I will start with three broad convergences.

The Human Dilemma – The first convergence lies in the concern with depth. Depth relates to what is profoundly inside and not always apparent in human beings, on the one hand, and yet also to how they really live, and existentially engage the world, on the other. In both senses, depth psychologists prefer 'life' over theory, although this is not to say that, fallen human nature being what it is, people do not become proud of and addicted to their models. In distinction to so much of academic or scientific psychology, whose methodology condemns it to investigation of the surface – the how rather than the why – modern depth psychology tackles people's lived story, with its inner potentials and outer revelations, both heavenly and hellish. It tackles, in short, what would be recognizable to any religious person as the 'dilemma' of being alive.

Those who are closest to the Greek Fathers, especially in this regard, are the existential depth psychologists, a fact that the current generation of Greek theologians have noticed and made much of in their various writings. The concepts of angst, commitment, choice, passion, vision, and the absolute primacy of the 'person' over any and all psychic mechanisms, has a distinctly patristic flavour. Depth psychology is almost alone in Western culture in giving Westerners permission to speak of a whole host of human experiences. This includes what can be described as the central dilemma of being alive, in an existence where meaning is present in footprints rather than cast in concrete, and where uncertainty and pain are the human lot.

None of this fits with the technocratic and greedily ambitious thrust of science and business to conquer the world. Nor, or course, does it fit with the model of religion that one cynic (rightly) called, 'comfort for the already comforted'. The depth of life, outside us in what we meet, inside us in what is dredged up to meet it, is both agony and joy; but it is, most of all, unfulfilled promise. Like a call we have to answer, or a hint we have to pursue. The 'depth' orientation is valuable *per se*, and profoundly Christian, and that held in depth psychology would be at least recognizable to the ethos of the Greek Fathers. It is recognizably the same 'problem' of being human that both are talking about.

The Dynamic of Change – The second convergence concerns a second meaning of depth. If the first meaning of depth implies that we cannot get comfortable, religiously or materially, 'on the surface of existence', because of our psychology, with its inconvenient lacunae, needs and incompleteness, then the second meaning implies a strong orientation toward a dynamic in human life that demands we change – in fact, change or die. Though this may not be apparent to those who cannot see under the surface, this is basic to the life of the Holy Spirit in us. In hidden ways, the Holy Spirit urges, guides and pushes us deeper, approaching ever closer to the divine image – and for those who tacitly or explicitly say 'yes' to Christ's sacrifice, toward the divine likeness.

Depth also means journey. This journey is many things: venturing forth, adventure, discovery; but it is also crisis, loss and death. 'It is a fearful thing to fall into the hands of the living God.' It is a desert, indeed, where we are put in an inner furnace, and proved by its burning. True self-examination – as opposed to the use of techniques to rationalize one's current psychology – is a hard struggle through a hard place. St Isaac of Syria spoke truly when he said: 'He who knows himself is greater than he who raises the dead'.

The point is that there is a kind of knowledge which we only acquire as a by-product of real change, as a result of going on the journey, with its oases of living waters, dark clouds of fierce revelation, and burning deserts of purging. Such self-knowledge, in being bound up with human change, is never merely academic, theoretical or abstract. It is highly personal and highly dynamic. It pertains to the deepest movements of the heart and soul, the deepest beliefs, the deepest roots and constitution of who we are and how we are taking our stand in existence. This conjunction of change with self-knowledge is, of course, also recognizable to Orthodoxy, as a version of the ascetical life that is central to the Orthodox understanding of what it means to live in the Spirit. (This should be sharply contrasted with the emotionalism and general surface-ness of the charismatic approach to having the Spirit.)

An Orthodox might be more clear than a depth psychologist that this dynamic of change and self-knowledge is intended to re-forge us, bringing us closer to God and our own true image of and likeness to God. However, as with the way of seeing the dilemma of existence, there is here too a common orientation to the lived truth, in that depth demands profound testing and proving that 'exposes hearts', as part and parcel of its alteration of them.

Mission Against Dehumanization – The third convergence, which follows from the second, is that at its best, there is in modern depth psychology a sort of mission, a crusade almost, against some of the dehumanizing trends of the culture from which it has sprung. The best in modern depth psychology is a true kind of humanism, in the right and orthodox meaning of the term. It is a response, not only to the popular (and often non-sober) idea of human potential, but also to the sense of being bent out of shape by the very way we live and arrange ourselves and the world 'on the surface'. One might put it in this way: depth psychology channels a cry of the human heart, and so long as depth psychology remains respected in the culture, some of that cry actually does get heard. This cry tells us that there is another life in us which we are not living, another person and another story, more worthy of being human than the strangled existences that pass for 'success' or 'adaptation' or 'comfort' can understand.

This cry of the psalmist, the hearing of which depth psychology has inherited in the absence of anyone else wanting to listen, is the true gateway to the real human potential. Therefore, anything in the culture that takes the cry seriously is on the side of a Christian humanism which, for Orthodoxy, is founded not on nice sentiment about human beings, but on the revealed truth of the divine image in us. The very fact that all our religious and secular 'answers' still leaves that image in us pained, restless and dissatisfied, is proof both of its existence, and that dis-ease is often a better pointer to where we are coming from and where we should be going than the satisfactions which are shallow.

These are three very broad, but vitally important, convergences brought about through the shared reality of 'depth' in modern psychology and in Orthodoxy. They are: the human dilemma; change imposed upon us, via life struggles and honest self-examination (confession and repentance), and the true meaning of defending the 'human' against all the de-humanizing strains which threaten to overwhelm it.

However, there are more specific convergences, although these invariably present a mixed picture of divergences alongside the convergences. I am thinking here of specific schools of depth psychology which have rediscovered, and maybe sometimes even pressed further, areas of experience well known to Orthodox Tradition. All these schools can be seen as reflecting different aspects of the Holy Spirit's economy in us.

1. Freud and 'the Passions'

There is an obvious link between Freudian psychology and the teaching of the Desert Fathers on 'the passions'. The overlaps here are stunningly precise. If you read St Maximus on pleasure and pain, and then Freud, you can almost substitute the literal words of one for the other. (A nice joke to play on a humourless Freudian scholar is to substitute St Maximus for Freud on 'the pleasure principle', and see if he notices!) I have seen Orthodox people who shudder at Freud, but this must mean that they also shudder at the equally sober, tough-minded and rather saturnine psychology of the passions presented unequivocally by the ascetic Desert Fathers.

Although the descriptions given by Freud and the Desert Fathers diverge on key points, they converge in many, many respects. Both see human nature as driven, from the depth; both see us as covering over, and lying about, this fact, so that we have powerful resistances against facing it. Both see us as even less likely to do anything to

136

change it, as this wounds the ego image we have slowly built up, and requires a peculiar kind of effort, involving renunciation. Both see us using morality not only as a defence, but also as a cruel attack on the failings of others. (Christ discusses what Freud called 'projection' in his 'beam in the eyes' saying.) Both see that the passions elicit fantasies, and that the satisfaction of the passions involves indulging the imaginative scenario laid out by the fantasy. Both see fantasy as a background psychic process, exerting the utmost power against reason, and any self-control allied with reason.

Even what Freud called 'complexes', borrowing Jung's term, can be found in St Maximus's description of the way passion-fantasies interweave, and group themselves around key deep themes. Maximus even agrees with Freud that deep passions fall basically into two groups – the erotic ('libido'), and thymotic ('aggression') – with the two engendering different kinds of sickness of the soul. Both agree that the energies of passion-fantasy are engines of the human heart and disturb our peace all the time, during the day, and at night in our dreams.

No human, however rational or self-controlled on the surface, is without them; they are simply covered up, deflected, or dressed up. But they are constantly active and there is no way to transcend them, or to bury them by trying merely to subjugate them. Both Freud and the Desert Fathers agree that only by wrestling with them consciously can their role in driving our psychic economy be seriously challenged. Doing this is one of the hardest and bravest efforts a person can undertake, a true heroism.

Freud thought that in the absence of such effort, civilization will remain a compromise between what we really desire, deeply buried, and what we profess to aim at ideally on the surface. This split in civilization is reflected as a split in the human heart, in the personality. The ascetical tradition would say: we have to know the real evil to get closer to the real good. Greed versus pride, and materialism versus idealization, dominate an endless, unsatisfactory condition of divided loyalties in the human breast. What the right hand wills, the left opposes.

Despite the fact that the Desert Fathers and Freud have clearly uncovered the same area of human nature, there are vital differences between them. These are differences both in view and experience, which can only be put down to the difference brought about in our relation to the passions through ascetical practice and divine grace. Without being able to take the space to develop the point more fully, it can be said that the Eastern Christian experience of 'the passions' is that they are a fallen version of an essentially singular passion. This passion is not to be stoically renounced and rationally contained, which is Freud's final answer, but instead offered to God so that it can be transmuted. When this is done, the authentic, redeemed passion finally becomes what it is, implicitly, in its primordial innocence right from the beginning: an energy of love, and as such, a life of the heart not unlike the divine energies that stream from the essence of God. Energy is the capacity for work, the goal and aim, the motive force, the synergy with grace.

Freud had endless trouble situating the passions ontologically. Although his theory demanded that they were an inherent, biological inheritance, his clinical practice taught him that they were much more. Orthodoxy sees the passions as a fallen version of love, work and creativity, the authentic life of the human heart. Here, Freud's pessimism is in stark contrast with the ascetical *podvig*, or 'exploit'. To endure, to sacrifice, to let go, to embrace death is also passion; and there is thus in the ascetical path, as there is not in Freud, a transformative and indeed transfigurative suffering within passion, through which the fallen energies that drive us are purged, through the frustration and restraint of their fallen aims. A new energy is resurrected from the ashes, whose power, directedness and vitality expresses not only an innocent love, but a final, mature love, whose very struggles have educated and deepened it into a state of holiness.

Passion comes through this purgative process as the very fire of love that, suffering everything and enduring everything, is finally proved. Mention should also be made of the fact that the Desert Fathers found a practical way of not allowing fallen passion to develop, by not indulging its fantasies in the mind. This makes room for grace, and thus precisely for that truer and more 'burning' passion unknown to Freud. (One equivalent to this known in the modern world is the meditation practice of the Buddhists.)

Only at the end of his life, in his distinctly vague but poetic theory of *eros* versus *thanatos*, did Freud move closer to the true and final ethos of ascetical wrestlings with the passionate life. This is to free the body from the flesh; not to abolish but transfigure that energy in us which William Blake said, 'is the only life'. It is the only life because passion is the *action* of the heart, and as such, is the engine of the body. It determines whether materiality dictates the heart's agenda, or whether spirituality drives the heart and causes it to stand, and act, for love's extremity in the world, as in the passion of Christ (see Romans 8.14-25, 31-39).

2. Jung and 'Symbol, Sacrament and Mystery'

There is a less clear, but no less obvious link between Jung and the contemplative aspect of the ascetic tradition. This is, in fact, a bigger and more difficult subject than that of Freud's relation, and even some Orthodox have succumbed to the temptation to think of Jung as 'more Christian' than Freud. This is a mistake. The Desert Fathers would say, as would many modern depth psychologists, that you do not get to the 'Jungian area' in the right way unless you do the hard task of working in the Freudian area first. Thus the spiritual warfare of wrestling with the passions must precede what the Fathers called contemplation. To bypass the former and seek the latter as a sort of escape from it, or as a refuge from the existential obligations of life, is to 'angelize' – that is, to attempt to rise above the physical instead of transfiguring it – and thus to fall prey to serious spiritual deception.

This, I believe, was the fate of Jung himself, and it is the fate of many who follow a Jungianism divorced from the Freudian root. This issue of where contemplation stands in the spiritual economy of Christian salvation is too big to go into in detail. For a full account of Orthodox ecstatic contemplation, see Oliver Clement's *The Roots of Christian Mysticism*, and Father Sophrony's *A Monk of Mount Athos*. With this in mind, the following needs to be said.

Orthodoxy is in a very good position to assess the strengths and (dire) weaknesses of a figure like Jung. This is because Orthodoxy wrestled, in bringing together the Jewish and Greek traditions, with so many hellenizing proto-Jungians in its ancient history. Though Jung at times sounds Platonizing, and is certainly at other times entirely Gnostic, his consistent philosophical framework is neo-Platonic. Plotinus's dialectic of one/many is the same as Jung's dialectic of collective unconscious/individual ego consciousness. But Jung came finally to rest in an alchemical esotericism that both agrees and disagrees – as with Freud on the passions – with Orthodox tradition.

On the plus side, and very markedly so, is a stress on the imagination as revealing, transmuting and opening up the mundane, pragmatic and literal to those dimensions of life where divine and human energies intersect (I am putting this in an Orthodox rather than a Jungian way). We can find parallels between Jung's work on symbols and the writings of St Maximus on 'symbol, sacrament and mystery'. As in Kierkegaard, symbols are a vital force that beckon us to venture forth, and which open up a sense of possibility. Jung also saw, as did the Greek Fathers, that symbols can transmute passions, and thus (again in Orthodox language) 'cleanse' fantasy. They can provide self-knowledge, and articulate accurately wisdom about human psychology – as in myths, legends, fairy tales, and our own dreams. And they certainly provide a way of invoking the many-layered 'trans-ego' potentials of our nature – the gods and goddesses – which would otherwise remain buried.

Jung saw that symbols are energy carriers, and as such they can dynamically change the psychic economy of personality. They open up to it genuine avenues of change: change toward new goals, change toward less fragmentation and bifurcation, change toward a sense of the existence of the meaningful and numinous. The soul is the pilot of our movement towards change and transformation, and this is because of the pull exerted by the symbols that arise spontaneously and naturally in the soul. Thus symbols are organs of perception for formulating and understanding the deeper story of human life, to which we have very little access in our fallen state. They tell us that there is something else besides the surface life of safety, comfort, status and power over the external world.

Symbols, for Jung, are given to us, rather than being merely our creations, and that numinosity which they possess, in contradistinction to that which we invent, guarantees that they speak of something vital and real. Symbols are a sort of guarantee of life's inner landscape. As such, they are part of that in the soul which 'knows' or has intuitive inklings about life's deeper meaning and purpose.

All this is well and fine, and contains nothing either new or contentious. Indeed, given the enormous importance attached to the symbolic in Orthodoxy – not just as a dimension of the Bible, but also as part of the Liturgy, the way in which nature is viewed, and in the concept of 'spiritual gnosis', as defined especially by St Ephrem and St Dionysius in the early Church – several lines of overlap, or at least strong parallel, do open up. An Orthodox friend has even suggested that Jung's archetypes are, in fact, best seen as a modern re-description of the *logoi* of St Maximus. This is an interpretation which I think is almost but not quite right, although the similarity is undeniable. But just here the differences emerge.

The simplest way in which I can summarize these differences is to say that Jung confuses the unconscious psyche, in which symbols are written as a given imprint, with many other mysteries beyond the psyche that can in no way be reduced to it. Thus Jung runs together symbols of the psyche, vision, and mysticism – a conflation not acceptable to Orthodox hermeneutics. Nor is this confusion merely academic: these differences of experience correspond to steps in a spiritual path that Jung did not walk.

Symbol is both the first and easiest step. After that it gets harder, and more testing. Symbol is a menu – but Jung confuses the menu with food. Thus he fails to understand the realism of religious life, which is not an innate unfolding from our own psychic gift, but an existential engagement of increasing intensity and purity with the otherness of God, as of other people, creatures and, indeed, the very earth. It is this step beyond the seeing of possibility that Jung cannot take. To see possibility, but not realize that one must yoke oneself in faith to something real beyond what is only 'hypothesized' in imagination, is to fall prey to that characteristic danger of spiritual arrogance and immaturity combined in one.

Thus I would correct my Orthodox friend by saying that symbols as Jung describes them are only reflections in us of the *logoi* beyond us. These reflections ought to point us beyond reflection to try to stretch out into that state of vision where we can actually 'see' the real thing. The primordial intersection point between God and creation is not in the human psyche, but above and outside it in the heavenly temple of God's sacred wisdom. This is the place of true contemplation, the sacred space where God takes the soul to show us his vision of how the divine and the creaturely are to relate and interweave. Therefore, the *logoi* are, as Black Elk, the Oglala Sioux holy man, calls them: 'the spirit shapes of things as they should be'. They are the points of intersection of the infinite and the finite, pre-ordained and pre-established by God.

Equally missing in Jung is what St Maximus called *typoi*, or 'types', which is a hermeneutic reality complementary to that of the *logoi*. These refer to the actual revelations of God's movements and deeds in history, which culminate in the incarnation, cross and resurrection of Christ. They are places where the divine and human energies intersect, each having gone out of itself. Jung, basing everything in the psyche, can have no way of dealing with the realism of such visionary events. Equally if not more problematic is Jung's dangerous and absurd conflation of psychic forces with genuine mysticism. The intimacy, love and personal participation – what Metropolitan John of Pergamon calls 'being as communion' – of true mystical union between God and humanity, and between one human and another, finds no echo in Jung. His solipsistic psyche-ism condemns him to the contemplation of his own inner universe. There is no Other to bring risk, vulnerability and the dynamic of personal love.

This leads us to ask: what really is the difference between reflecting upon the symbolic reflections in the psyche, and the vision of the great and terrible images, types and *logoi* involved in contemplation? The difference is that the former can remain confined to and focused upon us, where the latter demands that we go outward to confront a non-subjective otherness, which is by no means within us even as a gift. Jung's mistake is to misread the call in symbols as if it were only to an undiscovered depth or source in us. This is why he thinks that we are answering that call when we try to put the depth in us together with the surface in a single, larger, but enclosed whole. To do this by way of response to symbols is in fact to kill the very life they inaugurate.

Symbols do not tell us that the answer is within us. On the contrary, they expand our inner horizon precisely by telling us to move towards that greater reality of which they are only the reflection. Indeed they are numinous, and indeed we have in no way invented them: they are other to any power of invention we can command. But we sense them in this way because they are a gift to us from the greater reality, and the gift is not meant to be clutched to our bosom, as an inner garden which we can cultivate according to our lights, which in effect makes us 'God' to ourselves. Rather, the gift is meant to call us back to its giver. Jung's fatal misunderstanding of symbols allows him to use them to avoid making this commitment of our inner selves to that Giver. There is no *eros* in Jung, as Orthodoxy understands it. *Eros* draws the soul out of itself and allows it to be brought both to God's love and to the Wisdom that expresses that love.

Yet the irony is that, savage though the Orthodox critique of Jung must be, it is also through Orthodoxy that Jung's psychic solipsism can be cast in a different light. Thus, Jung's alchemic esotericism can be developed in an Orthodox Christian way. Alchemy – unlike Platonism, Gnosticism and neo-Platonism – raises the authentic issue of the ultimate and final transfiguration of all of human and indeed created nature as the 'secret' carried in the soul. A symbol read in this way is an anticipation of the final marriage of the psychic matter, or substance, of the creation with the transfiguring of the Holy Spirit. But the danger, as Martin Buber pointed out, is that Jung divinizes the soul without first sanctifying it. By contrast, the true purpose of the soul's *exstasis* is to be initiated by God into the Sacred Wisdom which operates by the mutual offering of love. In true contemplation, we participate in this offering and discover what it costs. Thus it can be said that the divine love wounds the soul and breaks the soul open, rather than making it whole.

Orthodox hermeneutics knows not one, or two, but three great metaphors concerning the world as imagined by God. The world is 'a sea of symbols', 'a book of light' and 'an ineffable and prodigious fire hidden in the very essence of things, which one day will burn away the dead crust of ash that lies over everything'. We have to understand contemplation as graded, with symbol (water), image (light), and icon (fire), in increasing eschatological fullness (see 1 Corinthians 13.9-12).

3. Adler-Existentialism and 'the Person and the Community'

Of course, there are many other schools of depth psychology besides the Freudian and Jungian, with things to contribute. And even scientific psychology, with its caution, offers sobriety of a kind often needed to cool down, and slow down, the sometimes confused and un-self-critical stances which some depth psychologies assume almost as a matter of course (the Freudians are the worst offenders in this regard). This does not necessarily produce depth, but only arrogance and a willingness to believe that a thing is true because one likes it.

I would recommend any Orthodox who wishes to find the strongest links between depth psychology and Orthodoxy, especially with the Greek Fathers, to investigate existentialism in authors such as Rollo May and E.G. Howe. Howe's book, *War Dance*, asserts that we must live in paradox and contradiction, always on the edge where known and unknown meet, and that neurosis is the 'shadow crucifixion' which comes about when we avoid this.

These authors have, like the Greek Fathers, made the mystery of personhood deeper than any conception of the unconscious, ruling out any notion that we are driven by passions, or lived by images, at depth. At depth, we stand before the otherness of existence – of God, of neighbour – and thus passion and imagination are communications, synergistic energies, binding persons together.

Also close to the 'priority of the person' found in Orthodoxy is the revisionist neo-Freudian H. Kohut, whose view of the 'self' is very close to the patristic *hypostasis*. This self is therefore born with a sense of its own greatness, which Kohut calls 'healthy narcissism', but which in Orthodox terms is the first intimation of the image of God in us. On Kohut's view, the true self is ready to love and be loved, and is willing to grow out of its primal loves, rooted in the need that others reflect back what it lacks as parts of its identity,

145

into a self-esteem in which self-belief, self-respect and self-sharing grow into self-giving.

'Love thy neighbour as thyself' recognizes the clinical truth that frustration and hate towards oneself only produces repudiation of the adventure of life's 'otherness'. This alerts us to the Orthodox teaching that, given love as the real driving force, then person and community are both equally absolute and primal. This teaching also makes a distinction between the 'person', as created by God in his image, and the 'individual', which is a fallen state.

While the person always lives in a fundamental ontological relation and connection with all others – God, persons, creatures and things – the individual is enclosed in a boundary of self-preoccupation and self-serving that cuts him or her off from the original ability to commune with all others. This communing should exist whether we are alone or with these others. It is not a psychological disposition, but a state of being. 'To love is to acquire another self' is the real meaning of the binding together of persons in community, and this community includes not only humans but all created things.

I should also mention at this point the work of Alfred Adler. His teaching on 'social interest' or 'social feeling', and sickness as the person's abuse of this via a false individualism of power, rather than communal contribution, is a huge step towards understanding the Holy Spirit's task of creating a communion of persons (see 1 Corinthians 13.1-13; 14.1).

4. Conclusion about the Schools

It seems clear that we can in a rough way see the three domains of modern depth psychology – Freudian, Jungian and Adler-existentialist – as paralleling the three steps of Orthodox spirituality.

- Freud parallels the spiritual warfare.
- Jung parallels contemplation (*theoria physiki* and 'spiritual gnosis').
- Adler-existentialism parallels union with God, or that state of affairs which makes mysticism no mere individual rapture or individual illumination, but entry into that community life where there is a love in which persons share their very selfhood, so that 'being' becomes 'communion' in the powerful way in which Metropolitan John of Pergamon has put it.

Each of these domains allows us to see from a different angle a certain facet of the human dilemma. Thus through Freud, we see the deep problem of man as guilty; through Jung, we see the deep problem of man as arrogant, and through Adler-existentialism, we see the deep problem of man as tragic, having lost his true self.

The spiritual path must address these deep problems, and that is precisely its hallmark in Orthodoxy. We have to suffer through guilt, in the spiritual warfare, to reach holiness; we have to suffer through arrogance, in contemplation, to reach knowledge; we have to suffer through alienation from God, neighbour, self and the very earth, to be restored to and grow in the community of all living in union.

We have looked at broad points of convergence, and at some key figures whose similarities and differences to Orthodoxy have been pointed out. We need now to look at points of divergence. I will then offer a suggestion concerning the meaning of this convergence-divergence. This offers a suggestion about the real way in which the Holy Spirit works 'psychologically' in the depth of human beings.

Divergences Between Orthodoxy and Depth Psychology

The many broad similarities, and even the overlap of modern schools with areas of depth charted 1600 years ago in the Egyptian

147

Desert, are surely enough to suggest that the Holy Spirit works outside the Church. But does it follow then, that Tradition hardly matters, if the Holy Spirit may blow where he will and cannot be confined to such Tradition?

The answer to this question is that the Church could not anticipate the final divinization of all flesh and the final defeat of the ancient sorrow, if the Holy Spirit were not at work in the Church in some fuller way than he is in the world. In the Church, the Holy Spirit is at home, or is among friends. The Church, by virtue of its permeability by the energies of God, is an earthly sacrament, now, of a divine reality that is still far off, but coming for the rest of the world. And the Church exists to demonstrate this concretely, existentially and in a lived way – not as a theory or as words.

The truth of this claim can, I think, be demonstrated by pointing out what is the truly profound, basic difference between Orthodoxy and modern depth psychology. Quite simply, the important thing about Holy Tradition is that it explicitly, consciously, with effort, suffering and will, always leaves open a space for God. This is not necessarily the case with modern depth psychology. This is a major difference that matters in practice.

I do not mean by this that the God of otherness, the Creator, is not explicitly recognized and invoked. Nor do I mean that therapy lacks any declaration of belief in, or sacramental communion with, the incarnate Logos, the Redeemer. I mean something simpler, and I think more basic. No place is left for the Holy Spirit. Therefore there is neither any way for the Spirit to manifest the Father as Creator, nor reveal the Son as Redeemer, to those who may be in search, yet not know what they seek. But most fundamental of all, many therapists and their therapies offer no 'substance', no 'matter', to the workings of God, however hidden. Their space is closed, not open. So it is not a 'sacred' space. In twelve years of therapy practice with all sorts of people – troubled, neurotic, borderline, psychotic – I have come to the following conclusion.

In each of us is a child who is inherently religious, not in the sense of acknowledging the Father, nor yet recognizing the Son, but in a manner that is permeated by the presence of the Spirit, through whom the energies of God penetrate the world and render it profound, beautiful and naturally meaningful. This child in us is naturally religious because it serves something greater. It hears a call that is in the world but not of it, and whatever aspect of the world it 'puts' this call upon, it is really the call of the Spirit and this child answers it. It ventures forth; for this child, to use Kierkegaard's phrase, has a thirst for the prodigious and mysterious. This child goes out of self. In the original Greek and theological meaning of the word, this child is 'ex-static'.

Equally, however, there is inherent to the fallenness of existence a condition that destroys this true child. This condition causes it to get stuck, to retrench and live by its wits, with all sense of life's call to something greater jettisoned and replaced by strategies designed to feed, protect and aggrandize the self. This selfishness is at the root of all sickness, and my experience is that no force on earth – no wit, technique, or subtle influence of any therapist – is sufficient to challenge it. People only change if they are truly religious in the way that the child is originally religious: in love with the world, and full of the *élan* that can only come from reaching out of oneself, in interest and concern. Those people who retain a spark of this religiousness, and who therefore still serve something greater than themselves, will because of that 'something' open their selfishness to life and healing. Only such people will repent of selfishness, and let life show them that it is wrong as a basis for existence.

Those who lack religion in this sense, who are only selfish and acknowledge no force greater than themselves – a force whose truth, beauty and responsibility tells them they cannot persist in their selfishness – have no motive for change and do not change. No amount of insight, challenge or compassion can 'move' the essential in-static mode that we fall into, moving ever more into self, as opposed to being able to go out of self. It is truly a heart of stone, as the Jewish mystics describe it, and not a heart of flesh.

The sick are relentless in their egoism, and the more sick, the more self-centred. That is the sickness. Not the suffering of life, but what it does to us, or maybe what we do to ourselves in the way we deal with it. It closes us down. It causes us to abandon our inherent trust in what is more than us, and beyond us, as calling us out and supporting and helping us as we go. Instead, we close down and close up, and will risk nothing, surrender nothing. We offer ourselves not one jot. The egocentrism of our self-preoccupation is a force far stronger than anything in this world – and no holy person can shift it. It is, as the Jewish mystics put it, a stone in the heart which nothing can break.

Because of this, my argument is startlingly simple and radical. People who leave a space for God – even for the 'hidden' God, which is what the Holy Spirit is: God's humility – can be helped, and can change. They can learn to live with the most extreme damage and suffering, and yet still find joy in life. That they do not even know they are religious is probably a huge advantage. Their faithfulness to the call may take the form of dedication to their children, or to their work, or love for persons, or a true contribution which they make. But people in whom the selfishness that is ultimately the fall has won, abuse all help and will ultimately reject it. This is because they always come to the crunch point, where they have to change by taking action, and that action always entails a loss to the system of selfishness, because something has to be given up, and this they will not tolerate. So they discontinue the help they are receiving at the point where it is proved to them that it is not magical, but demands a change of heart which entails a change of action.

People who leave a space for God are able to make that change of heart, not for any sentimental reason or out of any moral superiority, and certainly not because of what is conventionally called piety, but because and only because, despite their selfishness, they truly acknowledge and have faith in a force that is greater than themselves. They are willing to open their selfishness up to that greater force, and in opening its closed system, to begin to let life teach it its mistakes and heal its wound, and comfort its genuine suffering.

In my experience, there are a few therapists who leave this space for the Holy Ghost in their practice – but they are few indeed. What many others might call 'religious', or worse 'spiritual', is merely sentimentality that does not challenge – and so does not disturb – the essential, deep self-enclosure.

Given that the Holy Spirit works in secret, does it matter that this space should be left open? Jung quoted an old saying – 'The God is present whether invoked or not'. In one way, the Holy Spirit is present all the time, in everyone. Were this not so, the real fruits and values of depth psychology would not have accrued. It is not mere decoration that one of the Holy Spirit's titles is 'counsellor'. He blows where he wills, and ignites with fire those who offer their substance to his burning, as St Dionysius said. Another Orthodox saint has said God does not coerce. He puts his splendour in the world and seeks to seduce man through its beauty.

But this is the precise point. The Holy Spirit does not follow the 'who's in, who's out' prescriptions we put on God, but neither does he work where the door is closed against him. This is an inner attitude. Some who say, 'Lord, Lord', have closed hearts; while others who say nothing outwardly are open inwardly, and so closer to God. The problem in therapy, however, and especially in the whole ethos and culture of its practitioners, is the widespread sense that doors are closed to the Spirit. No space is truly left open for mystery. Instead, various kinds of humanism, whether mundane or supermanish, are relied on. A feeling that we do not need God, and that we can 'solve problems', 'delve', 'integrate the whole of us', or 'journey toward the lost treasure' by ourselves, becomes the unstated article of faith believed by the therapist and conveyed to the patient. This creates a closed system between the two, and that creates innumerable further problems. This includes the problem for which Freud has no solution, namely that of analyses or therapies that become lifelong, that never end or resolve anything, but become ends in themselves. They become a substitute for restoring the true child to life, risk and faith.

Hence therapy engenders, as a cultural movement in Western society, a sort of higher-order childishness, an endless quest which abandons and trivializes our mission and duty to the world. The Sioux people say that the difference between childhood and adulthood is this: in early childhood we think the world revolves around us. The mark of the adult, by contrast, is that we become someone on whom the world can depend. The child who hears the call, and goes out of self, is precisely the one who will be the real adult: who will give himself, whatever the cost and consequence, and so will live. But the child who uses damage and suffering to remain the centre of the universe is the one whom no amount of self exploration will really change. A therapy that shuts out the call will, in some subtle way, merely help us to find the way to live with ourselves at the centre, in a world whose centre, the Holy Spirit is trying to show us, lies elsewhere: in the theandrism and sacrifice of Love.

This wrong ethos of therapy as a movement therefore entails a final tragedy. Going round and round in ever-decreasing circles in search of a 'self' determinedly put at the centre, we lose faith in the call, leave the true child cramped and unrestored to life, unable to make its contribution. Therapy unwittingly contributes to saving the self, when life's adventure, and salvation, consists in spending and losing it. As Jesus said: 'Unless a seed falls into the ground and dies, it cannot bear fruit.' The lesson is clear. It is not quite enough to say that the God is present even if not invoked. Orthodox synergy – collaboration between God and mankind – requires that if God will not be invoked, at least a space left open should be offered to him.

People can be more religious in depths than they consciously know. But if openness to religion is truly lacking, if the door has really been closed, then the human depths which can be heaven when God enters and dwells in them show themselves as hell. And hell is far stronger than any so-called 'healing' or 'caring' can cope with. Psychology can therefore move people onto the road, but only if in concrete practice – even if not always in the words of its theories – it lets the Holy Spirit lead the way on that road. God does not have to be invoked, but as the consciousness of all 'primordial' people knows, a sacred space has to be consecrated and given to God.

The second major divergence is over the Church. Virtually all modern intellectuals, reacting against Christian history in the West, see the Church as merely an external institution. They have no idea of the Eastern Orthodox view of the Church as a mystery with real ontological force.

I have in various writings tried to identify this churchly reality with the figure of Sophia in the Old Testament wisdom literature, and also with her typological parallels: the paradise inside each of us, from the beginning in our birth, and the new Jerusalem that will be between us all at the end, in order to show that the Church is a mysterious power that cannot be reduced to any other category, cosmic, natural, social or psychological. Indeed, the Church is in my view the woman who dances before the throne of God (in Proverbs 8), and who is created before the world so that she can be its foundation, its true original innocence and singularity in the secret recesses of the soul, and its final holiness in the open and declared halls of the heart.

Virtually no modern depth psychologist has even the inkling of an idea about the mystery of the Church, which can also be understood in Red Indian terms as the sacred circle that holds the world. In its centre, where the Great Mystery has made the good and bad roads to cross, lives the sacred tree of life, the holy fire, and the hoop of the people which reflects the spirit shapes of things as they should be. All of these guarantee and point to the holiness of the earth, and the earth as the final locus of the coming kingdom of God. This sacramental and transfigurational mystery of the Church is 'hid from the world' and yet is the real hope for the world, its origin and end. The only tradition I know outside Orthodoxy with a similar belief in and experience of the mysterious power of the Church as a unique ontological category is indeed that of the Red Indian peoples in their approach to the sacred circle. This circle is in one sense everywhere, yet in another is constituted by those who consecrate themselves to it.

The Tension Between the Church and the World

Is there then, any way to understand the tension between the fact of the Holy Spirit working in the world, outside the Church, creating convergences between the two, and the fact of the Holy Spirit working inside the Church in a fashion he does not in the world, creating divergences?

In my view, both poles of this tension are valid and necessary. It is not the intent of the Holy Spirit that all should be in the Church, nor all outside. Real dangers exist on both sides. I have just pointed out what I think these are for the world: the danger of losing the call of the Spirit, and disregarding the eschatological and sacramental and transfigurational mystery of the Church, as a reality which is tied to the future destiny of the very earth. From this follows the danger of not realizing that the centre in things is not 'in' us but 'between' and 'outside' us, in the place where God has made the two roads to cross, the tree to flower, the fire to burn, and the hoop to reflect the real constitution of things. To centre our hope for the whole world on society, on our own depths, on nature or on the cosmos will not do. The sacred place of centre is the Church, whether anyone knows this or not. This sacred space is special, and its substance is open to the revelation and workings of God's energies in a way that no other place is. The dangers of disregarding Holy Tradition are, therefore, to lose the call and become centred on society, oneself, nature or the cosmos, when the true centre is a place where God and humanity meet.

Yet for those in the Church, the danger is of the false notion of 'salvation' that has disfigured all Western traditions, high church, low church, middle of the road, conservative or radical. This is the mistake of seeing the Holy Spirit as little more than Christ's messenger, and confining his work to extracting the 'saved' from the rest, who can – literally it seems for some misguided Christians – go to hell. The Orthodox view – once that of the whole, undivided Church – has always been very different.

Against this 'Churchianity', Orthodoxy has always seen the Holy Spirit as equal to the Logos and equally constitutive of the Christic mystery, not merely the postcard on which the message is sent. More than this, since the Holy Spirit is the irrational economy of the Holy Trinity (the Father's being trans-rational and the Son's rational), which manifests the divine energies, it follows that from start to finish the Holy Spirit is engaged in truly making divinization inclusive: a community, not an individualism; a shared reality, not a private acquisition. This affects the way the Holy Spirit is 'in' the Church, and how even from inside he guides the Church's relationship to 'the outside'.

From an Orthodox perspective, the spirit of 'we are saved from the world' is not holy, but Satanic. No religious body whose relation to the world is that of a superior 'we're in, you're out', possesses the Holy Spirit. This being so, what is this way in which the Spirit works to include all, safeguarding at the same time the difference of those already dedicated now to what will be for all later? This is the crucial point and reveals to us how the tension works.

Clearly, if the Holy Spirit were not at work outside the Church, no one outside would ever come in. But the point is more profound than that. The work of the Holy Spirit in resolving the tension between these two poles testifies to the true universality of that which comes from the Father, is effected by the Son, but perfected by the Spirit: the Church of Jesus Christ. Because Christ is the God-man, the Saviour and transfigurer of humanity, recreating our possibility to grow into the divine-humanity described by St Maximus, the Church cannot exist as a separate haven for the saved. It can only exist as a prophetic and sacramental anticipation of the coming parousia for all mankind – indeed for all flesh, and for all matter.

This role contains unavoidable tension because, on the one hand, it means standing firm for what the Church has, but the world does not yet possess. We cannot point to where the world's destination is, as a foretaste and prefiguration of it now, unless we stand by the difference. Yet, on the other hand, since we only taste now what others will taste one day, it follows that we must always open the hugeness of Christ's regenerative deed to one and all, like the sun and rain which fall on the just and the unjust alike.

This is manifest, I feel, in two basic ways. First, we must recognize all those places where the Holy Spirit is present in those who embrace what the Church declares without knowing that they do. Second, we must do as Christ did, and by suffering those who really do reject divine things, suffer for them, carrying the burden they have put down. Our suffering of those who are really 'against' is a standing in for them; our suffering of the world is a suffering *for* it, and this has a redemptive power. It opens up a more mysterious possibility of inclusion and extension of the Church to all. By our willingness to embrace the truly unholy, in holiness, we open a door, a wound, through which it may still enter.

This was Christ's sacrifice on the cross. The unwillingness of the Holy Spirit to let the Church become militant, and succeed in dominating the world through coercion and threat, or promises of 'better experiences' than those available in the world, is a sign that only by the cross will the mysteries of the Church be extended to the world. The Church suffers the world, and generously sees friends where it finds them; but the Holy Spirit also maintains and prospers the Church, giving it more profound life even though that life is hidden from the world. This, it seems to me, is roughly how the tension between the Church and the world works, and must do. The relation of depth psychology to Holy Tradition is one example of such tension, with its convergence and divergence. But many others could be found in all areas: politics, art, society and other branches of enquiry.

Having said this, depth is the place where the tension stands its best hope of finally being resolved, because depth is the place where all need salvation, where all need God, and where all hunger and thirst for the mysteries, beauties and powers which God entrusts to the safekeeping of the Church. There is a wider Church in formation, out of the aspiration and cry of the deep human heart, in one and all.

The Final Meaning of Depth

Despite the undoubted difference between Church and world, the real conclusion is that no human being escapes the depth of existence. In every human life, at depth, is not just a core or centre, but the place where the two roads meet and cross. This is the place where inevitably we lose our self-fulfilment and our self-development, because our destiny crosses and is crossed by the destiny of every other – every other human, every other living thing, and the earth itself.

Depth does not mean the 'potential' of the individual. It means the paradox that we are involved in the life of the other and they in us. There is no Jungian individuation, because there is no self free of damage, nor a spirituality able to cultivate its garden and complete itself independently of the fate of all others. We damage each other. We suffer each other. We suffer for each other. In this sense, there is a place in every human being where they are already on the cross. It is this existential meaning of depth that Christ came to redeem.

Christ's deed is universal because the tragedy and possibility it addresses is the same in everyone. Depth psychology knows this human dilemma, but it remains in the hands of the Holy Spirit as to how far and in what way depth psychology might go deeper into the reply to it God has given – the decisive reply: the incarnation, death and resurrection of Christ.

But then, would that not apply just as well to all of us in our life?

'It is the Great Spirit who has made the good road and the bad road to cross, and the place where they cross is holy' (Black Elk, Oglala Sioux holy man).

'Even if I make my bed in hell, thou art there with me...' (Psalm 139.8).

'But we preach Christ crucified, unto the Jews a stumbling block, and unto the Greeks foolishness' (1 Corinthians 1.23).

9

Orthodoxy and Art

Dr Andrew Louth

In considering the question of Orthodoxy and art, it is not long before one encounters a paradox. On the one hand, it is the place of art and beauty in Orthodoxy that is probably most striking to those who look at Orthodoxy from the outside – the icons, the beautiful singing, the solemn splendour of the Liturgy. And this is something that is important to the Orthodox themselves. The story which the newly-Orthodox Russians told about their conversion in the tenth century laid stress on the beauty that the envoys of Prince Vladimir of Kiev experienced in the great Church of the Holy Wisdom at Constantinople: 'For on earth there is no such splendour or such beauty, and we are at a loss how to describe it. We know only that God dwells there among men... For we cannot forget that beauty' (*Russian Primary Chronicle*).

Despite this, anyone who is interested in Orthodoxy soon discovers that the Orthodox are not at all happy about using the language of art to speak about their devotion and worship. In particular, in relation to icons, the Orthodox often seem quite defensive. Mother Thekla, in her recent book on icons, is quite firm: 'Ikons are not works of art.' The reason for this is not far to seek. The Orthodox are defensive about the aesthetic because they feel, quite rightly, that the whole realm of the aesthetic is something immensely seductive. There is a danger that their own appreciation of the importance of beauty will be drawn into a way of looking at things that is fundamentally at variance with Orthodoxy itself. This is part of a wider problem.

Christians in the West, dismayed at what they feel is a lack of orientation and even conviction in their own tradition, sometimes look to the East for solutions, and sometimes think that they find them. But we Orthodox must be wary of letting disaffected Western Christians think that we have the answer to their problems. This is not because that may not in fact be the case, but because if we are not careful, we shall ourselves come to see Orthodoxy as an answer to the problems of the West. If we allow that to happen, our conception of Orthodoxy will become merely a mirror-image of the problems of the West. We will be defining Orthodoxy in terms drawn from the West.

The truth is not that Orthodoxy is an answer to the West's problems, but that Orthodoxy *transcends* those problems altogether. So with icons and art: the truth is not that icons are a more satisfying form of religious art than Western art has been able to evolve (after it deserted the common tradition); the truth is rather that if icons *are* art, then this poses questions about the very nature of art that are quite different from those that have come to be taken as fundamental in the experience of the West. And that is what Mother Thekla's uncompromising negation affirms.

The Distinctive Features of Art in the West

One way of developing this – this is an example, not an exhaustive analysis – would be to look at what is distinctive of art in the West. I would suggest that what is distinctive is the notion of artistic creativity: that in his art the artist is in some way analogous to God, in that he creates something. The notion that the artist is creative in this way can be traced back no further than the Renaissance, and only comes into its own in the Romanticism of the eighteenth and nineteenth centuries.

The germ of the idea is found in Nicholas of Cusa's concept of the created mind as a *secundus deus* that creates a conjectural world in imitation of God the creator. In Nicholas, this is only a minor theme and is never properly developed. Scaliger, the great Renaissance humanist, in his *Poetica*, says that whereas the rest of the arts only imitate, and like an actor or performer bring to expression what has already been composed, the true poet is creative like a second God. Other Renaissance influences – especially that of Giordano Bruno – combine to make the poet, the true artist, a kind of Prometheus: 'one who from the inner apprehension and experience of the divine, creative, universal nature and from the fullness of this ethical personality becomes himself a creator... from "inward form"'.[1]

In the eighteenth century, these ideas invaded Germany. To begin with, the use of the word *Schöpfer*, or 'creator', for the poet caused offence to Christian ears. By the time of Goethe, however, the idea of the poet as a kind of divine genius who is essentially creative, creating from the inner depths of his being, had become an accepted notion. As this idea was increasingly taken for granted, the understanding of what it is to appreciate art changed: it became a kind of echo of the creative process of the artist. To understand a poem (or in principle any work of art) is to enter imaginatively into the creative process of the artist and relive his experience. In a way, art is displaced and the artist himself assumes the focus of the experience: it is the artist's inner life that we are to attempt to penetrate and share. Such a conception of what it is to understand was worked out with genius by Schleiermacher, the great theologian. His other hat – and perhaps more important hat – was that of a philosopher of the process of understanding and interpretation, an area that has come to be called 'hermeneutics'.

If this is a true, if somewhat oversimplified, analysis of developments in Western thought, then it is not difficult to see why Orthodoxy has a problem with art. For the notion that the artist is essentially creative has scarcely any roots in the Tradition that is the treasury and touchstone of Orthodox theological reflection. It is something that has grown out of the ideas of the Renaissance, the Enlightenment and the Romantic movement – all movements of thought and sensibility that bypassed the historical continuity of Orthodox Christianity.

This is a familiar problem for any Orthodox thinker in the West. For although in my first paragraph I spoke rather lightly about a divide between the West and Orthodoxy, for most Orthodox Christians in the West this divide goes right through us. We Orthodox in the West in various ways find ourselves compelled to be amphibious. We are pulled by our faith in Holy Tradition, but our ways of thinking have been shaped, and inevitably so, by traditions of thought that are quite independent of the Tradition of the Church. We cope with being amphibious in all sorts of ways: trying to forget our own nurture in the West is one extreme, trying to translate Holy Tradition into Western terms is perhaps the other, and in between there are various other kinds of bridge-building, some rather impressive, some very makeshift.

To reflect on Orthodoxy and art is to be forced to bring all this into the limelight. For the language of artistic creativity is absolutely basic currency for anyone who cares about art and poetry. But the roots of this notion are tangential to – or perhaps it would be better to say independent of – the historical course of the Tradition of the Church. Further, to attempt to translate talk of creativity into language that has a place in Tradition is hazardous, because the notion of creativity in the West is not innocent. It is part of a development that substitutes the individual for God. It is right at the heart of the process of secularization that has proceeded apace in the West. If we accept that agenda, then we will have insuperable difficulties in keeping in touch with Tradition.

However, if the idea of artistic creativity, as it has developed in the West, is foreign to the Tradition, artistic creation itself – or at least the creation by artists of holy images of Christ, the Mother of God and the saints – has an important role to play. It is not, of course, just a matter of the visual arts. Music, poetry and architecture have all found a welcoming home within Eastern Christianity. But the visual arts led to the crisis of iconoclasm and thus to a definite affirmation of and analysis of their value.

In fact, historically conceived, Byzantine culture, and the Slav cultures derived from it, are distinctive in being cultures that have evolved an explicit understanding of the place of visual art. Although something similar is true of Islamic culture, it is not true of the West, which has used art in a variety of ways but has never, as a culture, articulated any justification of art as such. Byzantine culture did develop a justification of art, as a result of the iconoclast controversy of the eighth and ninth centuries. So it seems to me that it may be profitable to look back at the Byzantine rejection of iconoclasm, and its justification of icons and their veneration, to see if this gives us any context in which to develop an Orthodox understanding of art.

The Eastern Christian Justification of Art

One of the arguments of the iconoclasts, incorporated in the definition of the Iconoclast Council held at Constantinople in 754 and refuted at the Seventh Ecumenical Council, held at Nicaea in 787, was this: 'nor is there any prayer of consecration of it [the icon] to transpose it from the state of being common to the state of being sacred. Instead, it remains common and worthless, as the painter made it'.[2]

The Orthodox refutation of this is interesting: it simply admits the fact, but finds no difficulty in it. Not only are icons made and venerated without being sanctified, so is the sign of the cross (which is simply made in the air or on the forehead) and the sacred vessels used in the Liturgy (which then were not consecrated either). What the artist makes is worthy of veneration; it is not something 'common or worthless' that needs to be blessed. Although, in the course of time, a form of blessing of icons did develop, this response of the Seventh Ecumenical Council seems significant. The artist, in making an image of Christ, the Mother of God or the saints, is making something that is holy. In this case, artistic creation is within the realm of the sacred, it does not need to be brought into that realm. An icon is holy because it has been made to disclose one who is holy; it is not holy because it has been blessed. The work of the artist is itself a sacred activity, a sacred work.

If we look at St John Damascene's defence of the divine images, we find him responding to very similar objections to the veneration of icons. The iconoclasts seem to have objected to such veneration on the grounds that icons are just bits of wood (or mosaic, paint or whatever). Icons are just matter. Again the Orthodox response is to concede the point – icons *are* just matter – but to refuse to accept it as an objection. So St John says: 'I do not worship matter, I worship the creator of matter, who because of me became matter and consented to live in matter and through matter worked my salvation, and I will not cease from venerating matter through which my salvation was worked.'[3]

The icon is material, but that is no objection to venerating it, because God created matter (St John goes on to accuse his opponents of Manichaeism),[4] and even more because God became matter in the incarnation. For St John, the ultimate justification of the veneration of icons is the incarnation. This means that although veneration of icons is understood as veneration of those who are depicted by the icon (for 'the honour paid to the image passes to the archetype', as the endlessly-quoted passage from St Basil the Great has it), this does not mean that the materiality of the icon is to be played down. On the contrary, the materiality of the icon – its 'thingness', so to speak – is stressed. The icon recalls the value of matter established by its creation and revealed in the incarnation.

Right at the heart of St John's theological defence of the holy images lies his understanding of what is involved in the image, or icon. In both the first and the third treatise, St John dwells on the meaning and significance of the notion of the image. His thought is most fully developed in the third treatise. There he defines the image as 'a likeness and paradigm and imprint of something showing in itself what is depicted', and he says that every image 'reveals and shows something that is hidden'.[5]

He then gives a list of different kinds of image.[6] First, there is a natural image: the example he gives is the way the second person of the Trinity, the Son, is the image of the Father, and the Spirit the image of the Son. The notion of image, then, can be traced right back to the uncreated Godhead. The relationships between the members of the Trinity are relationships in which one is manifest and shown forth in another as an image.

Secondly, there are the Ideas: the Platonic Forms that exist in the mind of God and are the models of everything that has come to be as a result of God's will. This Platonism has, however, been modified in that St John sees this second type of image as the idea in God of *what is to come*. In other words, it is tensed, and so it is naturally identified with God's eternal will that predetermines all things. These 'images and paradigms' in God are what St Denys the Areopagite called *prohorismoi*, predeterminations.[7] Everything that exists, everything that is to take place, is – in some way – mirrored in God's will.

The third kind of image is the human person, who is created 'in the image and likeness of God' (Genesis 1.26). St John explains how the human person is in God's image in a rather unusual way. As mind, reason and spirit (*nous, logos, pneuma*), he reflects the Trinity of Father, Son and Holy Spirit. This idea occurs in St Gregory the Theologian, and was picked up by St Maximus the Confessor, whom St John is reflecting here. The human person is also like God because he is free or self-determined, and because he rules creation.

A fourth kind of image is to be found in the shapes, forms and types used by Scripture to depict the invisible God and the invisible angels, something in which St John acknowledges his debt to Denys the Areopagite.

A fifth kind of image is constituted by the types and figures of things to come. For example, the burning bush (Exodus 3.2ff.) and Gideon's fleece (Judges 6.36ff.) are both seen as types of the Virgin Mother of God, and in particular of her virginal conception.

The sixth and final kind of image is that which arouses memory of past events or persons. Of this sixth kind of image there are two varieties: accounts written in books, and those images that are perceived by the sense of sight, the icons or images to which the iconoclasts objected. St John draws his examples from the Old Testament, thus outflanking the iconoclasts who had themselves appealed to the Old Testament and the second commandment.

The important thing about St John Damascene's exposition of the meaning of the image is that the kind of image he is immediately concerned to defend is only a very small part of the whole spectrum of theological meanings of image. There are images within the Godhead; images are involved in God's loving providence; man, who as microcosm reflects in himself the created cosmos, is in the image of God; images are used to make the invisible world known to the visible world; images mediate between the Old Covenant and the New Covenant, as the images of the Old are fulfilled in the New, and images are used to awaken the human memory. Images mediate; images bring one thing into relation to another; images make possible meaning. And they do this because this is the way things are; this is the way God has made the world. It all relates and interconnects, and images reveal this relationship and interconnection.

When the artist makes an image or icon, he is contributing to the symphonic unity of the world or cosmos in all its senses: the world that embraces the invisible and the visible; the world that embraces the material and the spiritual; the world that is reflected in the inner reality of the human being; the world that moves from creation to consummation by way of the paschal mystery of Christ; the world that is the communion of saints of both the Old and New Testaments. In the icon or image that he makes, the artist both reflects and effects the harmony that exists in the heart of things. The artist reflects, because he does not make something imaginary, but helps us to see something real. And he effects, because the icon draws us into this harmony, and through being regarded and venerated it extends that harmony to those who respond to it.

There is clearly a lot that could be developed here. One might reflect on the way in which icons do not just depict past events, but depict those past events that are celebrated in the Liturgy – the events connected most clearly with the establishment or re-establishment of the harmony, the cosmos, that God has made. But the main point I want to make is this: an icon does not stand alone; we do not understand it simply by understanding what it depicts and how it manifests it. Instead, we can only fully understand an icon by seeing it as part of an iconic world, a world whose symphonic harmony is established and manifest in the manifold relationships and reflections that link everything together.

The Spiritual Senses

Perhaps now we begin to see why the Western emphasis on artistic creativity skews our understanding of art as manifest in the icon. If art is a kind of sign-making that seeks to read the manifoldly iconic nature of the cosmos, then the notion of artistic creativity perhaps puts the emphasis in the wrong place. It directs our attention to the artist's world – the mind's conjectural world, as Nicholas of Cusa put it.

But why should we be interested in this? Not because it is the *artist's* world, unless we think that art is a kind of higher gossip – which is, I confess, very much the impression given by the weekend supplements – a higher gossip which is entertaining and diverting because artists' egos are so much bigger than ours. If creativity as such is the criterion of art, then that is the direction in which we shall be heading, or drifting. But the artist's world might be interesting for another reason – although in this case we might find that to talk of the 'artist's world' is a rather odd way of putting it.

There was in my exposition of St John of Damascus earlier something that will have made an attentive reader uneasy: all this language of 'symphonic unity', 'harmony' and so on in relation to the cosmos. How can we go on using such language in the world as we know it to be – wounded, divided, fragmentary? St John uses such language for two reasons: first, God created a cosmos, a beautiful and harmonious world; and secondly, through the incarnation – which is a mighty bringing together of opposites – God has restored the world to the unity and harmony that it lost in the fall.

St John – and indeed all the Greek Fathers – speaks of the cosmos as a harmony both protologically (that is, with respect to its first condition) and eschatologically (that is, with respect to its final condition). In between there is brokenness, but it is a brokenness that is being healed and restored. The heart of this restoration is the healing of the image of God in men and women. As the image is restored, so the first and last harmony of the world is revealed, which we call paradise.

One of the effects of the fall is fragmentation. From being persons living in and out of one another, we become individuals, isolated from each other. As individuals, we see the world as centred on me. Our 'worlds' conflict, because I am not you, and we either attempt to establish the hegemony of our own world, or shelter under the hegemony of someone else's, or retreat into a small world that we hope no one else will notice.

If there is no God, then there is no reason why such fragmentariness should not simply be the way things are. Why should there not be, as a simple matter of fact, competing worlds or competing visions? (It is this truth, it seems to me, that lies behind Dostoyevsky's extreme dichotomies: either God or anything goes, either immortality or immorality.) But if there is a God, such fragmentariness is a sign of the fall. It is not ultimate, and finally it is founded on falsehood, because no created being is really the centre of the world.

I suggested earlier that the individualism that lies behind the notion of artistic creativity is at the heart of secularization. In such a secular world the imaginative vision of a great artist can be fascinating. It points to something beyond the pettiness and destructiveness of our competing worlds, and does so in a way that is much more appealing than the claims for hegemony of a Napoleon or a Hitler. The imaginative vision of a great artist might remind us of a lost harmony, of values – like love – that seem fugitive even within the small circle of those who are close to us and irrelevant in the wider world. Such an imaginative vision might properly be called 'creative', for there is no world – real or ideal – of which it could be a copy. Unless, that is, God exists, and there is a paradise we have lost, and a paradise to be regained.

If that is so – and that is what we try to believe – then artistic creativity should perhaps be approached in a different way. Concentration on artistic creativity leads to a focusing on the creative act. Hermeneutics, as understood by Schleiermacher, is concerned to analyse and relive that creative act, as I mentioned earlier. But there are a number of reasons for thinking that this approach is bound to be pointless. In a lecture on 'Watching Artists at Work', E.H. Gombrich remarks:

When the artist intends to realize a novel idea which he has in his mind he can transcribe it as little as he can transcribe the motif he sees in front of him. This view may well run counter to prevailing beliefs, but I think it could be experimentally

169

confirmed. I once asked a group of artists whether they felt able to visualize a single stroke of the pen or the brush so exactly that they could put it on paper or canvas without any deviation. There was not one among them who felt sure that that was possible.[8]

What Gombrich is suggesting is that making something new is a process that is worked out in the making: there is no prescription. One might think, too, of T.S. Eliot's remarks on John Livingston Lowes' *The Road to Xanadu*, which sought to explore the making of Coleridge's 'Kubla Khan' and 'The Ancient Mariner'. Eliot said that it was a 'fascinating piece of detection', but that at the end of the book, 'how such material as those scraps of Coleridge's reading became transmuted into great poetry remains as much of a mystery as ever'.[9]

Another example might be Rilke – of all people! For Rilke believed deeply in the creativity of the poet. But in the first of his letters to a young poet, the main burden of his advice is: 'Ask yourself in the still hour of the night: do I have to write? Dig into yourself for the deepest answer. And if there should be heard agreement, if you can meet this earnest question with a strong and simple *"I have to"*, then build your life around this necessity...'[10] Taken seriously, the notion of artistic creativity means that what the artist does is unique, unrepeatable. Therefore, the idea that the critic recreates the creative experience, as the criticism of the Romantics envisaged, is simply absurd.

Let us put the matter the other way about and ask: what is the poet trying to say; what is the artist trying to depict, and how does he know? It is something he or she has seen, glimpsed, understood. We read or look to capture for ourselves something of the artist's vision. Put this way round, what comes to the fore is not so much the creative act, and for the reader or spectator, the experience of sharing in that creative act, instead what comes to the fore is what is perceived and how it is perceived. And what is perceived is not just what is there, there is something more: some insight, some aura. But it is perceived.

Now there is something in the Orthodox Tradition that offers itself here. It is the idea that the bodily senses are not all that we have got, that there are also spiritual senses. Origen was the first to develop the notion, and from then on the doctrine of the spiritual senses was developed in a whole variety of ways. Spiritual senses are contrasted with bodily senses, sometimes in terms of a crude dualism of Platonic inspiration, but more deeply in terms of an understanding of the human person as a unity. Our experience of the fallen world through our bodily senses is one end of a spectrum that reaches at its other to an experience of paradise through senses that have been transfigured.

The pull of the fallen world through the bodily senses is very strong, however, and is not so much a matter of our actual use of bodily senses, but rather a matter of how we value the world and relate to it. Fallen man experiences a fallen world in terms of externals: the world is something outside him, to be possessed, used and dominated. At the other end of the spectrum is an experience of the world as no longer external and alienated, as no longer exploited for my pleasure, but instead as a source of delight.

I have spoken of a 'spectrum', but that gives a misleading sense of continuity. The earliest accounts of the Christian experience of paradise are to be found in the *Acts of the Martyrs*. The martyrs, by their union with Christ in his death, have broken with this world and are received into paradise. So asceticism, a living martyrdom, is required, if we are to pass from this world to paradise. Prayer, fasting, acts of love and compassion: these are the ways in which the fallen bodily senses are starved and the spiritual senses begin to stir and awaken.

Perhaps, at its deepest, the question of art is concerned with the spiritual senses, both for the artist himself and for the understanding and appreciation of art. If so, it would lead us to look for a much greater sense of objectivity in art. By that, I do not mean that the question of what is good art would be simplified, and certain recognized patterns of aesthetic value established. Rather, what I mean is that our attention would be drawn away from the subjectivity of the artistic experience (for both artist and admirer) and focus on the world disclosed by the artist.

This takes us back, I think, to what we were exploring in St John of Damascus. There we found an understanding of art that connected with a world of symbols and images disclosing the interconnectedness and history of the cosmos that God created. And that perhaps reveals more of the nature of the problem. Take one strand in St John's world of symbols and images: that of what one might call figural reality. In this strand, sacred history has put together a treasury of symbolism (to borrow an idea from Paul Claudel) that can be used to bring out the significance of later events in the history of the Church, or in the life of the individual or group. This was something that was available in the West at least until the time of Dante. Auerbach thought – and he is still, I think, convincing – that it was the collapse of such a sense of figural reality in the fragmented world of the Renaissance and the Reformation that led to the quite new ways of representing reality found in the modern world. These are ways that he felt have become increasingly private – to the point of virtual mutism.[11]

It would, I think, be a possible reading of twentieth-century literature to see it as a variety of ways of seeking to establish a matrix of symbol and reference of sufficient density to enable one to say something significant. In very different ways this is true of both James Joyce and David Jones: Joyce with an elaborate playfulness bordering on the cynical, David Jones with a seriousness tinged increasingly by despair. Despair is present in Jones because there seemed to him to be fewer and fewer people who could make contact with the various patterns of symbolism that he could take for granted. As he put it to Harman Grisewood in

1962: 'Unless *certain* things are taken for granted it's well-nigh bloody impossible for my sort of stuff to mean anything. I don't resent this, and I see why it must be so, but it does account for my smallness of production.'[12]

Between the Spiritual and Material Worlds

I am conscious that there are more than a few loose ends in all this, and there is not enough space left to do much about it. But I want to approach my conclusion by quoting from Hermann Broch's novel, *The Death of Virgil*. In the course of this remarkable novel, there is a great deal of reflection on the nature of the poet's task. At one point, fairly early on in the novel, we find Virgil reflecting thus:

And it could not have been otherwise with Orpheus and his poem, for he was an artist, a poet, an enchanter of those who hearken, singer and hearer enshrouded in the same twilight... the enchanter, but not the saviour of man – a privilege never to be his: for the grace-bearing saviour was one who has cast off from himself the language of beauty, he has reached beyond its cold surface, beyond the surface of poetry, he has pushed on to simple words which, because they come close to death and to the knowledge of death are able to knock on the imprisoned souls of his fellowmen, to appease their fear and their cruelty, and make them approachable to real help; he has attained the simple language of spontaneous kindness, the language of spontaneous human virtue, the language of awakening. Was it not this very language for which Orpheus had striven when, in search of Eurydice, he made ready for the descent into the realm of the shades? Was he not also in despair, one who perceived the impotence of the artist in his discharge of human duty? Oh, when fate has thrown one into the prison of art, he may nevermore escape it; he remains confined within the unsurpassable boundary on which the transported and beautiful occurrence takes place, and if he is incompetent he becomes a vain dreamer within this enclosure, an ambitious trifler with un-art; if, however, he is a real artist he becomes despairing, for he hears the call beyond the border, and all he may do is to capture it in the poem but not to follow it, paralyzed by the injunction and bound to the spot, a scrivener this side of the border...[13]

I have several reasons for quoting this passage. First, it gives some sense of what might be meant by regarding the artist as a *seer*, one who has glimpsed beyond the everyday, rather than as a creative personality.

Secondly, it suggests some of the ways in which art differs from religion; the icon, if you like, from the sacrament. The artist glimpses and beckons: the saviour passes beyond the beautiful and 'makes them approachable to real help'. But it also suggests parallels. Notice, for instance, the parallelism of death and despair. If the martyr is the paradigm of the one who enters paradise from this fallen world, it is beyond despair that the artist finds it possible to articulate what he has seen.

And then finally it suggests what it is that the artist does. He makes something: a poem, a painting, a musical work. He makes something that moves in the realm of the imagination and appeals to the memory. The imagination: perhaps we make too much of it, or maybe we misconceive its nature. Gombrich's remarks quoted earlier suggest to me that the imagination is not so much a faculty as a process. It is a process of trying to picture, and then correct. Rather in the way a poet writes one draft and then corrects it, perhaps several times, or the way a musician plays a piece, listening to himself and trying to find what sounds 'right', meaning by that something not at all easy to define, but including faithfulness to the score and faithfulness to the inner dynamic of the music. Someone playing a piece of music is, of course, not only an executant of the piece (the French say that a piece of music is interpreted rather than simply played by a performer), but a mediator, midway between the composer and the hearer, responding and recreating.

But it seems to me that the same tentativeness checked by the objectivity of the *poiema*, the thing made – the sonnet or sonata or whatever – is involved in any attempt to respond to a work of art, and that process is the imagination at work. Similarly, perhaps, with the memory. It is not so much a cavity in the mind, like a cupboard full of memories that we cannot always find, but a process of recovering links and connections, and reforging them. To remember something is to awaken to the links and connections of which the thing remembered is a focus. Seen like this, a work of art draws us into a world of links and connections indicated and established by symbols.

Perhaps it is also worth making the point that understanding our response to art is often, it seems to me, foreshortened by a tendency to see the process as a single, instantaneous 'pure aesthetic experience'. I read a poem or look at a picture, and have such an aesthetic experience. I wonder if this is so. Sometimes I do, but often I don't. More often I need to read a poem more than once, look at a picture on several occasions, listen to (or play) something over again. It seems to me that a thing of beauty is to be frequented. And it is, of course, only beautiful things that will bear such frequenting. Think how irritating and frustrating it is to use a prayer frequently that is badly expressed or awkwardly worded.

This last point brings out how an understanding and appreciation of art belongs to time. However much art may be a window on to eternity, it needs time for us to be able to see anything through that window. Just as Rilke insists that the first, last and always necessary virtue the poet needs is *Geduld*, or 'patience', so with our grasp and appreciation of art. Time – and space: art belongs to the realm of spatio-temporal reality, although it has seemed to many that music can more and more elide from space. Something like this lies behind Schopenhauer's conviction that all art aspires to the condition of music. And this takes me back to some ideas of David Jones, whose spirit has brooded over these reflections even if I have hardly followed exactly any of his lines of thought. In his essay, 'Art and Sacrament', David Jones says at one point:

> A man can not only smell roses (some beasts may do that, for lavender is said to be appreciated in the Lion House) but he can and does and ought to pluck roses and he can predicate of roses such and such. He can make a *signum* of roses. He can make attar of roses. He can garland them and make anathemata of them. Which is, presumably, the *kind* of thing he is meant to do. Anyway, there's no one else can do it. Angels can't nor can the beasts. No wonder then that Theology regards the body as a unique good. Without body: without sacrament. Angels only: no sacrament. Beasts only: no sacrament. Man: sacrament at every turn and all levels of the 'profane' and 'sacred', in the trivial and in the profound, no escape from sacrament.[14]

This picks up all the ideas introduced at the beginning from St John of Damascus. Art is important; it is concerned with *things*; it makes of these things signs or symbols whence they derive meaning. But David Jones suggests something else. The unique position of the human being as poised between angel and animal, as a *methorion*, to use the Greek word, a 'being on the borders', is brought out by pointing to the human capacity to make signs – to make things that are not useful, but which re-present something else in things.

According to some of the Fathers, it is only human beings, not angels or beasts, who are in the image of God. (According to other Fathers, all spiritual beings are images of God, and the difference between angels and men is simply that men are embodied. However, this seems to me an aberration, doubtless due to an overdose of Platonism.) Only human beings are in the image of God, and only human beings stand on the border, as a *methorion*, between the spiritual and material world.

Perhaps both these facts about the human condition are affirmed when we say that human beings are sign-making beings – that they do not simply make things for use, but they use things as signs. And perhaps it is this very capacity to make and use signs – which is the premise of art – that reveals our condition as created in the image of God. We are created, that is, as signs that point to our creator, and, familiar with signs in our very being, able to make and use signs.

One of David Jones's favourite quotations – he uses it as a motto for his book *Epoch and Artist* – is from the Jesuit theologian, Maurice de la Taille. He says of Christ: 'He placed himself in the order of signs', meaning primarily that at the Last Supper, by the use of bread and wine as signs pointing to what he was to do the next day on the cross, he created a set of signs to interpret and effect his work. But more deeply, as we have come to see, to place himself in the order of signs is equivalent to saying that he became man: man who is a sign and uses signs and thereby lends meaning to things and discerns meaning in them.

10

Man the Priest of Creation

A Response to the Ecological Problem
Metropolitan John of Pergamon

The subject of this chapter is one of the most critical and urgent problems which the world faces today. There is no doubt that whereas all the other problems faced by humanity have to do with the well-being of the world, the ecological problem has to do with the very being of the world. It is not a question of whether the world will be better or worse off, but whether the world will survive or not. This makes the ecological problem an issue which the Church cannot ignore or bypass, because the Church and theology are there precisely in order to witness to the saving Word and Act of God for his whole world. Therefore, if the world is in danger of ultimately disappearing, as it is today, the Church cannot remain silent.

Unfortunately, the Church has done very little so far about this problem. However, we are now beginning, thanks to certain initiatives particularly of the Ecumenical Patriarchate, to realize that the Church has something to say on this subject. The late Ecumenical Patriarch Dimitrios issued a message on 1st September 1989 drawing attention to the seriousness of the problem of the protection of the natural environment. He asked that 1st September each year – already the first day of the ecclesiastical calendar – be the day on which prayers are offered by the Orthodox Church to God for the protection of the natural environment. He also commissioned one of the monks of Mount Athos, a hymnographer, to write a special service for the environment to be used in the Orthodox Church on 1st September every year.

In addition, the Ecumenical Patriarch organized a pan-Orthodox Conference in Crete, which took place in November 1991. This conference had the participation of all the Orthodox Churches, who sent representatives, including bishops as well as theologians and scientists. We were privileged to have Prince Philip, the Duke of Edinburgh, present to deliver the opening address to us, which was deeply appreciated by the Orthodox participants of the conference. The findings and conclusions of this conference will, I think, have a great significance for many years to come, especially as the Churches realize more and more that it is time they should do something about this serious problem.

As the title of this chapter indicates, the real contribution which Orthodox theology can make to the problem of the environment is to emphasize what is so central to this theology, namely, that man – the human being – is the 'priest of creation'. What does this mean, and what in particular does it mean for the problem we are facing concerning the protection of the environment?

What is Man?

We cannot tackle the subject of man as the priest of creation without first having an idea of what man, the human being, is. (When I say 'man', I mean both male and female, and I hope that I will not be misunderstood, especially nowadays, when people are so sensitive about this matter. What I have in mind when I say 'man' is what we call in Greek *anthropos* – both male and female. I will therefore refer to the human being as 'man' with this explanation in mind.)

What is the being that we call 'man'? It is not only theology that tries to answer this question, but also science and philosophy. Although each of these three disciplines has something different to say, they cannot but have something in common about this matter. Otherwise, they would contradict one another on basic ground, and there would be no possibility of a dialogue between them.

179

For science – and for biology in particular – the human being is very closely connected with what we call animals in the world; he or she is another animal. This view has prevailed in biology ever since Darwin produced his theory of evolution. Although this may sound rather disturbing to theologians, we must bear in mind, as we will see later on, that it is important for all of us to remember this connection of the human being with the rest of the animals. Biology approaches the human being as another animal with higher qualities than those of the rest of the animals, but with many things in common, including intelligence and consciousness. Attributes such as these used to be attached exclusively to human beings in the past. But for biological scientists today, the human being is, in a certain sense, basically an animal.

Philosophy tries to give a different view of the human being. Although it admits that the human being is an animal, it distinguishes it from the animals in one important way. In the past, philosophers made this distinction by saying that humans were specially characterized by intelligence or rationality. However, ever since Darwin showed that intelligence can also be found in other animals, and that the difference is a matter of degree and not of kind, philosophy no longer insists on rationality as the special characteristic of man.

The difference seems now to lie in the fact that whereas the animals adjust to the given world – and sometimes they manage that very well, much better than the human being – the human being wants to create its own world, to use the existing world in order to make something specifically human out of it.

This is why the human being produces tools of its own, which are used in order to exploit nature. But more significantly, it treats nature as a raw material from which it creates new realities, as is evident particularly in the case of art. Only the human being can see a tree, for example, and make another tree out of that, a tree which is 'his' or 'her' tree, bearing the personal seal of the person who painted it. Thus it is creativity that characterizes the human being, and this we cannot find in the animals. Man is a creative being. This is very important, as we will see later, for theology as well.

In his attempt to be creative and to create his own world, man is normally frustrated, because he tends and wishes to create, as God does, out of nothing, and to be fully free from what is given to him as his environment, his 'world'. It is because the human being has this tendency to use the natural world for his own purposes that he can be both good and bad for creation. The human being can exploit creation in such a way as to subject it to himself, and in this way make the natural environment suffer under his dominion.

All this indicates that what distinguishes the human being from the animals is freedom expressed as creativity, as the free creation of something new. There are two ideas here to remember which will be very important for our subject. The first we draw from biological science, and that is that the human being is organically and inseparably linked with the natural world, particularly with the animals. The second is that although he is united with the rest of creation, man tends to rise above creation and make use of it in a free way, either by creating something new or sometimes by simply destroying what is 'given' to him.

With these thoughts from science and philosophy in mind, let us now ask what theology thinks the human being is. For theology, the human being is not only related to the rest of creation, but also to another factor, which science does not want to introduce, while philosophy sometimes does, but very often does not – namely, God. For theology, God is crucial in order to know what the human being is. The human being must emerge as something different, as a different identity with regard to the animals, with regard to the rest of creation, and with regard to God. Thus man is a link between God and the world. This is what is expressed in theological terms through the idea of the 'image and likeness of God'.

In the Bible, when man was created, God said: 'Let us now create man in our image and likeness'. What does that mean? What does it mean that the human being is an image of God? This has been discussed throughout the centuries, and I will not bother you with all this complex discussion. Instead, I will simply mention that one of the elements that the Fathers saw as expressing this 'image of God' in man is rationality (*logos*), that man is a *logikon zo-on* ('rational living being'), and that it is through his rationality that he reflects the being of God in creation.

However, *logos* or 'rationality' had a particular meaning at that time, and it had mainly to do with the capacity of the human being to collect what is diversified and even fragmented in this world and make a unified and harmonious world (*cosmos*) out of that. Rationality was not, as it came to be understood later, simply a capacity to reason with one's mind. Instead, as the ancient Greeks thought of *logos*, it is man's capacity to achieve the unity of the world and to make a *cosmos* out of it. Man has the capacity to unite the world.

There is also another element that was stressed by the Fathers as expressing the 'image of God'. This is what Gregory of Nyssa calls the *autexousion* – the freedom of the human being. The animals do not have a *logos* in the sense of acquiring a universal grasp of reality, nor the freedom from the laws of nature; whereas the human being has to some extent both of these things, and that is very important for him in order to be, as we shall see, the priest of creation.

Another aspect of the image of God in man – or rather, another aspect of what man is or represents for theology, particularly Orthodox and Patristic theology – is that man is the 'prince of creation', and the microcosm of the whole of creation. One of the Fathers who wrote in the seventh century, St Maximus the Confessor, developed this idea in particular, namely that in the human being we have the whole world present, a sort of microcosm of the whole universe. Because the human being has this organic link with creation and at the same time the drive to unite creation and to be free from the laws of nature, he can act as the 'priest of creation'.

What is a Priest?

The priest is the one who takes in his hands the world to refer it to God, and who, in return, brings God's blessing to what he refers to God. Through this act, creation is brought into communion with God himself. This is the essence of priesthood, and it is only the human being who can do it, namely, unite the world in his hands in order to refer it to God, so that it can be united with God and thus saved and fulfilled.

This role of the human being, as the priest of creation, is absolutely necessary for creation itself, because without this reference of creation to God the whole created universe will die. It will die because it is a finite universe, as most scientists accept today. This is theologically a very fundamental belief, since the world was not always there, but came into being at some point and, for this reason, will 'naturally' have an end and come into non-being one day.

Therefore, the only way to protect the world from its finitude which is inherent in its nature, is to bring it into relation with God. This is because God is the only infinite, immortal being, and it is only by relating with him that the world can overcome its natural finitude and its natural mortality.

In other words, when God created the world finite, and therefore subject by nature to death and mortality, he wanted this world to live for ever and to be united with him – that is, to be in communion with him. It is precisely for this reason that God created the human being. This underlines the significance of man as the priest of creation, who would unite the world and relate it to God so that it may live for ever.

183

Now, the human being did not perform this function, and here lies for theology the root of the ecological problem. The human being was tempted to make himself the ultimate point of reference, and not God. By replacing God with himself – that is, a finite created being – man condemned the world to finitude, mortality, decay and death. In other words, the human being rejected his role as the priest of creation by making himself God in creation.

This is what we call in theology the 'fall of man'. When this occurred, God did not want the world to die and brought about a way of restoring this lost communion between him and creation. The incarnation of the Son of God was precisely about this. Christ is the one who came in order to do what Adam did not do: to be the priest of creation. Through his death and resurrection, Christ aimed precisely at this unity and communion of the whole of creation with God, at the reference of creation back to God again. It is for this reason that Christ is called the 'second Adam', or the 'last Adam', and that his work is seen as the 'recapitulation' (*anakefalaiosis*) of all that exists.

Thus we must see Christ not simply as an individual who died on the cross for our souls, since his mission – his life, death and resurrection – was meant for the whole universe, and not just for the human being, although it was achieved *through* the human being. Christ came so that the whole world may live, and the human being may become that which he was meant to be when he was created by God, namely the priest of creation.

Now it is this role, which Christ performed personally through his cross and resurrection, that he assigned to his Church, which is his Body. The Church is there precisely in order to do the work of Christ, namely to act as the priest of creation who unites the world and refers it back to God, bringing it into communion with him. This takes place in the Church particularly through the sacraments.

The meaning of the sacraments, for example that of baptism, is that through it the attitude of the fallen Adam is reversed. Man dies as to his claim to be God in creation, and instead recognizes God as its Lord. Through the path of asceticism, the Church educates man to sacrifice his own will, his self-centredness, and subject himself freely to the will of God, thus showing that man has reversed the attitude of the first Adam. Finally, through the eucharist, the Church proclaims and realizes precisely this priestly function of humanity. The eucharist consists in taking elements from the natural world, the bread and the wine which represent the created material world, and bringing them into the hands of the human being, the hands of Christ who is the man *par excellence*, and the priest of creation, in order to refer them to God.

At this point, it is important to remember – especially those of us who belong to the Orthodox Church and are familiar with the Orthodox Liturgy – that the central point in our Liturgy is when the priest exclaims: 'Thine of thine own we offer unto Thee'. This means precisely that the world, the creation, is recognized as belonging to God, and is referred back to him. It is precisely the reversal of Adam's attitude, who took the world as his own and referred it to himself. In the eucharist, the Church does precisely the opposite: the world belongs to God and we refer it back to its Creator through the priestly action of Christ as the real and true man, who is the head of the Body of the Church.

Theology and the Ecological Problem

When we come to the ecological problem, we see that its roots lie in the fact that human beings have separated themselves from the rest of creation. This is really the root of the problem: that man cut himself off from the rest of creation and regarded himself as self-sufficient. An entire theology developed out of this idea, especially in the West since St Augustine, who seemed to believe that the human being consists essentially in the human soul – in the human mind or reason.

This essentially Platonic view was, I am afraid, bought very easily by many Christians in the East as well, who came to devalue the material aspects of the human being. And yet our Orthodox faith stresses that the body which unites us with the rest of the animals in the material world is an essential part of our identity as human beings. The human being is not only a spiritual being, it is a psychosomatic being, as it is rightly called today, and therefore our link with the material world is absolutely necessary for our identity. We cannot exist as human beings without this link.

This is why we believe that in the kingdom of God, when Christ comes again, and as we confess in the Creed, we will see the resurrection of the body: 'I believe in the resurrection of the flesh'. Without the resurrection of our bodies we are not complete human beings. Father George Florovsky, one of the greatest theologians of our time, used to say that a body without a soul is a corpse, while a soul without a body is a phantom – a ghost. The human being must retain its connections with the material world, and that is important also for the sake of the material world, since man is the link between creation and God.

It is for this reason that the Son of God became man, and not an angel. He took upon himself human nature because he wanted to save the whole of creation, and not just souls and minds. Therefore, when theologians stress the spiritual aspect of the human being at the expense of the material, they contribute to the appearance of the ecological problem.

Furthermore, particularly in the West, the commandment of God which we find in the book of Genesis, that man should 'multiply and dominate the earth', has been exploited. As a result, man was understood as the being who could do anything he wished with the rest of creation in order to dominate all the earth.

It seems, therefore, that such theological attitudes have greatly contributed to the appearance in our culture of the position of the human being which could be expressed like this: 'I do not care about what is going to happen to the material world. I am the centre of the world. I am here in order to please and satisfy myself, and the world is there in order to satisfy me, the human being.' This shows that the whole problem of ecology is basically a *spiritual* problem, not simply a practical or scientific one. It is the egocentricism of the human being – 'I am the lord of the world, the world is there in order to serve me' – that underlies the ecological problem. If we do not abandon this attitude, the human being will go on destroying the world, and will of course suffer the consequences.

These consequences today are becoming more and more obvious and threatening. The human being is now beginning to worry: 'What is all this? I had thought that I was the lord of nature, and now nature revolts against me. What shall I do?' Man uses science in order to exploit the natural world even more, but this leads to further problems and complications, and the more science advances, the more nature revolts and the more problems are created.

Faced with this, man turns to other solutions, such as legislation. This leaves the ecological problem with the politicians, who are expected to pass laws in their parliaments forbidding this and that in the hope that nature can be saved in this way. But this does not work because all the democratic parliaments depend on votes, and the people who vote, owing to their wrong spiritual attitude of self-centredness, want to take more and more for their own benefit and are seldom prepared to lose their privileges and make sacrifices. Thus political power and proposals for legislation cannot in themselves lead to a resolution of the ecological problem, without a widespread spiritual transformation.

The same can be said about ethics, because ethics again is a set of rules by which we are called to abide. However, there are such contradictions between the various systems and rules of ethics that one does not know what is right and what is wrong at a given time. Is it right, for example, to reduce production for the sake of avoiding air pollution, if by doing so we increase unemployment with the risk that some people may even go hungry? Where does the answer lie?

In Greece, there was a big problem a few years ago in Lavrion, a town not far from Athens. The government passed laws forbidding factories and industry in that area in order to save the environment. As a result, unemployment rose to such a level that there were demonstrations against the government for closing down the factories. The government is now considering re-opening them. What is the right thing to do in a case like this? Is it better to let people go hungry, or to let them die from polluted air? You often have to choose between different evils.

This leads us to the view that neither ethics, nor legislation or science can solve the ecological problem. This is why the role of the Church becomes absolutely essential today. What we need is a new attitude, a new mentality, a new ethos, and this can be created with the help of the Church. This has happened throughout the centuries, at least in the Orthodox Church, where the faithful were brought up on fasting, on respecting the material world and acknowledging through the Liturgy that creation belongs to God. In this way, people were less self-centred than we are today. Unless we attack man's self-centredness, by stressing that man is there in creation not in order to possess it, but in order to refer it to God, the ecological problem will increasingly be with us, and its consequences will be very serious indeed.

Only when man learns to be the priest of creation, in the sense explained above, can we hope to adopt the right attitude to the solution of the ecological problem we are facing today.

11

The Holy Trinity, the Church and Politics in a Secular World

Costa Carras

Politics uses several well-developed vocabularies, which can be classified under such headings as: liberty; rights and obligations; equality; utilitarian ethics; national, class or individual interest; state sovereignty, and so on. Christians soon find that such concepts do not marry easily with those of Christian theology or teaching, even if a few of the words used – for instance, 'freedom' or 'kingdom' – are the same.

There can be three responses to this. The first is to operate with one or more such vocabularies, as do most citizens and indeed most Christians. Implicitly, this would be either to accept that the Christian faith has nothing distinctive to say about politics, or alternatively to affirm that it should be totally separate from political life. The second is to look for entry points, namely areas of convergence between political and theological vocabularies. The third response is to deduce from fundamental Christian beliefs whatever conclusions regarding the relationship between Christianity and politics may emerge.

I believe that it is the third path that should be followed. For the Christian God is the supreme reality on which our created world is in every way dependent. Orthodox Christians believe that the one God exists as three persons in a communion of love. Although the word 'person' is a concept, we believe that this reality of three persons in a free and eternal communion of love is in every way prior to and indeed the basis of all human concepts. It is also the cause of the existence of the whole glorious panoply of the material world, within which humankind has evolved and subsists.

This belief emerged from the witness of the Apostles and was elaborated by the Fathers, both of whom were grafted on Christ and inspired by the Holy Spirit. From it two conclusions may be drawn, one only true in a simple sense, the other giving a picture both more complex and more complete.

The Holy Trinity and Society

The simple conclusion is that the Holy Trinity should be the pattern of our societies. It is indeed fundamental that the truth of three divine persons existing in a free and eternal communion of love provides the pattern and the explanation for the realization by many – if not most – human beings, and not just Christians, that their deepest experiences are of communion with others. This can be seen in friendship, in the love of husband and wife, or in meeting strangers and finding oneself in an unexpected unity of spirit with them. All these are for Christians relationships of personhood. Their common feature is that we grow in depth by going out of ourselves towards others, and in so giving ourselves to others we ourselves receive in return a hundredfold.

Because this point is so fundamental, however, the first conclusion cannot stand except in its roughest form. God, who is three persons in a free communion of love, is to be firmly distinguished from human societies made up of families, professions, classes and so on, which are inevitably based to a large extent on institutions and bonds that are anything but freely chosen. Even where any group of human beings forms a single society, that society does not represent a communion, but a series of interlocking relationships between individuals, groups within the society, and the society as a whole. Such relationships at all times display a mixture of collaboration, competition and conflict, far more so where separate societies are concerned. The Trinity bears no analogy to the structures of power, or to the systems of law, administration and markets, which are fundamental to all human societies.

Not only are our human societies quite different from the divine communion, but the two came into direct conflict in the trial and crucifixion of Christ. Christ's mission on earth was to serve others and thus show the road to salvation in the kingdom of God. Each person he met he treated as valuable in themselves. It is noticeable that he employed severe language chiefly towards those who were satisfied with their moral state. Any legalistic morality is defined by external limits and is hence automatically prone to hypocrisy, while openness to God and to other human beings entails the impossibility of ever being self-satisfied or secure in a sense of our own merit.

Let us now compare this challenging teaching with the very rational stance (in worldly terms) of those who followed the logic of earthly power. On one side the dispensability of the individual as against the interest of the preservation of the nation, as presented by Caiaphas; on the other, the dispensability of the individual in the interest of the preservation of state power, as presented by Pontius Pilate.

The alternative, more complex, but more complete picture preserves the distinction between a communion of persons and the normal workings of human societies. In so doing it makes one preliminary negative point about politics in general, and one positive point about the life of the Church that is relevant to politics.

The negative point about politics is that if personal communion with the Trinity and with other human persons brings us closest to the relationship of the divine persons among themselves, then the activity of politics, though crucial for human societies, cannot represent the highest value for human beings. This again tallies with human experience: the proclamation of absolute ideals that so frequently reverberates as a sardonic echo from the rock-face of reality; the comradeship of a political movement that is often betrayed at the first conflict of ambition or of will; the deliberate – and indeed often in worldly terms necessary – use of misleading arguments to turn people, and events, in the desired direction. These are such common phenomena of political life that there is inevitably some mistrust even of democratic politicians. This is a point that has been made by satirists from the fifth century before Christ to our own.

However despondent or cynical human beings may become about the politicians of their age, no one will deny that their decisions can be of immense significance – often creative, and often tragic.

The life of the Church, centred in the eucharistic worship of the Holy Trinity, presents a very different picture. It is simultaneously concerned with this world and centred outside it. It emphasizes not the manipulation of political forces or masses but the existential stance that will help free each human being of passions in learning to reach out towards others in love. And if it is a 'society', it is one in which the communion of persons is meant to take precedence over any institution or collective group.

Such a statement invites the immediate response: 'But the Church is not like that at all. It is highly institutionalized. It represents a centre of power which can at times be most worldly. And far from freeing human beings, it is concerned to bind them to particular patterns of behaviour.'

This objection can be approached from two angles. First, the Church herself has always insisted that she is perfected in her communion with God, but most imperfect in each of her members. Therefore, to be constantly straying away from perfection, and to be constantly called onto the path of the true Tradition by the renewing call of the Holy Spirit, is a confirmation and not a denial both of Christ's teaching and the experience of his immediate disciples in response to it.

Secondly, however, we must clearly distinguish between this inevitable and continuous failure of the Church, intermittently more or less serious, and the infinitely more serious distortion of her very nature. This may occur if the inverted pyramid of service based on Christ – in the phrase of Metropolitan Anthony of Sourozh – instead becomes identified with the secular pattern of a ground-up organization presided over by men. It may also occur if the law becomes a master rather than a guide, for when this happens, hypocrisy will be close at hand and the attainment of freedom from passions sacrificed to the limitations of an externalized morality. It may occur finally if the siren songs of individualism and corporatism respectively tempt the Church away from her divine basis of personhood, in the interests either of individualistic self-assertion, or disciplined effectiveness in the search for institutional power.

Thus, while some failure of the Church is inevitable, the distortion of the Church's nature is more catastrophic even than the failure of a political system. It deprives the world of what it most needs, namely the witness of the possibility of a community based on the coming together of persons in a liberating communion of love, in the worship of God, who is himself three persons in eternal communion.

The Church and Society

In such a form, the Church, without uttering a word about politics, displays a creative political stance, offering both an alternative and an inspiration to society as a whole. Such a stance was radical enough for the Romans and Hellenes in the first centuries to have understood that despite genuine protestations of civic loyalty, Christians could not bear ultimate loyalty to any worldly institution. Totalitarian regimes in our own century have been equally and correctly clear in the perception that even when externally subdued, the Church is their most insidious and persistent enemy. Past apostles of secular perfectibility, as also their heirs, less keen on future perfection than on present satisfactions, have hoped that where persecution has failed, tolerated indifference and finely modulated scorn might succeed. They have all had cause to suspect or fear the Church, even when it is overtly unpolitical.

A related difference between the world of politics and that of the Christian faith stems from their very different concepts of power. These share one trait: the ability to act freely and effectively in order to achieve one's ends. There follows radical divergence: the Christian concept of power verging on that of authority, with no necessary connotation of domination; that of the world leaning to success in achieving domination, from which the desired consequences will flow even if authority does not. At the extreme, this is summarized by the Latin adage: *odent dum timeant* – 'let them hate so long as they fear'!

The Christian concept is based on the example of Christ himself. He specifically rejected any position of leadership in worldly terms during the temptations in the wilderness. Yet he spoke with what many who met him considered unparalleled authority. His acts of power, chiefly healings, display a going out from himself which drew forth an acknowledgement of authority even from demonic spirits, and still more from natural forces and the natural world.

It follows that even when human concepts of power have so affected the Church that a hierarchy of service has been perverted into one of domination, analogous authority within the body of the Church as a whole has seldom followed.

Nor is there a correlation between worldly power and spiritual achievement in Church history. Even in our own century, the history of Orthodoxy can give examples of this. Perhaps the most dramatic and creative instance of theological renewal in the Tradition in this century has stemmed from a group of Russian intellectuals forcibly exiled by the Revolution, and those who continued their work. Who would have imagined that a spiritual tradition seemingly dependant on national power, but then humiliated and discarded in its homeland, could not only be transplanted but flourish in very brambly foreign soils?

More recently, at a time when persecution has left successive Patriarchs of Constantinople without a local flock adequate to staff even their secretariat, the Patriarchate has yet proven able to reach out to non-Orthodox Christians in a way that nationally established jurisdictions have not. Similarly, in the Diaspora, it has often been the smaller rather than the numerically or financially stronger dioceses that have most effectively communicated something of the openness and depth of the Orthodox Tradition. In the nature of the spiritual life, these phenomena would not be expected to last forever, but they serve as illustrations of the difference between the inverted pyramid of Christian authority and the seemingly more logical and effective standard pyramid of worldly status and power.

We can thus see a formidable distinction between the Church and the world even as things are, let alone as things should be. It follows that the Church should be far more central to our concern as Christians than most of us consider her to be. The concept of a professional clergy, with the laity as 'consumers' of the service they provide, on the model of a secular profession, stands in opposition to the Tradition of the Church as the people of God, a body of believers joined in communion with one another and with the Holy Trinity. This emphasis on the communion of believers represents a point of unity held in trust for all humankind among the world's divisions, and an abiding witness of eternity in a world whose precious spring freshness is ever a prelude to autumnal decay.

If the Church is so crucially important simply by being as she should be, it becomes easily comprehensible why, despite her fundamental concern for the world, her role cannot be political, in the specific sense of an involvement in earthly politics. Doubtless, in a modern civil society Christian bodies should have the same right as others to express their views. Whether and when that right should be exercised is the issue. The Church has a different purpose: not of coming out in support of one opinion, or in opposition to another, though that may sometimes be necessary, but to be – if only in expectation and by anticipation – a reference point displaying the possibility of combining freedom and unity.

By contrast, lay Christians may well be obligated, as individuals or in groups, to take part in political activity. It is hard to hold a position of some status in society and to deny an obligation to join with others in helping bring that society closer to Christian values, or to prevent it moving yet further away from them, or, more usually, such being the complexity of the ebb and flow in worldly affairs, both simultaneously.

There are situations in which this may not apply. In a militantly anti-Christian society, to help make up the Church may well be sufficient political witness in itself. In non-democratic societies, those without power or status may have neither call nor opportunity to become involved outside their local community. By contrast, in a democratic society that is not militantly anti-Christian, the opportunity given to all creates an obligation on every lay Christian to take some part in political life.

Behind this lies the more fundamental truth that the Church is the point of communion between human beings and God because it follows Christ in being a saving presence and example in and for the world. It does this both by its existence as a community and through the service of its members in the world. Christ himself set this pattern of service to those outside: no Christian may refuse, in some way at least, to follow.

The substantive question which then arises is this: in what directions should that witness be exercised?

Eucharistic Life as a Pattern for Action in the World

The Church gathered together in worship has certain distinguishing features which are clearly relevant to Christian witness in the world. Among these are the emphasis on freedom, understood simultaneously as freedom from external constraint (including religious) and freedom from internal passions, which can limit freedom quite as dangerously. This internal and not just external struggle for freedom necessitates a firm opposition to hypocrisy: opposition not only to the use of force against human beings, but also to any fraudulent means of presenting ethical or other attainments. Fraud and hypocrisy are actually far more effective than the crude use of force in denying human beings their internal freedom. Such freedom is extended by a combination of self-discipline and the exercise of love and friendship in self-giving.

Each human individual's self-realization can be achieved only in becoming a 'person'. This means entering into a relationship of giving and receiving love, friendship or altruistic service with one or more other human beings. This development of personhood in relationship with others is what brings us primarily into the image and likeness of God. The highest and most demanding such relationship open to us is that with the divine persons of the Holy Trinity.

Other distinguishing features of the Church are evident in the celebration of the eucharist, presided over by the bishop or his representative, who is chosen in relation to a specific community, and also simultaneously unites it with other communities in space and with the Apostles in time. Around the celebration of the eucharist, there is an ordered outpouring of thanksgiving and praise toward God expressed in prose, poetry and chant, in architecture and art, all of which have been made Spirit-bearing.

This is true even more literally of the bread and wine, which human hands create from the grapes and grain found in nature.

197

These are offered in thanksgiving to God the Father, and are received again, after invocation of the Holy Spirit, as the body and blood of Christ. Here is a second way in which human beings may display God's image and likeness, as creators. Human creation is blessed by God, but, within the Church at least, not in a spirit of self-assertion or self-satisfaction, but as service offered towards an ongoing exploration of truth and as a feast of joy and thanksgiving in which all may share.

In working out what such features of the Church might mean in terms of Christian witness in the world, however, we must accept some inevitable limitations. The values which flow from the mystery of the Trinity and the nature of the Church will not be given the same weight by all Christians as they consider specific situations in a sinful world, where by definition we cannot expect perfection.

Nevertheless, the exercise of examining the implications of Christian thinking for political life is by no means academic. As will be seen, it does not produce anodyne generalities. Instead, it uncovers real differences of approach from secular points of view that should tend to unite Christians, and also genuine dilemmas which will explain inevitable differences of approach between Christians. In the sections which follow, we will look at ten of these implications for political life.

1. Hypocrisy and Integrity – We begin where Christ's teaching is most disturbing to many, including past and present members of the Church. This is in the severity of his judgment on hypocrisy and that legalistic morality which embraces this form of deceit as 'vice's compliment to virtue', in the revealing English adage. Hypocrisy and deceit debase language, which is the currency of social relationships. They proffer a fine front under which every sort of passion, such as power-lust, envy and greed, can operate with little impediment within the 'rules of the game'. They degrade human beings, as does the use of force, but by more insidious and persuasive means.

Hypocrisy and deceit are not identical with falsehood, since they are often present even when no directly false word has been uttered. Hence they contrast not just with honesty, but with truthfulness and integrity, pre-eminently social virtues, which indicate a genuineness of approach and response to others. These virtues are all the more valuable in our age, when vast resources have been devoted to identifying the fundamental motivations of human beings, and then to skilfully moulding the messages of politicians, entrepreneurs and managers – who often have little choice in the matter – to meet these motivations. The result is that public figures say less what they intend, even when this has merit, than what will most effectively appeal to the passions and prejudices of the message's recipients, so as to secure their preference or custom.

In the game of politics it was, to a considerable degree, ever thus. Themistocles is said to have sold the Athenians on a war-fleet for use against Aigina, which was always intended against Persia instead. However, the power given by the understanding of deep human motivations and prejudices has made the battering waves of messages so powerful that one sometimes wonders whether our societies might lose the ability to come to the surface for a gasp of truth. In short, there has seldom if ever been such a need even in free societies, not chiefly of questioning – which in itself can be just as loaded, hypocritical and exploitative of human passions as the positions questioned – but of a sound currency of social and political intercourse, based on integrity, and an honest examination alike of ourselves and of the arguments we employ.

Even Christian views will vary on the possibility and nature of any response. Wider respect for two fundamental Christian values, control of our own motivations, and a genuineness of approach towards others, would help; as does the constant struggle to maintain sound institutional frameworks, especially in respect of the judicial system and the media, that permit false currency to be exposed. Some limitations on political techniques such as advertising might also be considered. The notorious Willie Horton television advertisement in the 1988 United States election campaign is by no means the only example of a cynical exploitation of base human passions beneath the fair cover of acceptable political campaigning.

2. Power and Authority – This leads us to the question of the Christian approach to the exercise of worldly power. Christians have overwhelmingly accepted that in applying orderly constraint on the extremes of human behaviour it usually reduces disorderly constraint on human freedom overall. This is particularly so with protection from external aggression. Furthermore, because those in positions of power are more exposed than most to the temptations associated with its acquisition and maintenance, but also because they must take decisions which raise the harshest ethical dilemmas under the stress of unpitying immediacy, the Church has always prayed for those in authority.

There is another Christian tradition, stronger in some sections of Western than Eastern Christendom, that is hostile to the arrogance of state power. This tradition is connected with that Christian vision which sees the world, stripped bare of compromise and subterfuge, as a direct contest between the forces of good and evil. And there are occasions – who could honourably deny it of the twentieth century? – when this vision, so often reasonably criticized as crude, corresponds all too accurately with reality.

The tensile balance in the life of the Church between equality and hierarchy has something to suggest about the correct balance in secular societies also. All Christians are members of the people of God, with an identity of nature; each has particular gifts; there is a uniting hierarchy of service, respect for which stems not from innate status or power, but from its relation to the Church community as a whole.

If these attitudes were to have an influence outside the Church, we would expect to see the following characteristics in society. First, an overriding emphasis on equality between human beings in terms of the law, because of the identity of human nature. Secondly, an encouragement of open access to positions of relational leadership in society, because of the variety of gifts. Thirdly, a respect for those who have assumed such positions of leadership. And finally, a strong preference for the elements of authority and service, rather than of domination in the exercise of power. In these respects, one might indeed suggest that there has been a healthy long-term influence of Christianity on some societies.

3. A Christian Approach to Modern Democracy – Christians have frequently had to live under, and have often justified, non-democratic systems. Is there a Christian basis for democracy in the sense of ultimate popular sovereignty with universal adult suffrage? Although the observance of hierarchical order in itself exercises some restraint on the arrogant exercise of power, vesting ultimate power in all citizens seems likely to be far more effective in protecting ordinary people from actions expressing a desire for arbitrary dominance.

This is a strong Christian argument for democracy, but one must immediately observe that there are three exceptions. First, where there is a clearly identifiable minority which is unpopular with the majority; secondly, in respect of citizens of a neighbouring but weaker country; thirdly, the exercise of overall power by a majority may be oppressive not just to an identifiable minority, but to particular individuals. It is therefore not every democratic constitution, and specifically not those which concentrate power over life, liberties and property in elected officials, which are most likely to achieve the diminution of the undesirable exercise of power. Rather, it is those which, to a greater or less extent, balance the exercise of power and leave ample scope for the exercise of human freedom and collaboration in voluntary institutions and enterprises.

If such a Christian attitude is one justification for a balanced democratic constitution and a civil society, another is that one of the fundamental principles of action laid down by Jesus – 'act towards others as you would have them do to you' – is likely to have its greatest influence on society as a whole in a democracy. For this is a principle that, within any particular society, fewer people are likely to oppose than to support – at least as an ideal, if far less frequently in practice!

A third and specifically Christian justification for democracy might be based on a prophetic understanding of history. As peoples feel mature enough to determine their destinies, so they take responsibility before God both for their own land and for their relationship with the rest of the world. The thought is troubling, because far from providing a comfortable, self-justificatory basis in securing popular rights and serving our own interests, it suggests that we are under God's judgment in the exercise of our citizenship, as in all else.

4. Power and the Current Crisis of International Order – One area where a Christian might today argue that all humankind, and our more democratic prosperous societies in particular, stand under judgment is our inability to build up an international order based on a consistent upholding of the rule of law, with supporting institutions. This inability has been particularly marked since the end of the bipolar world – which gave some excuse for the situation – until 1989. Reliance on a nineteenth century network of great power initiatives and alliances is more convenient for the powerful in the short term, but more dangerous in the long term, especially in a nuclear age. Nor has the stench of hypocrisy in international affairs diminished as powerful states intervene to punish aggression and injustice wherever either their own interests are affected, or their own favourites are challenged, or their peoples' consciences are effectively moved by the media; but otherwise turn the other way on the road to Jericho – and earn good money in arms sales to the thieves on the side!

The main focus of our concerns is shown by the contrast between this lack of interest in gradually building up an international order based on the rule of law, and the immense effort successfully contributed to opening the world for freer trade. Even if the motive force of many who argued for this course was self-interest, its objective effect has been different. It has given an opportunity to those countries whose standard of education makes them able, and whose social values make them willing, to absorb Western technology and methods of organization and to make dramatic progress in approaching wealthier nations. It thus tends to diminish, if not for all, then at least for many, the notable inequality that has marked the world community in recent decades.

This focus on economic growth as one of the chief purposes of human societies has therefore had an altruistic aspect, that of reducing the constraints of poverty, communicating the benefits of material progress to more people, and stressing peaceful rather than military competition. However, making the acquisition of wealth and property – or alternatively, status and power – the primary ends of human life, increasingly places a question-mark over our sense of civic and human responsibility.

5. Prosperity and the Current Crisis of World Ecology – This widespread attitude has been based on a false premise, that of human autonomy from the rest of God's creation. This runs against the early Eastern Christian tradition in which our role was to be co-creators with God, guardians of his world and priests called to offer it to him, in the words of Metropolitan John of Pergamon. Today, despite increased general concern by some, and widespread anger if our neighbourhoods are affected, most human beings continue to stand in relation to nature as a whole principally as exploiters and consumers.

This situation is scarcely surprising, given the marked preference for the short term in a world dominated by educated agnostics ('in the long run we are all dead'!), the increased atomization of societies, the scientific tradition of objectifying the natural world, and above all the revolutionary increase in knowledge and technical skill. We are witnessing a phenomenon which might be described as 'the idolatry of the technological fix', which makes it an article of unexamined faith that a technical solution can be found for any problem in good time. This gives human beings a false sense of security and a self-image of overpowering autonomy in relation to the natural world.

Changes in Christian and secular thinking over the centuries provide the historical background to this situation. Given the Eastern Fathers' cosmic vision of salvation, however, it is a particular responsibility of Orthodox Christians to re-express that vision, whose long neglect has been a sin, in the sense of a failure to hit the mark. Even in the many areas where technical solutions will prove to be available, their timely implementation is unlikely, unless our atomized sense of human existence is rapidly transformed into one of eschatologically immediate responsibility of each person for others, and for the cosmos as a whole.

It remains true that the balance of importance between such a consideration, especially if it is interpreted in terms of the need for constraint, and others, such as preserving and expanding human freedom, can very well be argued on the political level. In each of our lives, however, creativity and freedom should increasingly coincide so as to express a sense of responsibility for our world as a whole.

6. Human Creation Outside the Church – We have seen how creation by human beings is blessed and sanctified within the eucharistic Church, not in a spirit of self-assertion or self-satisfaction, but as acts of service offered towards an ongoing exploration of truth, and a feast of joy and thanksgiving which all may share. Ideally, this should also be the model, doubtless only rarely to be attained, outside the Church.

Likely differences between a Christian and non-Christian approach is that the former would be less likely to admire display for its own sake, and more likely to acknowledge the creation of beauty where the attempt is made to relate, whether in harmony or as a challenge, to its surroundings, or to the wider society for which the work is created.

Very similar has been the attitude of Christians to creativity displayed in human institutions. Here too human creation can be distorted by self-appropriation and self-glorification. Still worse, the service of human institutions – as indeed of the Church when mistakenly seen in a primarily institutional manner – may all too easily combine humility towards such institutions with an arrogance of pride on behalf of the institutions served.

Christians accept also, in the face of human creation that falls short, the frequent need for an ascetical willingness to endure either ugliness or hardship, since even the abuse of creation can be redeemed by suffering freely chosen.

Yet the main thrust of the Church's teaching has always been positive. From the earliest days of the apostolic Council of Jerusalem, related in the book of Acts, the Church has distanced itself from the idea of a single culture, which would in those days have been a continuation and extension of Judaism. Instead, consistently with fundamental Christian beliefs, there emerged a sense that despite the obvious dangers, different languages, cultures and ways of life could coexist in the Church. In the early centuries, Latin, Syriac and Coptic flourished together with Greek. In the ninth century, St Cyril and St Methodios fought against the theory of three 'sacred languages' – Hebrew, Greek and Latin – to establish the Slavonic tradition, and in so doing kept open the road for many more.

7. The Ministry of Reconciliation Between Peoples – We have seen that the most central feature of the eucharistic community is the combination of love and freedom as two interacting existential values, a never-ending paradox for the non-Christian. Their relationship stems from the spiritual reality that there is no firm ground within the individual. It is by the simultaneous process of on the one hand freeing ourselves from the bonds of passion and attachment, together with an automatic adhesion to various natural and institutional identities, and on the other hand a reaching out beyond ourselves towards others, that we root ourselves in the Body of Christ and can be renewed by the Holy Spirit.

This has further implications. One concerns the ministry of reconciliation, which has its firm foundations in Jesus' saying, 'Blessed are the peacemakers'; in his concern to bring back into the fold of Israel those groups which were despised and excluded by the religious of his age; and in the very difficult but on the whole successful attempt of the early Church to hold together as one Church – but not one language or culture – people of many different backgrounds.

Reconciliation is not the same as compromise, still less surrender. It is by no means certain that where such a need comes into conflict with one of the other Christian approaches already or soon to be touched on, reconciliation should necessarily take priority. This indeed was also true with Jesus, whose challenge to many of the religious of his day was deeply resented, and who proclaimed his teachings' ability and destiny to divide every natural category, including the family itself.

However, what is true is that even in the sharpness of dispute and conflict, we should never forget that there are human beings on the other side of the divide. Thus any victory, particularly any victory involving the loss of human life, is not only a victory but a defeat, unless and until reconciliation has followed.

The ministry of reconciliation is genuinely respected in many quarters in our world today, and it is also acknowledged that its exercise may sometimes, in a sinful world, involve tough language or action, and the countervailing exercise of power. It is also true, however, that the bonds of racial, national, religious and communal feeling have seldom proven as widely murderous as in our century. Far from preventing such developments, the most acceptable of all political ideologies of our time, namely democracy, has in many instances made matters not better but worse.

The reason is obvious: the competitive element in democracy is held in balance with the collaborative within states whose populations share their basic identity. Where this does not occur, however, political divisions may come, even after a long period of peaceful symbiosis, to reflect an ethnic, religious or communal fault-line. The majority group may exercise its power provocatively, or the minority may nurse fears based on almost inevitable past or present grievances. If the minority has power at its back, especially in the form of a neighbouring friendly state, even the form of democracy may suffer. Either way, the fundamental rationale of balanced and libertarian democratic government will be injured.

Here is an indubitable example of the dangers of exalting one political principle above all others. Like an ancient Semitic idol to whom all first-born sons were sacrificed, hundreds of thousands have lost their lives and many more their homes and properties in our generation not just because of the inability of whole groups to seek reconciliation rather than domination, but because the seeming apostles of reconciliation themselves have been grossly negligent in adjusting their standard prescription to meet the needs of multi-communal societies.

What has already been said regarding the need for an elaboration of a system of international order is relevant here. Also relevant is the acceptance that in multi-communal states, democracy needs to be modified so that each community has a substantial say in the election or choice of the representatives of the other or others. Thus part of the leadership of each community would depend on the support of those 'others'. If reconciliation and cooperation are not enshrined as values no less important than popular sovereignty, the faultline in multi-communal societies will always be in acute danger of becoming a yawning chasm.

8. The Ministry of Reconciliation Within and Between Societies – Another implication of the central feature of the eucharistic community, the combination of love and freedom, shows in a whole range of issues which arise both within and between countries. There have always been peripheral groups beyond societies' normal constituents. These are the people denied natural social intercourse, among them the hungry, the destitute, the prisoners, the abandoned, the seriously ill. Jesus' words and actions were of a piece: his ministry and his teaching alike held them at the centre of his concerns.

Recently, it has been widely held that his attitude validated political action to help these and other such groups. Jesus actually spoke of personal rather than instrumental (including political) action. There are indeed many instances where only personal and not political action can be effective; but it is true that effective political or administrative action which releases people from suffering usually also enables them freely to enter into personal relationships. This is therefore an area in which Christians should and do play a very prominent role, both in voluntary work and as members of political pressure groups.

Increased prosperity in many parts of the world, and in most sections of Western societies, will tend to increase rather than diminish this role in those parts of the world where the Western 'recipe' for prosperity may be inapplicable, and in those sections of Western society where the Western 'recipe' itself must inevitably increase disintegratory tendencies.

9. The Paradoxes of Freedom and Constraint – Beyond this point, the issue of whether reducing external constraints effectively extends the range of human freedom becomes more complex. Jesus' warning that much worse could befall human beings than the diseases he healed sounds a note that is all too relevant to societies such as our own. In these, external constraints on human beings have now been lifted – except for small and shifting minorities – to a degree inconceivable in any previous period, but even the possibility of gradually acquiring internal freedom is widely questioned.

This freedom from external restraint, the only worthwhile freedom in practice rather than theory for most modern libertarians, has led to an increase in altruism. On its own, however, it could not result, and indeed has not resulted, in that degree of personal engagement with others, whether in need or not, that one would have anticipated from increasingly prosperous societies still leavened by the Christian message. Instead, an emphasis on increased consumption and the satisfaction of the senses has become the dominant note in society. This is perhaps inevitable, given the secular values that even most Christians uphold in practice. In the process, the secular vision of progress has been drained of its once attractive optimism. It is now confined largely to numerically quantifiable data like per capita GNP. We should never be ungrateful in respect of the increased freedom obtained from greater prosperity. Is it a coincidence, however, that the sense of a dead end can be glimpsed in the widespread unwillingness of the most prosperous generation in history to bear children who would form the next?

A Christian cannot propose a purely ideological or policy response to a spiritual problem, and here one must again insist on the centrality of the Church's existential role. This does, however, imply support for the principle of freedom of action in general, wherever it does not infringe on equivalent freedom for others.

Seriously to constrain freedom of action in the cause of an allegedly Christian morality represents a contradiction in terms, for a 'Christian morality' is not met by the formal fulfilment of certain commandments, but by a genuinely free response to and love for others that cannot co-exist with external constraint.

There are, all the same, some ways in which society might legitimately be more cautious. One is in regard to the purveyance and exploitation of fantasy. Certain types of advertising, as also of sadistic and pornographic imagery, are defended as expressions of freedom of action, but are more accurately to be seen as attempts to profit from the enslavement of human fantasy. The falsehood their purveyance involves – in contrast, say, to the provocative work of an avant-garde artist or writer a century ago – is no less dangerous than the false description of foodstuffs on the market. We should be as determined to limit the one sort of falsehood as the other. Both, in the name of freedom of action for their initiators, actually reduce the freedom of the recipients.

This reinforces the well-known point that in order to reduce the constraints on some it is often necessary to increase constraints on others. This is most controversial where measures to reduce the evident constraint caused by severe poverty may lead to further constraint on economic freedom and creativity.

Is there a 'Christian' view on this? Not in the sense of a view generally valid for all situations. Christianity is neither a religion that demands the legal enforcement of what is in general at least correct action, nor one which ascribes a divinely ordained or sacral character to life as it finds it, nor yet one which turns away from and is indifferent to the world.

There are, however, certain powerful lines of Christian thinking on the subject. The first we have already set out – it is favourable to freedom to create in the economic as in other spheres. The second would argue that acute deprivation – as of food, shelter, medical care or health itself – represents a constraint on freedom of action far more severe than laws preventing an unhindered acquisition of property, even if the acquisition of property increases the potential for freedom of action among those who acquire it. Furthermore, this argument is valid for a Christian not just within a particular state, but also between states.

This argument has proven very persuasive in recent generations both within some of the poorer countries, as in the development of 'liberation theology', and in the wealthier countries, encouraging the creation of huge institutions to ensure people's welfare, and even, to a smaller degree, encouraging aid to poorer lands.

The severe limitations to this argument from a Christian point of view do not end with the point already made and partly answered above that such activity often has no personal element.

A second limitation is that the Gospels' concept of poverty is not one of relative deprivation, as it is within the political and social dialogue of most modern states, but of destitution or other forms of exclusion from normal society. Otherwise, there can be no automatic assumption that the immediate advantage of the relatively poorer is morally preferable to that of the relatively richer. This would depend on a wide range of extraneous considerations – saving and investment by the wealthier might well be of greater advantage to the poorer also. Nor is envy any less dangerous a passion than is greed.

A third limitation on the validity of the argument is that constraints on human freedom and creativity in the economic sphere have usually involved an increase in the range and power of the chief constraining institution, the state. The state and its employees are scarcely neutral. Powerful state machines habitually misallocate either to their political masters, or to their employees, or to those who exercise influence on them, a disproportionate share of available resources. Thus countries with opposed economic ideologies, but similarly powerful state machines, have faced similar situations where a bloated state distributes largesse to comparatively few, while at the same time constraining the creativity of many. This is not simply economically undesirable; it is a situation corrosive of the fabric of society.

The final limitation concerns effectiveness. In the last generation, the argument, after long, slow swings of the pendulum, has turned decisively in favour of 'free' markets, which are thought to offer greater general effectiveness in reducing poverty within an arguably acceptable time-span. Free markets usually combine strong elements of competition with other elements of collaboration and regulation, in contrast to economic systems that place emphasis on a combination of collaboration and command. Where the absence of one constraint – on economic activity – may also be the most effective way of combating another – poverty – the only economic dilemma that remains is that of the timescale within which this may be achieved.

Even where this conclusion is valid, however – and it might be valid in some places and at some times, but not others – there remains another danger. The spiritual temptation for the successful is reinforced by a sense that the wider economic effects of their success provide a conclusive justification for a style of life often associated with social consequences which are very questionable.

10. The Success and Crisis of Secular Individualism – Thus the end of one argument also signals the opening of another. Since about the sixteenth century, if not before, the process of acquisition of property in Western society has been associated with the growth of individualism. This also depended on family structures that encouraged energetic risk-taking and a value-system that was simultaneously favourable to individual ethical responsibility and individual success. As individualism has become secularized and has reached the zenith of its influence in the atomization of societies, it is breaking down both these presuppositions. With the breakdown of the family, there are many individuals who do not have the psychological or educational possibilities of playing this increasingly competitive game, but who are open to exploitation by all the modern means of persuasion. What place can be found for this new, non-industrial proletariat in democratic communities remains a troubling question.

Furthermore, with all the unquestioning confidence of success, some of those inspired by the wonderful modern engine of economic growth have increasingly ignored the frameworks of collaboration, the legal ground rules, and the ethical values such as integrity, which were meant to characterize market systems at their best. Instead, they are turning increasingly to a new, semi-religious 'idolatry of the invisible hand', which in its crudest form claims that the shortest road to the best of all possible worlds is to let markets do all the work.

The combination of two modern idolatries, that of the 'technological fix' and that of the 'invisible hand', both devoid of ethical content in theory, and frequently anti-ethical in implementation, seems to be creating greater problems with every year that passes. Placing primary emphasis on the acquisition of consumer goods and sense satisfactions inevitably diminishes the priority of human relationships and acts as a solvent on those ethical guidelines that help give societies their sociability.

Then again, there are many who cannot win the game if they play by the rules. And as these are held to have no ethical significance, but simply to reflect the current state of positive law, they play instead by their own rules. It should be no surprise therefore that whole sections of societies now live by crime, as for instance by trade in the various drugs that provide a very temporary bliss to some of the new proletariat – and many others! Nor should it be a surprise that organized crime can assert a share in power in all too many countries, including even some democracies.

The Unity of the Church and the Secular World

The preceding discussion should have demonstrated that the Christian faith is relevant to economic or social questions, but cannot be tied to a specific set of policies at any particular moment. Usually individual Christians may validly prefer one or another course even with solely Christian arguments in mind.

However, discussion within the Church in terms of such Christian arguments is essential, because the Christian Tradition is likely to find itself in opposition to the logically consistent operation of most secular formulas. This is because it seeks above all to preserve human freedom from any slavery, external or internal, and simultaneously to give priority to the development of those personal relationships, which, rather than the acquisition of goods, justify human life.

It can also be seen more clearly why the Church as a body, in distinction to individuals or groups of Christians, should not be seen as a religious collectivity that operates largely like secular ones: merely urging on society policies that appear more moral at the time. This would be tantamount to a secularization of the Church, which represents an existential and not a moral unity of its members, a place of actual and potential communion between all human beings and God.

The exceptions to this general rule, therefore, must be when this existential unity is at risk. What places it most at risk is not moral weakness, but inhuman behaviour, which turns communion in the body and blood of Christ into a hypocritical sham. To defend this unity, St John Chrysostom attacked the greed of the court in Constantinople, and St Philip of Moscow the cruelty of Ivan the Terrible, at the cost of effective martyrdom for the one and actual for the other.

A far harder instance is where inhumanity is displayed to members of the Church in a particular country by foreigners who are outside it. Given the sacrificial element in the Church's nature, it is almost inevitable and usually justifiable that the Church as a body should react, and this type of response creates a powerful bond between Church and nation. It has occurred in the majority of Orthodox countries as the result of repeated attacks from both East and West between the seventh and fifteenth centuries.

This development had both healthy and unhealthy consequences. Christian self-sacrifice gained the implicit trust of a wider proportion of people than might normally occur. Also, an identity defined less in terms of this world than of eternity gave them infinitely greater strength to endure oppression while remaining creative. The unhealthy consequences were first that those inflicting the oppression came, with reason, to see the Church and the opposing ethnic groups as one. Thus, from being a faith of potential unity open to all peoples, as in the early centuries, Orthodoxy gradually became a faith effectively closed to most. Little or nothing could have been done about this at the time.

However, far worse occurred when influence started flowing in the opposite direction, from increasingly secularized ethnic bodies towards the body of the Church. This was all the easier, because the initial impetus came in the form of a demand for freedom from oppression, and this found an answering chord in the Christian Tradition. It seldom takes long, however, for physical conflict to reverse the positions of oppressors and oppressed, even if only temporarily. When this occurs, the Church is in danger of appearing to be merely the ecclesiastical aspect of a state that behaves like any other.

The Orthodox heartlands have witnessed a process of intense secularization, brought about by nationalism, and also by both Communism and consumer capitalism. This, combined with the evident bankruptcy of a model of the Church that simply blesses the activities of a secular state, means that the Church must think again. Not all Orthodox Christians in the heartlands have realized this, but it is as necessary for them as for Orthodox Christians outside the heartlands.

To be true to the Orthodox Tradition, any answers should come neither from an absorption of secular concepts, even if with hierarchical blessing, as has happened too frequently in the last two centuries, nor should they come from an attempt to find accidental points of convergence between systems of thought that are based on premises of a quite different order. Instead, answers should come from a careful consideration of the implications for the world of the mysteries of the Holy Trinity and of the eucharistic communion of the Church, which Orthodox Christians hold central to our existence.

12

The Prophetic Role of Orthodoxy in Contemporary Culture

Dr Andrew Walker

Since the Middle Ages until recently, prophecies in the West have ranged from portentous prediction (for example, the fifteenth-century Girolamo Savonarola) to pretentious presumption (the nineteenth-century Mormon founder Joseph Smith). Today the prophetic role tends to be interpreted in three ways.

In liberal churches, it is usually interpreted politically. The prophets in this line need to be supporting one party against another party, or one cause against another cause. The legitimate biblical concern for the poor and the oppressed becomes a legitimation for a social or liberation gospel which all so often ends up being a different gospel. Prophets of such a religion take on the characteristics of an *agent provocateur*, or a romantic activist – more a follower of Marcuse than Moses.

In fundamentalist and conservative Protestant circles, prophecy is prey to religious enthusiasm, seen either in millenarian or ecstatic terms. Millenarians, such as the American televangelist Jack Van Impe, interpret eschatology not as the final judgment but as a second advent. Adventist prophets search the Scriptures, notably the apocalyptic passages, in order to help them look for and recognize the signs of the 'end-time'. Charismatic churches tend to stress divine inspiration over and against Tradition and sacred text – as if one could somehow distinguish *rhema* from *logos* – or they insist on the legitimacy of immediate and unmediated revelations alongside revealed Tradition. The prophets of such a religion are more in the line of Montanus than Mark the Ascetic.

The Prophetic Function

As a matter of fact, both of these conservative Protestant traditions reflect – though refract – strands of Orthodox teaching. St Irenaeus, for example, included a millenarian section in his apologia *Against the Gnostic Heretics*, and St Simeon the New Theologian stressed that the inspirational side of spiritual life should be normative for the Christian. But these lesser known prophetic traditions are not the core prophetic concept in the Orthodox Church. In order to discover what that might be, we can do no better than begin with the Russian catechism, where we read the following:

'Anointed' was in old times a title of kings, high priests and prophets. Why then is Jesus, the Son of God, called 'the anointed'? Because to His Manhood were imparted without measure all the gifts of the Holy Ghost, and so He possessed in the highest degree the knowledge of a prophet, the holiness of a high priest and the power of a king.

In the Patristic era, the interconnection between Christ as king, priest and prophet was continually held in creative tension. However, all these titles shared in common the generic feature that they are charisms of Christ's humanity, conferred by the anointing of the Holy Spirit.

Fr Schmemann, drawing on earlier literature, reminds us in *The Water and the Spirit*, that when Jesus came out of the waters of Jordan at his baptism, there was the first public demonstration of the true nature of the Son of God. The Trinity was revealed, and Jesus coming up out of the water was a way of showing, as it were, the divine stature of who he really was. The full stature of Jesus as a human being, however, was that in receiving the Holy Spirit from the Father, he was anointed to be the greatest of the prophets, our one true high priest and supreme mediator between God and humankind, and our everlasting king – one who rules with intrinsic authority and absolute justice.

Fr Schmemann makes the claim – as daunting as it may be for us to accept this – that when we too are baptized, and immediately afterwards chrismated with oil, this is also a trinitarian action and a threefold calling, that we may be like Christ in our anointed humanity. So we are grafted into the Body of Christ through the waters of baptism in the power of the Holy Spirit, and affirmed by the Father to be joint-heirs with Christ. And we too are called to be a prophet, a priest and a king.

This is why St Irenaeus is so foundational for Orthodox theology. He stressed the incarnation as the event which enabled men and women truly to become what they are called to be: not merely restored to the innocence of paradise and the (forever lost) unfallen flesh of Adam, but recapitulated in Christ's new humanity as co-heirs with him of God's future kingdom. We are permitted to be co-heirs in this kingdom only because we have become members of this new race through adoption into Christ's divine life.

The New Testament calls our Lord the second or final Adam (1 Corinthians 15.45) because he is both the origin and fount of this new race, but also its apotheosis or fulfilment. To 'put on Christ', therefore, is to acquire through grace what he alone among men and women is by nature. This grace allows us also to acquire the charisms of Christ's anointing.

We might say that the incarnation initiates the future kingdom because it marks the beginning of 'eschatological' time: the end-time when God from the future (the eschaton) enters the space-time continuum of created existence. Through that decisive moment of history – when eschatological time entered ontologically into the human situation – the future of the created cosmos, and of all men and women who have put on Christ, is destined to be greater than anything Eden knew.

Eden, however, was a world in which human beings knew something of prophecy, priesthood and kingship. Before the fall, man and woman were in communion with God. They were stamped with God's character or image, and made in his likeness. Adam and Eve, in Fr Schmemann's memorable phrase, were 'matter made articulate': God's prophets or 'spokespersons' to the world. They were priests too because it was a unique function of human beings as bearers of God's image that they could mediate between the created earth and God himself. They offered God to the world and the world back to God: 'Thine of Thine Own' in the words of the eucharistic prayer. Human beings were kings also, not as overlords, but as regents or royal stewards of the Lord's good creation.

The prophetic role is the one I want to dwell on in the rest of this chapter even though, as we have seen, it rightly belongs in concert with our priestly and kingly functions, given us at the birth of the world and now restored to us in Christ.

The prophetic function is very simple and I would like to spell it out if I may in a simple sentence: to be a prophet is to know and speak the mind and will of God. It was the fall that hid this knowledge from us, just as it perverted our God-given kingly power, and weakened our natural propensity for mediation between the created order and God.

Throughout the Old Testament, we read from time to time of men and women who had flashes of insight – people who seemed to be able to re-connect with the original created human being who knew God's mind, and who could speak the will of God. We think specifically of Moses and Elijah, or of Jeremiah, Amos and the other prophets. But in the New Testament, it is the Lord Jesus who is supremely our prophet, and we are called as baptized disciples to follow in his footsteps. The words of St Paul make this quite clear: 'Therefore, if anyone is in Christ, he is a new creature, a new creation. Old things have passed away, behold, all things have become new' (2 Corinthians 5.17).

Strangely enough, many people find it difficult to associate prophecy with our Lord, because we think of Jesus as our Saviour, or as divine, or as the God-man. While the epistle to the Hebrews draws our attention to Christ as our High Priest, and Orthodox Tradition has long associated Jesus with the Judge-King (*Pantokrator*), whose kingdom shall have no end, the word 'prophet' is not automatically a word that comes to our lips. I suspect that this is due also to the fact that we tend to distinguish our Lord from the last of the great Old Testament prophets, St John the Baptist, the forerunner to the expected Messiah. But clearly it is right and proper to see Christ in his humanity as being a prophet, a new creation, a new creature, one who knew and spoke the mind and will of God. St Luke is the most important of the four Gospels when it comes to the prophetic role of our Lord, for in his Gospel we read that Jesus identified himself as a prophet (Luke 4.24). Speaking in the synagogue at his home town of Nazareth, Jesus said:

The Spirit of the Lord is upon me because he hath anointed me to preach the gospel to the poor; he hath sent me to heal the broken-hearted, to preach deliverance to the captives, and recovering of sight to the blind, to set at liberty them that are bruised. To preach the acceptable year of the Lord (Luke 4.18-19).

In the Old Testament, taken as a whole, it is more accurate to say that the prophets were not so much *foretellers*, as *forthtellers* of God's mind and will, the ones who proclaimed God's word. Jesus begins his ministry forthrightly in Mark's Gospel with the words: 'Repent and believe the gospel'. Jesus, the Son of God made Son of Man, is therefore revealing to us the mind of God. God's will for us, which is nothing less than the gospel, is that like the prodigal son we must turn from our failure and degradation and return to the

Father who is always ready to re-affirm and cherish us. It is the Son who reveals this to us, who alone speaks the truth from the mind of God, who is the way home, life itself (John 14.6).

The Prophetic Role of the Diaspora

I am mindful, following the example of St John Chrysostom, that Holy Tradition needs to be applied to our contemporary condition. So having grounded the role of prophecy in the life of Christ himself, I would now like to turn to the role of the prophet today, writing as a Western member of the Orthodox Diaspora.

But first there is something that we must make clear, and it is something that I believe we Orthodox already know in our hearts. It is that we must try to avoid individualistic notions of the 'prophet': he is a prophet, she is a prophet, I am a prophet. There may be individuals whose utterances are more prophetic than others; we know also from the writings of St Irenaeus that there were still institutional prophets in the late second century. However, what makes the prophet significant is not the novelty of individual insight, but the faithful recollection of Tradition. Tradition is the divinely inspired – though human, and hence fallible – mediation of the mind and will of God.

A better way of understanding this is to recognize that Orthodoxy distinguishes individualism from personhood. Individuals are disconnected persons, separate islands of consciousness, solipsistic beings, lost selves; whereas persons are ontologically constituted by their relation to others in communality, and supremely through the Holy Spirit. The Holy Trinity may be the only true, perfect communion, where relationships are unbroken between the distinct, though never separate, divine persons, but members of the Church are by definition joined one to another. We are what we are as persons because, as St Paul puts it, we are 'joined together' (Ephesians 4.16).

We are prophets precisely, and only, because together with our Lord we are the *totus Christus*. We are prophets because we are 'little Christs'. We are prophets because we are adopted by the Spirit into a new personal creation – this newly constituted humanity of which Christ is the firstborn through the incarnation and resurrection (see Colossians 1.18). In one sense, therefore, the Church cannot help but be prophetic. I think it was Fr Justin Popovic who said that the past is always present in the Church, and therefore the Church is always contemporaneous. That is to say, it is not really possible for the Church not to be prophetic today, or at any time. But what does it mean to be prophetic? To reiterate: it is to know and speak the mind and will of God.

I would like now, as I promised I would, to point to something rather more concrete and specific that affects us all. I would like to talk about the prophetic significance of the Orthodox Diaspora in the modern world. We could be reductionist and say: 'Well, of course, we can understand the Diaspora entirely in terms of war, civil strife, sociology and economics', and that is perfectly true on the political and cultural level. But prophets are called by God, and I think it is also true, on the spiritual level, that God called the Orthodox Church into the West. With all its faults and weaknesses – and hopefully not blind to its faults and weaknesses – the Orthodox Church finds herself in a world both secular and religious that is becoming increasingly fragmented and polarized. In such a world, all that the Church is called to be is to be herself. To be herself is to be prophetic.

I would like to give you an example of what I mean. A colleague of mine at one of the American universities where I teach says that increasingly, Protestant Christians are beginning to understand that the history of fragmentation within Christendom goes back at least to the Reformation – and we would want to say much sooner. While the Reformers genuinely desired to return to the catholicity of the creeds and councils, instead they gave us reformation *ad nauseam.* What my colleague and some of his friends see when they look at the Orthodox Church is a body of Christians who have maintained the apostolic faith, because the canonical structures have been maintained and kept secure.

My friend claims that one of the greatest failures of the Reformation was precisely that it did not recover or recapture the foundational canonical structures of Christianity that were laid down, not only in the New Testament, but also by the Fathers of the Church. In that sense, what the Church does by being itself is pointing to unity and showing something of the mind of God. That is what Khomiakov's remarkable booklet, *The Church is One,* contends. It is certainly audacious, but it is also auspicious and prophetic in an age of disunity. It is not so much that unity is a question, as Roman Catholics might put it, of an unbroken apostolic succession, as if this were an entitlement to legitimate churchmanship – like a deed of property or a right to dominion. And it is certainly not a question of untrammelled holiness in the Wesleyan sense of perfectionism – God knows that have we sinned immeasurably.

To be cataphatic, unity for us is an ontological fact. In the language of Metropolitan John of Pergamon, we are the Church instituted by Christ and constituted by the Spirit, and yet apophatically, our unity is the mystery of our calling. For lest we should boast, we are reminded, paradoxically, that to be Orthodox is to be willing, if it is possible, as St Paul says, to be castaways that all may be saved. Our unity, then, is not an expression of smugness but of mission. The Lord Jesus himself makes this clear in his prayer for the Church: 'That they all may be one: as thou, Father, art in me, and I in thee, that they also may be one in us: that the world may believe that thou hast sent me' (John 17.21).

The Diaspora's role in mission, however, has been mixed and not always prophetic. Orthodox missionary shortcomings in the West have been elegantly articulated by Metropolitan Philip of the

Antiochene Church in America. He says that the Diaspora has arrived bodily in the West, but remains absent psychologically. He says that there are Orthodox Christians in North America who are still living elsewhere 'in their hearts'. The 'old country' naturally exercises a strong pull on the imagination and memory, but it can also lead to a perpetual daydream where Christian responsibility is negated by nostalgic longing for the past.

Metropolitan Philip argues that one of the problems with this is that members of some Churches have not spoken to the West with a prophetic voice because they have not seen themselves as missionaries or prophets, but merely as a ghetto, holding together that which they had lost in the past. His argument over the last ten years or so has been that the Orthodox Church must cease to be a Diaspora Church in the sense of a museum or an ethnic enclave, and become a missionary Church. For Orthodoxy to be institutionally present in the West is not enough, because it is not here merely to survive or even to wax strong. It is here to mediate the presence of God the Holy Spirit. Or to put it in the language of this chapter: its prophetic role is to speak the mind and will of God.

What Metropolitan Philip says may not be popular with all Orthodox Christians, but I believe it to be true. However, I would like to suggest that there is a rather more positive way to look at the role of the Diaspora over the last decades. First, let me look at this quite sociologically. I have been a member of the Russian Patriarchal Church in Great Britain for twenty-three years. When I joined it in 1973, I saw myself as a guest in the Russian Church. Being a guest, albeit a welcome one, did not distress me. I realized that when a new group arrives from one land to another, if it is going to maintain the structures and traditions of the Church, sometimes it has to be, as I think Metropolitan Anthony of Sourozh once said, 'sniffy'. It wants to put its roots down and create something firm and deep before it grows, otherwise we know what can happen: the plant will be force-fed and soon wither and die.

My own view is that the Diaspora has needed to be in the West for a while and bide its time before it reaches out in mission – although, like Metropolitan Philip, I think that time is now ripe. But there is an inbuilt strength of the Diaspora that feeds the prophetic role, and it is this. People who are refugees, who come from one land to another are, if you like, resident aliens. They are resident in the country, but they do not really quite belong. Strictly speaking, that is what all Christians are, regardless of whether they are actually in an historical Diaspora or not, for we are citizens not of earth but of heaven.

To a certain extent, to be a resident alien means that you are open to the prophetic. That is why C.S. Lewis, always out of sorts with modernity – rather like the anti-hero of Dostoyevsky's *Letters from the Underworld* – was the outstanding European Christian apologist in the twentieth century. We notice in literature and in the secular world that the outsider often has an interesting way of seeing things. He or she has a unique perspicacity that insiders do not possess, because things happen underneath the noses of insiders, but they cannot see the obvious staring them in the face. So I think there is a very positive sense in which the Diaspora, because of its marginality, its status as the outsider, is well positioned to be prophetic – as long as it remains attentive to the mind of God.

To be on the edge, or on the boundaries, as Paul Tillich liked to talk of it, is a curious experience demanding great discernment as well as faithfulness to the Tradition. Orthodox Christians who settle in the West discover a mystery. On the one hand, by being what we are, Orthodox, with all our weaknesses, we witness to the one Holy Catholic and Apostolic Church. On the other hand, we discover, to our amazement, that there is more of a family resemblance with the heterodox than we had imagined. We find brothers and sisters in Christ in many countries. Even if they are estranged family members, the family resemblance is unmistakable.

This was one of the great shocks for Nicolas Zernov when he arrived in Europe from Russia some years after the Bolshevik Revolution. He discovered that there were Christians everywhere and many of them were asking for Orthodox help and illumination for Western theological problems. He found (as do many Orthodox today) that there were heretics too, but he became convinced that the adage of Metropolitan Sergius Stragovodsky of Moscow is true: 'we know where the Church is, but we do not say where the Church is not'.

For many years in Great Britain, Metropolitan Anthony has supported what little trickles of Orthodoxy he has been able to find bubbling up in other Churches, even if they never fully flow into the Orthodox Church. He has been encouraged by the many Christian people who have been committed to the sort of historic Christianity which allows real debate to take place between East and West.

The Diaspora still has a long way to go before it turns from a siege to a missionary mentality, but I believe that the Orthodox Church is turning outwards as Nicholas Berdyaev wanted it to and is beginning to share some of its treasures with others. I think, for example, that the ecological dispute is one major area where the majority of Western theology really has little to say about the relationship between humankind and the material universe, because it does not seem to have a full, organic understanding of the relationship between priesthood, prophecy, kingship and the world. This is one major debate where we have something to offer, something prophetic to say.

I know there are some Orthodox who feel that it is not our job to help Western Christians solve their problems. I believe that we cannot take that view: this is not only exclusivist, it is Pharisaical. I believe the right attitude is much more that we are here, and that if we can offer help, then we will. One of the ways we can do this is by displaying for people what our theology is, what our spirituality is, not in a proselytising, declamatory way that always makes people feel uncomfortable, but simply by spelling out some of the problems we are all facing together as Christians in the modern world.

The World Council of Churches' Faith and Order Commission, incidentally, with all its faults, is better than it might have been precisely because of the contribution that the Orthodox Church has made to it. If anyone ever wants evidence that some good has come out of ecumenical dialogue, just look back over the last ten years and see how the Trinity, baptism and a high Christology are back on the agenda of the World Council of Churches.

And we could go further. A number of leading Reformed theologians, of which Bishop Lesslie Newbigin is one, were of the opinion that the Orthodox delegation at the WCC Conference at Canberra in 1991 saved the council from disaster, when they were urged by Chung Hyun-Kyung, the controversial Chinese feminist theologian, to embrace a syncretistic understanding of faith far beyond the boundaries of revealed religion. It is ironic that a number of radical thinkers, particularly those interested in women's and inter-faith issues, support the Orthodox on the *filioque* clause, so that they can free the Spirit from the Son and let him loose on the world.

The Orthodox response to Professor Chung, and by implication to all those who would turn the Holy Spirit into *Sophia*, or a deistic immanence, was to say: 'Our Tradition is rich in respect for local and national cultures, but we find it impossible to evoke the spirits of 'earth, air, water, and sea creatures'. Pneumatology is inseparable from Christology or from the doctrine of the Holy Spirit confessed by the church on the basis of divine revelation.'

Here the Orthodox Church – heartlands and Diaspora as one – faced with a theological crisis as deep as the paganism of early centuries, was unequivocal. Without a hint of the Erastian and pragmatic spirit that has sometimes bedevilled our witness, we spoke the mind of God.

Not all Orthodox prophecy has been so dramatic. Sometimes it has been a case of a gradual opening up of the Church's Tradition to the outside world. Metropolitan John's book, for example, *Being As Communion*, is now standard reading in many Evangelical colleges in Great Britain as well as in Reformed seminaries. And the Orthodox adherence to the Cappadocian understanding of the Trinity has had great influence in recent years, moving people away from a sterile modalism or impersonalism to a dynamic model of personal communion. Not enough has been made of it, but the accord between the Reformed tradition and the Orthodox Church on the *filioque* and the doctrine of the Trinity has been a major breakthrough in ecumenical dialogue.

Those Orthodox who say that Protestants and Catholics can never understand the Eastern Church are sometimes guilty of failing to learn the theological jargon of the West, or of seeing how far Orthodox concepts can translate into Western forms. Tell a Pentecostal that icons are images of the holy and he will turn away in disgust. But talk to him of the synergy of God and man and tell him that icons are paintings of the Holy Spirit and he will prick up his ears. Or try telling a radical feminist, without due care and attention, that the Orthodox Church will not reconstruct Father, Son and Holy Ghost into a functional triunity of Creator, Redeemer and Sustainer, and she may lose interest or take offence. But make the effort to explain to her that there is no gender in the Trinity, and that the Father is not male (nor the Spirit female) and she will listen with respect. Sarah Coakley of Harvard University, an Anglican, will even argue that it is the Holy Trinity, properly understood, that is the best antidote to patriarchy – in the oppressive sense in which feminists use the term.

These examples remind us of the most neglected dimension to being prophetic: it is not enough to know the mind of God, one also has to speak it in the language and cultural context in which we find ourselves. This should also remind us that prophecy is not the obverse of ascesis. Just as the charism of discernment operates through the spiritual fruit of sobriety, so too does prophecy speak from the familiarity of ascetic attention to the mind of God on the one hand, and the culture in which we live on the other. Prophecy, in short, is hard work both in listening to and speaking from the mind of God.

Self-critical Orthodoxy

But now, if I may, I want to be less self-congratulatory about what Orthodoxy may be able to do for the West. This is because I think Orthodox Christians face what we might call in colloquial language an 'attitude problem' in their dealings with those outside their community. To be prophetic is to speak the truth from the mind of God to the Church and the world, but St Paul reminds us that we should speak the truth in love. Love can be stern or severe as well as gentle, but it is never a big stick with which to beat other people, who see things differently from us, over the head.

It is not necessary, and it is sometimes inaccurate, in talking about the West always to insist on using the language of heterodoxy or heresy to describe its religious beliefs and practices. To believe that there has been no richness of Christian Tradition outside Eastern Orthodoxy since the Great Schism is either ignorance or myopia. As if Calvin never once rang true. Or as if Charles Wesley never wrote magnificent trinitarian hymns. What allies the Orthodox would find if they scoured the West for fellow travellers, whether it be Edward Irving on the humanity of Christ, Ives Congar on the Church, or Jürgen Moltmann on creation.

The question I am raising here is not to doubt the richness of Orthodox heritage (for to do so would be to abandon the Church), but to ask whether the Orthodox are willing in their critical judgment of Western traditions also to look at themselves a little more closely.

I am not talking about importing Enlightenment rationalism into Church Tradition, with its concomitant cynicism and superior intellectual airs, nor am I suggesting a diminution of respect for the Patristic tradition. I am talking about ensuring that the Church speaks with a prophetic voice.

This needs nothing less than spiritual discernment: remembering to distinguish Tradition from customs; noting the gradations between dogmas, theological opinions, and pious opinions; knowing when either eirenic or polemical theology is called for; having the discipline not to quote canon law or the Fathers as indiscriminately as fundamentalists quote texts of Holy Scripture; not falling into the trap of liturgical legalism while (quite properly) distancing Orthodox Tradition from moral legalism.

It may be true, as my friend said, that Orthodoxy has preserved the form of the Church in its canons and in its theology, but in practice Orthodox Christians have often failed normatively to be the Church. That is to say, that the outward form of religion has been sustained in terms of rites and practices, but sometimes there has been very little inner reality of knowing the mind of God. Let me show you, if I may, what led to this critical train of thought, this self-examination. It begins in the passage from St Luke that I quoted earlier when Jesus said: 'The Spirit of the Lord is upon me because he has anointed me to preach the gospel to the poor...'

We later read (Luke 4.24) that Jesus makes it quite clear that prophets usually have no honour in their own country. It is St John Chrysostom who points out, in his homily on this passage, that Jesus is talking about his own brethren here. That is to say, it is we ourselves who often fail to hear the prophetic voice, and not other people. A similar point was made some years ago by the late Fr Lev Gillet, in a sermon in the Russian Cathedral in London. He was speaking on the passage in the Gospel where Jesus, struck by the fact that as a prophet he had no honour in his own country, among his own kin, or in his own house, could only marvel at the unbelief of his brethren (Mark 6.1-5). Fr Lev wondered why it was that the Orthodox of today, who know so much and have had so much given them, were so steeped in unbelief and sin.

Self-important and self-serving prophecy is prophecy without cost, without pain, without repentance. For to point the finger outside – at the West, at the heterodox – prevents us from having to look inside ourselves. When we do that, when we berate others for their shortcomings and neglect our own, we cease to be prophetic altogether and become stiff-necked Pharisees unable to bend our heads in supplication and prayer, and hence unable to know the mind and will of God. It was not for nothing that the Fathers rightly saw that the repentant publican was the true model of Orthodox spirituality.

There is no spirituality in Orthodoxy without repentance. It is repentance that gives to spirituality its route to the mind and will of God, not some vague cultural essence that we have somehow picked up and kept going over the years. Spirituality is something that we have to rediscover in every generation, in order that we remain prophets in fact and not merely in principle; that we are renewers of Tradition, and renewed by it, and not merely rehearsers of it.

I would like to give if I can some concrete examples of this. I do not wish to speak out of turn, but I think it is important that we understand that prophecy is bound to be uncomfortable for us if we are outside the will of God. The Orthodox Church has to weigh the wisdom of casting stones at other confessions, when it has the horror of the Balkans in its midst.

A journalist once rang me and asked, 'As an Orthodox are you embarrassed at what is happening in Bosnia?' I remember what struck me most about his question was this: what a terrible word to use – 'embarrassed'. The word that comes to mind when we think of the Lutheran Church and the Third Reich is 'ashamed'. Bosnia is not a question of embarrassment. It is a question of having to admit that sometimes even in the heartlands of Orthodoxy, as well as the hinterlands, sin abounds. There is no other word for it. We cannot dress it up.

Orthodox scholars and apologists might properly object that the Bosnian Serbs are not in fact from the traditional heartlands of Orthodoxy, nor are they a good example of a people who have been successfully socialized into the Orthodox Faith. This is a matter of historical fact. If Catholic Croatia was deeply influenced by fascism in between the two World Wars, Orthodox Serbs in Bosnia were subject to a surfeit of secularization under Marxist Socialism during and immediately after the Second World War. We could also properly object that the mass media are not objective in their reporting of the Bosnian war. Serbs, too, have been on the receiving end of 'ethnic cleansing', and they suffered as a people in the Second World War in their tens of thousands at the hands of Croatian fascists. Many of us know this, and it does help us to understand the present situation a little better, but it still does not make the Serbian conduct acceptable.

Of course, the Church is not institutionally responsible for atrocities, which have been rightly and courageously condemned by some of the hierarchs. But the fact remains that ordinary men from Orthodox churches have been involved in crimes against humanity. Sometimes the genuine light of Christian community throws shadows of ethnic exclusivity and tribal allegiance which can overcome that light, unless it burns brightly in the hearts and minds of ordinary men and women.

Russia provides us with perhaps a more pressing scenario for self-examination. When Russia was in the grip of Soviet rule, many Orthodox around the world were not slow to criticize the Church there at that time. But now, as Communism loosens its grip, will we also feel able to stand up to the present dangers: for there is a threat of a Slavophile neo-fascism within the Church itself, with its concomitant hatred of Jews and Freemasons. There is a national fanaticism hatching in some seminaries and parishes and a hatred of all things Western.

This danger is all the greater because much of what has been imported to Russia from the West is indeed evil: its consumer hedonism, pornography, greed, and its pragmatic triumphalism. All the more reason then that the Church should remain true to herself. When, however, a leading hierarch of the Russian Church can encourage the publication of a right-wing daily newspaper, of a virulent kind, saturate church bookstalls with thousands of unacceptable pamphlets, and watch while that old forgery much loved by the Nazis – *The Protocols of the Learned Elders of Zion* – rears its head again, it is time for the Church to speak out with clarion certainty.

Here the prophetic voice is unambiguous. There is Orthodoxy, the Church, and there is a counterfeit religion looking much the same. It has identical symbols and liturgical practices to the true Church, but its spirit is not the Spirit of adoption whereby we cry 'Abba Father' in repentance and reconciliation, but the spirit of discord. This is not to attack the Church, but it is to recognize that within the *ecclesia*, within the fold of God, we can and do find wolves in sheep's clothing.

Orthodox problems in the Diaspora are mundane compared to those in Eastern Europe, but they are nonetheless serious for all that. Cardinal Suenens once told me that Catholics in Belgium and France could no longer survive in the Western world without true Christian commitment, because there was no longer a benign Christian culture to encourage their faith. Nominal Christianity is a particular temptation for Orthodox living in Europe or North America, cut off from their Orthodox homelands, with their tacit cultural support for the Church.

How many Orthodox people, for example, have become like those Anglicans who put down 'Church of England' on the form when they are admitted into hospital, but who rarely attend church? Does

'Orthodox' mean any more than 'I belong to a particular denomination'? In Great Britain, perhaps our missionary work needs to begin with our own people. For many thousands of Cypriots who have been secularized by the forces of modernity, or who have married outside the Church, Orthodoxy has been diluted almost to the point of sterility. Even traditional rites of passage are becoming a thing of the past.

The purpose of such severe remarks is this: for Orthodoxy to be prophetic, it constantly has to remind itself that this is impossible without knowing the mind and will of God. To know and speak the mind and will of God is beyond human reasoning unless we are grafted by the Holy Spirit into the living Christ and his Church. In order to ensure that the graft is not rejected, we have to be daily renewed through repentance in the very life of the risen Christ.

Orthodoxy does not mean 'right belief' if by that we mean no more than antiquarian exactitude, learning dogmas by rote, or talking and preening ourselves like a parrot. Orthodoxy is better understood as true worship which is the overflowing of God's personal love into the Church. This overflowing is like abundant wine brimming in the cup from which we must drink deeply if we want new life, and drinking is both a physical act of opening our mouths and a spiritual act of surrender, of opening our hearts.

Let me end in this way. By the grace of God, the Orthodox Church came to the West. I believe it really is the true Church, spotless and holy in the mystery of its sanctuary, but also teeming in its empirical life with Judases and Pharisees as well as publicans and sinners. Orthodox prophecy is the voice of the mind of God to the world, but also to the Church. That same voice warns us that when Jesus says, 'I am the vine and you are the branches', it is quite clear that branches can wither and die if they are not grafted firmly onto the vine. There is no life in a dead branch, no Spirit-bearing sap, and the prophetic voice is silenced.

The Laos of God

Metropolitan Anthony of Sourozh

There is no such thing as a single Christian, an isolated Christian, an individual Christian. To be a Christian means to be a member, a limb – a real limb like a hand – of the Body of Christ. To be constituted in this way is a very earnest problem because in a body, as St Paul puts it, when one limb suffers the whole body is sick. When one of us falls, we do not say that 'my hand is painful': the whole body suffers.

We have lost this sense of being a body. Oh yes, we try these days to recapture it by saying that 'we must become a community'. No! We must *not* become a community. To become one of the many communities of people who are like-minded, who share the same tastes, who believe in the same God, who proclaim the same things, amounts to a sort of religious association. This is not enough! It is not enough to be Christ's own club! A body is not a collection of individuals who have nothing to do in common except share objectives while never caring for each other. And if we care, it should not be simply social caring, a sort of courtesy and kindliness and good behaviour. A body is not that!

Neither is the body the *laos* of the laity as contrasted with the clergy. The *laos* as the people of God is the total Body of Christ. A priest, a bishop, a patriarch, is part of this *laos*. There is hierarchy in the Church, but it is a hierarchy of service, not of power. We should be able to proclaim the gospel with conviction and authority because of what people see in us as a living body, and as persons connected one to another, not because we have power. A hierarchy

236

of submission, obedience and subjection on all levels is a heresy against the Church. We must recapture another attitude which is *sobornost*, conciliarity, unanimity – all united in the mind of Christ and in the guidance of the Holy Spirit.

To be the *laos* of God, as clergy or lay persons, is to recognize that in this world in which God has no recognized place, where he is an outsider, a tramp, we are the place of his indwelling presence. We are God's asylum – the place where he has a right to be. And yet God does not expect the *laos* to be a refuge, a place of safety for him, and more so for us. He expects his Body to be his presence in the world, and on his own terms: 'As my Father has sent me, so do I send you'. To be the *laos* of God is to be sent out into the world to bring joy, hope, light and newness of life. That is our mission.

Notes

Notes to Chapter 4
Orthodox Tradition and Family Life

1. There are even today many Orthodox Christians living as hermits; but they have contact with communities, and they usually have lived many years in a community before becoming solitaries. There are also those who live 'in the world' (a traditional expression for non-monastic life) alone, by choice or against their wishes. For the purposes of this article I include them as members of a family.

2. See his conversation with a fellow-traveller recorded in the Russian edition of *Saint Silouan the Athonite* (Essex: Monastery of St John the Baptist, 1990), p. 223.

3. I have written in greater detail on the education of Orthodox children in *Reflections on Children in the Orthodox Church Today* (Essex: Monastery of St John the Baptist, 1995).

4. The Orthodox Church only returns to the ancient practice of public confessions in exceptional circumstances. A remarkable example occurs in the life of the celebrated priest, St John of Kronstadt. See Bishop Alexander's biography, *The Life of Father John of Kronstadt* (Crestwood, NY: St Vladimir's Seminary Press, 1979), Chapter 6.

5. A marriage may be celebrated in the Orthodox Church between an Orthodox Christian and a Christian baptized into another confession.

6. Babies are given their name in a service which takes place traditionally on the eighth day after birth, cf. Luke 1.59, 2.21.

7. 'Secondary', in inverted commas, because details of daily life contribute to 'primary' issues. Christ said: 'He who is faithful in a very little is faithful also in much; he who is unrighteous in a very little is unrighteous also in much' (Luke 16.10). The point is that we should not 'strain out gnats' while forgetting mercy and justice and faith (Matthew 23.23-24); and we must have in consideration how each particular child is experiencing these fundamental realities at any time.

Notes to Chapter 5
Lent and the Consumer Society

1. Celia and Kenneth Sisam (eds.), *The Oxford Book of Medieval English Verse* (Oxford 1970), p. 120.

2. *Epistle to Diognetus* vii, 4.

3. *Against the Heresies* III, xxi, 7 (*PG* [= Migne, *Patrologia Graeca*] 7.953B).

4. *Dream and Reality: An Essay in Autobiography* (London 1950), p. 47.

5. On the Orthodox understanding of Lent, see the excellent and lively book of Archpriest Alexander Schmemann, *Great Lent* (Crestwood: St Vladimir's Seminary Press, 1969). Compare also the introduction to *The Lenten Triodion*, translated by Mother Mary and Archimandrite Kallistos Ware (London/Boston 1978), pp. 13-64.

6. Those with a mathematical turn of mind may wonder how Lent can be made equal to a tenth part of the year. One way used by Orthodox in calculating the length of Lent is to see it as consisting of seven weeks, each containing five days of fasting (for Saturday and Sunday in the first six weeks of Lent are not reckoned as days of strict fasting). Holy Saturday is then added to this, for it alone among the Saturdays of the year is kept as a fast day, and so one reaches a total of thirty-six days. While this manner of calculating

fits the notion of Lent as a tithe, in the Christian East, Lent is more commonly reckoned as containing not thirty-six but forty days, which are calculated continuously from 'Clean Monday' to Friday in the sixth week inclusive. Holy Week is then regarded as constituting a special period distinct from Lent itself. On ways of computing Lent in East and West, see *The Lenten Triodion*, pp. 31-33.

7. *The Mystical Theology of the Eastern Church* (London 1957), p. 171.

8. *On Baptism* (*PG* 65.1028BC).

9. Quoted in *Orthodoxy and the Ecological Crisis*, published in 1990 by the Ecumenical Patriarchate of Constantinople, assisted by WWF (the World Wide Fund for Nature), p. 10. Copies of this admirable brochure can be obtained from the World Conservation Centre, Avenue du Mont-Blanc, CH-1196, Gland, Switzerland. See also *So that God's Creation Might Live: The Orthodox Church Responds to the Ecological Crisis* (Proceedings of the Inter-Orthodox Conference on Environmental Protection, The Orthodox Academy of Crete, November 1991), published in 1992 by the Ecumenical Patriarchate.

10. *Homilies on Fasting* i, 10 (*PG* 31.181B).

11. This is in fact simply a more elaborate form of the ceremony of mutual forgiveness that takes place daily in monasteries at the end of *Apodeipnon* (Compline).

12. For fuller details, see *The Lenten Triodion*, pp. 35-37. The rules of Western Christendom were much the same as this until the later Middle Ages.

13. This passage is read in the Orthodox Church at Vespers on Friday in the week before Lent.

14. This is one of the *agrapha* or 'unwritten sayings' attributed to Jesus by the early Christian community, although not found in the Gospels.

Notes

Notes to Chapter 9
Orthodoxy and Art

1. Hans Urs von Balthasar, *The Glory of the Lord*, vol. 5 (Eng. tr., T&T Clark, Edinburgh, 1991), p. 296.

2. D.J. Sahas, *Icon and Logos: Sources in Eighth-Century Iconoclasm* (University of Toronto Press, Toronto, 1986), p. 99. Contains a translation of the refutation of the Iconoclast decree, read out at the sixth session of the Seventh Ecumenical Council.

3. St John of Damascus, *On the Divine Images* I.16 and II.14.

4. *On the Divine Images* II.15.

5. *On the Divine Images* III.16 and 17.

6. *On the Divine Images* III.18-23.

7. *Divine Names* 5.8.

8. E.H. Gombrich, *Topics of our Time: Twentieth-Century Issues in Learning and in Art* (Phaidon, London, 1991), p. 101.

9. T.S. Eliot, *On Poetry and Poets* (Faber & Faber, London, 1957), p. 108.

10. R.M. Rilke, *Briefe* (Insel Verlag, Frankfurt, 1950), p. 46.

11. Erich Auerbach, *Mimesis: The Representation of Reality in Western Literature* (Eng. tr., Princeton University Press, Princeton, 1953).

12. René Hague (ed.), *Dai Greatcoat: a Self-Portrait of David Jones in His Letters* (Faber & Faber, London, 1980), p. 191.

13. Hermann Broch, *The Death of Virgil* (Eng. tr., Routledge & Kegan Paul, London, 1946, reprinted 1977), p. 136f.

14. David Jones, *Epoch and Artist* (Faber & Faber, London, 1959), p. 166f.

The Contributors

Gillian Crow

Gillian Crow is an English convert to Orthodoxy. She contributes Christian articles to the national and religious press, and is the author of a number of Religious Education resources on the Orthodox Church. She is Diocesan Secretary of the Russian Orthodox Church in Great Britain, which she represents on the Council of Churches in Britain and Ireland, the Churches Together in England, and the Religious Education Council. She is the author of *Grains of Salt and Rays of Light: Reflections on St Matthew's Gospel* (St Paul's Press, 1994). She is married, with three adult children, and lives in Bedford.

Bishop Basil of Sergievo

Bishop Basil is assistant bishop in the diocese of Sourozh of the Russian Church in Britain. He was born in Alexandria in Egypt, and brought up in the United States. He studied for his first degree at the University of Buffalo, New York State, and for his doctorate studied classics at the University of Cincinnati, Ohio (where he also studied Hebrew at Hebrew Union College). Bishop Basil is one of the four presidents of the Churches Together in England, and is author, among other works, of a collection of sermons, *The Light of Christ* (St Stephen's Press, 1995).

Metropolitan Athanasios of Hercegovina

Metropolitan Athanasios (Jevtic) of Hercegovina was born in 1938 in Brdarica in central Serbia. He attended the ecclesiastical school of St Sava and immediately afterward took monastic vows. His postgraduate studies were at Athens University, and the subject of his doctorate was *The Ecclesiology of St Paul according to St Chrysostom*. Since 1972, he has held the Chair of Patristics and Ecclesiastical History of the Theological School in Belgrade, and was actively engaged in public discussion, publication and broadcasting, particularly in dialogue with the supporters of Marxism and materialism. He was ordained Bishop of Banat in Voivodina and in 1992 he requested to be transferred to Hercegovina. Metropolitan Athanasios has authored a number of books which have appeared in Serbo-Croat and Greek, including *Gladsome Light*, and *Christ: Beginning and End*.

Sister Magdalen

Sister Magdalen is a nun in the Community of St John the Baptist in Essex, which was founded by Archimandrite Sophrony in 1959. She graduated in theology from King's College, London, in 1975, and is the author of *Reflections on Children in the Orthodox Church Today* (St John the Baptist, Essex, 1995).

Metropolitan Anthony of Sourozh

Metropolitan Anthony (Bloom) is Metropolitan of Sourozh, the diocese of the Russian Orthodox Church in Great Britain. Anthony Bloom was born in Lausanne and spent his childhood in Russia and Persia. His family had to leave Persia during the Russian Revolution and settled in Paris, where he gained a doctorate in medicine at the University of Paris. During the Second World War, he served as an officer in the French army until the fall of France, and then worked as a surgeon in a Paris hospital, also taking part in the Resistance. Metropolitan Anthony first came to Britain in 1949 as an Orthodox chaplain, and was consecrated bishop in 1958, archbishop in 1962, and metropolitan in 1966. He is the author of several books, including *Living Prayer* (DLT, 1966), *School for Prayer* (DLT, 1970) and *Meditations on a Theme* (Mowbray, 1972).

Bishop Kallistos of Diokleia

Bishop Kallistos (Timothy Ware) is a Fellow of Pembroke College, Oxford, and teaches Eastern Orthodox studies in the University. He is an assistant bishop in the Orthodox Archdiocese of Thyateira and Great Britain (Ecumenical Patriarch) and he belongs to the Monastery of St John the Theologian, Patmos. He is the author of *The Orthodox Church* (Penguin, 1963) and *The Orthodox Way* (Mowbray, 1979).

Prof. H. Tristram Engelhardt Jr

Dr H. Tristram Engelhardt Jr is Professor of Medical Ethics at Baylor College of Medicine; Professor of Philosophy at Rice University; Adjunct Research Fellow at the Institute of Religion, and member of the Center for Medical Ethics and Health Policy in Houston, Texas. He is co-editor of the journal *Christian Bioethics*.

Dr Jamie Moran

Dr Jamie Moran was born in the United States of mixed Jewish, Scots-Irish and Cherokee Indian ancestry. He came to England when he was sixteen years of age, and became Orthodox when he was twenty-two. He was educated at Oxford and London Universities, and went on to do professional training in psychotherapy. He works as a psychotherapist and as Senior Lecturer in Psychology and Counselling at Roehampton Institute, London. He is deeply involved in North American Indian concerns and is at present writing a novel about the loss of the West in nineteenth-century America. He is also involved in writing on the qualitative or hermeneutic approach to science, and on 'spiritual psychology'.

Dr Andrew Louth

Dr Andrew Louth formerly taught patristics at the University of Oxford and Byzantine history at Goldsmiths College, University of London. He is now Reader in Patristics at the University of Durham. He is the author of many articles and several books, including *Maximus the Confessor* (Routledge, 1996).

Metropolitan John of Pergamon

Metropolitan John (Zizioulas) of Pergamon is a Bishop of the Ecumenical Patriarchate and also an academic theologian. Formerly Professor of Systematic Theology in the University of Glasgow, at present he is Professor of Dogmatics in the University of Thessalonika, and Visiting Professor in Systematic Theology at King's College, University of London. He has also taught theology in the Gregorian University of Rome and in the University of Geneva. His most well known book in English is *Being As Communion* (DLT, 1985). Metropolitan John also serves the Ecumenical Patriarchate as its theological adviser and official representative in many international bodies, including the World Council of Churches' Central Committee and the Faith and Order Commission, and the International Anglican-Orthodox Theological Commission, of which he is the Orthodox Co-Chairman. He has been particularly active in the Ecumenical Patriarchate's initiatives concerning the protection of the natural environment.

Costa Carras

Costa Carras was born in London in 1938 of Greek parents. He studied philosophy, ancient history, Greek and Latin literature at Oxford, and economics at Harvard. At the present time he is Chairman of the Assembly of the Diocese of Sourozh, and an Archon Notarios of the Patriarchate of Constantinople. He organized the conference on religion and the environment in Patmos (1988), which proposed that 1st September be declared a day of prayer for creation. In 1972, he was the initiator and first President of the Hellenic Society for the Preservation of the Environment and the Architectural Heritage, and is now Vice-Chairman of Europa Nostra, the confederation of European conservation organizations. For many years he was active in the shipping and other industries. The author of several articles on multi-communal states, culture and religion, Costa Carras was also the Orthodox Co-Chairman of the British Council of Churches' Commission on Trinitarian Doctrine (1983-88).

Dr Andrew Walker

Dr Andrew Walker is the director of Gospel & Culture, and Senior Lecturer in Theology and Education at King's College, London. He is also visiting professor in evangelism and culture at Perkins School of Theology, Southern Methodist University, Dallas, Texas. He is a lay preacher in the Patriarchal Russian Church in England. He is the author of several books, including *Restoring the Kingdom* (Hodder & Stoughton, 1985) and *Enemy Territory* (Hodder & Stoughton, 1987), and his latest book is *Telling the Story* (SPCK, 1996).